Readings: A New Biblical Commentary

General Editor
John Jarick

H E B R E W S

HEBREWS

Robert P. Gordon

Sheffield Academic Press

For Claire

Copyright © 2000 Sheffield Academic Press

Published by Sheffield Academic Press Ltd
Mansion House
19 Kingfield Road
Sheffield S11 9AS
England

Printed on acid-free paper in Great Britain
by Bookcraft Ltd
Midsomer Norton, Bath

British Library Cataloguing in Publication Data

A catalogue record for this book is available
from the British Library

ISBN   1-84127-113-6
          1-84127-114-4 pbk

Contents

Preface

When my Sheffield colleagues invited me to contribute a volume on an Old Testament book to the *Readings* series I confessed to a particular liking for *Hebrews* in the New Testament and was encouraged to indulge my interest. I am no expert on *Hebrews* but I am, in the postmodern way, an expert on my own understanding of *Hebrews*, and very willing to sail (for a while) under a postmodern flag of convenience. Some idea of my 'angle' on *Hebrews* can easily be gathered from the Introduction, but I suspect that New Testament specialists may well find the book's main claim to fame in its refraining from actually quoting what Origen said about the authorship of *Hebrews*. I was also attracted to the idea of a commentary in which I was to engage with the Greek text and keep interaction with secondary literature under strict control. (The modest bibliography at the end exceeds my reading for this commentary but includes those books and articles that I have at one time or another found helpful.) The enjoyable corollary of this—the curtailing of footnote references—I have pursued not only in the commentary but also in the introductory sections. Although I have worked with the Greek text (using my trusty UBS 3rd edn) I have regularly cited NRSV for the ease and comfort of the reader. When writing on Christian texts I normally use BC and AD. Here I use BCE and CE in accordance with the publisher's policy, but without much conviction.

Hebrews is as reticent about itself (author, addressees, date of composition) as it is vocal in its Christology, so although I use the term 'Hebrews' for the addressees from time to time this is mainly to ring the changes on 'addressees', 'recipients', 'friends' (and is it 'readers' or 'hearers'?). Despite my continuing suspicion that the addressees were originally converts from Judaism, in the main, the use of 'Hebrews' should not be taken to imply that the issue is settled. Names of biblical books have not been italicized, but I have made an exception with *Hebrews,* to lessen the chances of confusion between *Hebrews* and 'the Hebrews'. I should also say that at a very late stage I simplified Psalm references where the numbering in the Hebrew and the English Bible traditions differs. Now I simply give the latter unless there is special reason to be more detailed.

My warmest thanks go as always to my wife Ruth for carrying extra burdens while my writing and other duties have interfered with family life. I have also to thank John Jarick, the series editor, for his help and his patience, and for going away to Israel just when I had undertaken to send him the manuscript—so giving me a few extra weeks to mull over it. It is a pleasure to dedicate this study to our one and only daughter Claire (yes, it's your turn) who is currently completing her third year studying medicine at Queen's University, Belfast.

Cambridge
7 March 2000

Abbreviations

ANRW	Hildegard Temporini and Wolfgang Haase (eds.), *Aufstieg und Niedergang der römischen Welt: Geschichte und Kultur Roms im Spiegel der neueren Forschung* (Berlin: W. de Gruyter, 1972-)
ASV	American Standard Version
AV	Authorized Version
BIS	Biblical Interpretation Series
HNT	Handbuch zum Neuen Testament
JSNT	*Journal for the Study of the New Testament*
JSOTSup	*Journal for the Study of the Old Testament*, Supplement Series
MT	Masoretic Text
NEB	New English Bible
NIV	New International Version
NovT	*Novum Testamentum*
NRSV	New Revised Standard Version
REB	Revised English Bible
RSV	Revised Standard Version
RV	Revised Version
SBLDS	Society of Biblical Literature Dissertation Series
SNTSMS	Society for New Testament Studies Monograph Series
TynBul	*Tyndale Bulletin*
WBC	Word Biblical Commentary

Introduction

1. Who are these People?

The Author

Hebrews has no epistolary greeting and nothing else that would give a clear indication of the identity of its author. Little can be gleaned about him beyond that he was male (the natural interpretation of 11.32), and that he wrote in a style different from that of Paul and described his first encounter with Christianity in terms that, while also true of Paul, would hardly have been that apostle's preferred way of stating his relationship to the Gospel of Christ (cf. Gal. 1.11-24). The association of the letter with Paul goes back a long way, to the oldest extant text of *Hebrews*, in Chester Beatty Papyrus 46 (perhaps to be dated as early as 200 CE) which contains epistles attributed to Paul, beginning with Romans and immediately following up with *Hebrews*.[1] The elegance with which the author writes and his skill in handling the Old Testament with the help of Hellenistic concepts and terminology make Apollos of Alexandria, Luke's *anēr logios* ('learned man', Acts 18.24), a worthy candidate, but only as the representative of a certain class of individual rather than as the probable author of the letter. He speaks of the Gospel coming to 'us' in 2.3, thereby including himself with his addressees, but this does not necessarily mean that he was, or had been, one of their number. When he refers to the persecution that they had experienced after they became Christians he is aware of some of the detail but keeps to the second-person 'you', which may or may not be significant (10.32-34). That he was an absent member of the church, unavoidably detained, who had been asked by its leaders to intervene in a difficult situation is an interesting conjecture (but no more) by Lindars.[2]

We can be sure that the recipients of the letter knew the identity of its

1.   See B.M. Metzger, *Manuscripts of the Greek Bible: An Introduction to Greek Palaeography* (New York: Oxford University Press, 1981), p. 64. Metzger suggests that the presence of *Hebrews* in the codex reflects the high regard with which it was held in the eastern church. Its position immediately after Romans he explains as having been dictated by considerations of length.

2.   B. Lindars, *The Theology of the Letter to the Hebrews* (Cambridge: Cambridge University Press, 1991), p. 8.

author, and we may surmise that the absence of the expected epistolary greeting is not accidental, given the author's interest in divine speech as constitutive of both the Jewish and the Christian faiths. He may have wished to give prominence to God as the real 'speaker' in his letter. Accidental or otherwise, the absence of the greeting functions in this way for many readers. The common view that *Hebrews* is a written-down homily that has been adapted to letter form with the addition of a postscript in 13.22-25 illustrates how it may have achieved its present shape, even though the homily analogy is in danger of being overworked (see below).

The Addressees

The title 'To the Hebrews', which is, of course, a later addition to the text, is regarded as uncomfortably pre-emptive for much modern *Hebrews* scholarship, given that the letter itself is not strikingly forthcoming on the background and circumstances of the people to whom it was first addressed. With the title comes the easy and widely-entertained assumption that the addressees were Jewish converts to Christianity and that it was the possibility of their returning to Judaism that occasioned the writing of the letter. So obvious was all this to Dean Henry Alford that he devoted only a paragraph to the matter in the 87-page introduction to his commentary on *Hebrews*, published in 1864. With less than prophetic insight, he commented: 'The attempt to dispute this [*sc.* Jewish-Christian background] must be regarded rather as a curiosity of literature, than as worthy of serious attention.' Only one sentence is offered by way of argument about the background of the 'Hebrews': 'Not a syllable is found of allusions to their conversion from the alienation of heathenism, such as frequently occur in St. Paul's Epistles: but every where [*sic*] their original covenant state is assumed, and the fact of that covenant having been amplified and superseded by a better one is insisted on.'[3]

Alford is right insofar as there are surprising omissions in *Hebrews* if it is addressed to Gentile Christians with presenting symptoms of discouragement and lassitude sufficiently serious to worry the writer. For example, we might reasonably have expected to find the author exerting himself to encourage Gentile Christian friends to consider

---

3. H. Alford, *The Greek Testament. IV.1. The Epistle to the Hebrews, and the Catholic Epistles of St. James and St. Peter* (London: Rivingtons; Cambridge: Deighton, Bell and Co., 1864), p. 62.

themselves part of God's covenant people and in line to share in their blessings. However, when in 6.12 he expresses his hope that the recipients will become 'imitators of those who through faith and patience inherit the promises'—just like Abraham (v. 15)—he feels no need to justify his assumption on their behalf that they are among the inheritors of these promises. For people theologically weak in other respects they appear to have a remarkably strong grasp of the theology of participation with the Old Testament faithful. No hint of 'you [Gentiles] also…were marked with the seal of the promised Holy Spirit' (Eph. 1.13) strays on to the pages of *Hebrews.*

Admittedly, the argument from silence represents a precarious basis for theories about the religious background of the 'Hebrews'. At the same time, it must be conceded that if there are no convincing indicators of a Gentile background there is also no overwhelming evidence of a Jewish matrix for the addressees. It might be assumed from the author's detailed, sustained and sometimes rabbinic-style use of the Old Testament that both he and they were accustomed to reading it from a Jewish perspective. (That it is the *Greek* Old Testament that is quoted would not affect the case.) The point is neutralized somewhat, however, by the consideration that the Pauline letters to Gentile, or to mixed Jewish-Gentile, churches make comparable use of the Hebrew scriptures, if not quite on the scale, or always in the manner, of *Hebrews.* Perhaps a more material point is made by F.F. Bruce in this regard when he suggests that if the recipients of the letter were originally Gentiles their doubts about their Christian faith would easily have extended to questions about the validity of the Old Testament in a way that would not necessarily have applied to quondam Jewish converts to Christianity.[4] Whereas, the use made of the Old Testament in the letter is far from suggesting any such complication.

It is easy to read *Hebrews* in such a way that the Jewish-Christian explanation seems to find regular confirmation in the text. Which texts appeal most in this regard is to some extent a subjective matter. This reader paused over the statement in 2.16 that Christ 'did not come to help angels, but the descendants of Abraham'. This agrees with what the rest of the New Testament has to say on the 'Jewishness of Jesus', but the statement is surely also meant to embrace the circumstances of the

---

4.   F.F. Bruce, *The Epistle to the Hebrews* (New London Commentaries; Grand Rapids: Eerdmans, 1964; London: Marshall, Morgan and Scott, 1965), p. xxvii.

addressees as included among those who 'all their lives were held in slavery by the fear of death' (v. 15). It is true that the idea of descent from Abraham is elsewhere spiritualized or 'Christianized' (see Rom. 4.16-17; Gal. 3.29) and that modern commentaries tend to plump for this interpretation here in 2.16. But in this case the author of *Hebrews* would be using the expression 'descendants of Abraham' unnuanced and without further ado to denote spiritual descendants of Abraham. Other interpreters, Alford among them, have seen this reference to 'the seed of Abraham' as most naturally suggesting the physical descendants of the patriarch. (Perhaps they were guilty of over-refinement in insisting that the context 'speaks not of that *into which* Christ has *made* those redeemed by Him, but of that *out of which* He has *helped* them'.[5])

One might also look for a clue in 11.13-16 where the writer pauses to reflect on what motivated the patriarchs to give up the security of settled life for the uncertainties of pilgrimage. In v. 15 he suggests, with perhaps a glance at the circumstances of the addressees, that if the biblical worthies had given thought to the land that they had left behind 'they would have had opportunity to return'. For them return would have been to a pagan land and, presumably, to a commensurate life-style. Since for the 'Hebrews' such a return would hardly have been to Gentile religion and Gentile ways—the letter does not address such an option—'return' in any literal sense could imply the recipients' looking with favour again on their Jewish past. Again this falls far short of being conclusive and could at best be cited in the event of a more positive case having been established on other grounds. It may be that consideration of the problem with which *Hebrews* is concerned will provide stronger clues to the background of the addressees.

2. What is the Problem?

There was the general problem of spiritual torpor, which is well advertised in the letter, but there will have been other dimensions to this general problem and, in the absence of direct statements, these mainly have to be inferred from the lines of argument pursued by the author. At times he challenges the 'Hebrews' as individuals to ensure that they personally are not drifting away from the faith, which raises questions as to whether he discerned a community-wide problem or one affecting certain individuals only (see 3.12; 4.1, 11; 6.11; 12.15). These

5.   Alford, *The Epistle to the Hebrews*, p. 51 (commentary section). Italics original.

latter may have corresponded to the 'some' who had fallen out of the habit of regular meeting with the rest of the church (cf. 10.25). There is at least a designated church leadership to which he can refer the community—we might contrast the Corinth of the Pauline letters in that respect—and it appears that the leaders have his confidence (cf. 13.17, 24). The terms of his commendation of them in 13.17 hint at the possibility of tensions between the leadership and certain of the flock, which is not surprising in view of the dissatisfaction that appears to have set in. One area of concern is mentioned in the final chapter, when the author warns against 'all kinds of strange teachings' and especially teachings having to do with 'foods' that 'have not benefited those who observe them'. Since he immediately goes on to talk of the Christian altar 'from which those who officiate in the tent have no right to eat' (v. 10), and then builds on the idea in vv. 11-13, there seems no reason to doubt that it is Jewish food laws that are in question. The Graeco-Roman world was a complex one with no lack of sects, mixed creeds and half-way houses, but that does not warrant obscuring a relatively straightforward issue like the present one. It is just possible, too, that this issue of food laws was in the author's mind when, in 12.16, he drew attention to Esau's selling of his birthright 'for a single meal'.

The problem ran deeper than this, we can be sure. At a number of points throughout the letter, in the so-called parenetic sections, a series of interlocking dangers is exposed: of drifting from the faith (2.1), of turning away from the living God (3.12), of crucifying again the Son of God (6.6), or of spurning the Son of God and at the same time profaning the blood of the covenant and outraging the Spirit of grace (10.29). To judge from the christological emphasis of the letter, in respect of Christ's status as divine Son and of the sufficiency of his self-offering for the sins of humanity, we may judge that the community had problems in maintaining their original confession of Jesus as the 'Son of God'. The references to 'crucifying again the Son of God' in 6.6 and to 'spurning the Son of God' in 10.29 are as suggestive as they are heavy-sounding in this regard.

If we ask about the anterior conditions that produced or contributed to this situation two or three main possibilities suggest themselves, though here the temptation to excessive psychologizing as well as to exegetical overkill has to be checked. For a start, it is likely that the problem of the delayed parousia is somewhere in the background. The calls to endurance are explicable partly on this basis: the 'Hebrews' had made a good start, but had lost enthusiasm with the passage of time and the delay in fulfilment of what was promised (6.11-12; 10.36). So they are assured that 'the one who is coming' will come (10.37). Once more the earth and the heavens will be shaken (12.26-27). However, in the time between conversion and the as yet unrealized parousia there was opportunity for disenchantment. We could surmise that this community did not have any charismatic phenomena in the present to report; the reference to 'signs and wonders and various miracles' in 2.4 noticeably links these to the time of their conversion, and there is no other suggestion in the letter that these were a part of their present experience of Christianity. If they had been, it is not too difficult to imagine the writer appealing to them as Christian evidences in the way of Gal. 3.2-5, for, as that passage shows, the continuing experience of charismatic phenomena could be enlisted in the cause of orthodox faith. A combination of dearth in the present and a delayed parousia would understandably have been stultifying in its effects, just as it has been for all those individuals and communities that have replicated the circumstances of the 'Hebrews' down the centuries. In response to this situation the author not only commends patient endurance but also emphasizes the 'realized' aspects of the faith—the things that Christians possess in the present, and the sense in which they may be said to have arrived already at the heavenly goal of their pilgrimage (cf. 12.22-24).

However, in any discussion of the attendant circumstances of the 'Hebrews' there is one factor that calls for attention more than most, and that is the effect of hardship and persecution on the community. The calls to endurance have to be read in that light, as also the appeal to previous displays of fortitude (10.32-34) and the explanatory gloss put on their discomforts when the writer discusses God's disciplinary ways in 12.3-11. Whether this amounts to the scenario suggested by some scholars, that the problem was that of attraction away from Christianity and towards Judaism because only the latter enjoyed the status of a *religio licita* within the Roman empire, is another matter. There is, at any rate, a remarkable preoccupation with the idea of avoiding, or at any rate surmounting, death in the letter. The first text for consideration is 2.14-15, where the significance of the death of Christ is expressed in terms of his liberation of 'the seed of Abraham' from thraldom to the fear of death. Given the author's skill in orienting theological statement to pastoral need, this reference would almost be sufficient of itself to suggest something about the addressees' state of mind. Again, in 5.7 the Gethsemane (or Gethsemane-like) prayers of Christ during his earthly life are said to have been offered 'to the one who was able to save him from death'. The construction put upon the praying and the sequel is noteworthy in the present context: Christ's prayer was answered 'because of his reverent submission'. There is 'hidden text' in this, of course, for the answer came not in the avoidance of death but in deliverance out of it. Already the author is contributing to the sub-theme that he will develop in ch. 11, namely that, for the faithful, death is vanquishable in one way or another.

In ch. 11 the main thesis is, of course, that all those who pleased God in the past were characterized by their faith in God. The writer also appears to take every possible opportunity to point out where this involved the overcoming or the frustrating of death in whatever form it happened to present itself. Thus I do not altogether go along with Lane's emphasis on 11.35b-38 as celebrating the resolute stand of those who, tortured and sometimes done to death, were not rescued by divine intervention.[6] What these verses describe is undeniably a part of the picture, but the balance of the chapter is strikingly more upbeat in its treatment of the subject of death. However, we should first note that the writer prefaces his list of the heroes of faith with a reference to creation, even though creation was not brought about through the exercise of faith on the part of anyone. In that sense the mention of creation is anomalous in the chapter. However, the point of the reference appears to be that the same power that brought creation into being is believed to be at work in the lives of the faithful. In the commentary it is noted that the Maccabaean mother of the seven martyred sons encouraged her boys to face martyrdom by reminding them of God as creator: 'Therefore the Creator of the world, who shaped the beginning of humankind and devised the origin of all things, will in his mercy give life and breath back to you again, since you now forget yourselves for the sake of his laws' (2 Macc. 7.23). When she comes to encourage the youngest son she continues on the creation theme in a way that closely parallels Heb. 11.3: 'I beg you, my child, to look at the heaven and the earth and see everything that is in them, and recognize that God did not make them out of things that existed' (2 Macc. 7.28).[7]

---

6. W.L. Lane, *Hebrews 1-8* (WBC, 47a; Dallas, TX: Word Books, 1991), pp. lvii-lviii.

7. The NRSV footnote offers the alternative translation, 'God made them out of things that did not exist'; in other words, the same translation options exist as in Heb. 11.3 (see commentary).

The register of the faithful in ch. 11 begins with Abel (v. 4). Even Abel, the first to succumb to death in the biblical story-line, is said to be still speaking, despite having died. Enoch represents another angle on faith in relation to death (v. 5). His is one of the names in the genealogical list in Genesis 5, where the not quite universal refrain is 'and he died'. Enoch, however, 'was no more, because God took him' (v. 24), and Heb. 11.5 is even more specific on his circumvention of death. Twice the patriarch Abraham is depicted as overcoming death through the exercise of faith. The birth of Isaac came when Abraham was 'as good as dead' (v. 12), and the writer finds resurrection faith in the Akedah story in Genesis 22, crediting Abraham with the conviction that, even if Isaac had to be sacrificed, God could restore him to life— 'and figuratively speaking, he did receive him back' (v. 19). In this review of the faithful both Jacob and Joseph are remembered for acts done at the end of their lives: Jacob blessed the two sons of Joseph and worshipped (v. 21), and Joseph gave instructions about the deposition of his bones (v. 22). Moses also escaped the pharaonic edict of death because his parents hid him for three months (v. 23). The exodus and conquest traditions also contribute to the theme, since it was by faith that the firstborn among the Israelites were protected from the attention of the destroying angel on Passover night (v. 28), and it was faith that enabled the Israelites to pass through the Red Sea 'as if it were dry land' (v. 29) and that enabled Rahab to avoid perishing with the rest of Jericho (v. 31).

Verses 33-35a recount in more summary fashion how, by faith, others stopped the mouths of lions, quenched raging fires, escaped the edge of the sword, and even received their dead back to life again. Then come vv. 35b-38 which, as I have already noted, commemorate yet others who endured persecution to the point of death 'in order to obtain a better resurrection' (v. 35). This theme of death, its defiance and defeat, is continued into ch. 12 where the attention of the 'Hebrews' is directed to Christ who disregarded the shame of crucifixion and was exalted to the right hand of the throne of God (v. 2). The author makes bold to point out to the recipients that they themselves have not as yet been called to make such a sacrifice: 'In your struggle against sin you have not yet resisted to the point of shedding your blood' (v. 4). Verse 9 of this same ch. 12 seems to bring the issue to a head when, following some argument to the effect that God can use suffering as a disciplinary agent, it is suggested that just as human parents normally discipline their children for their good, so obedience to God as 'the Father of spirits' will result in life (and not death). This hardly amounts to a promise that if the 'Hebrews' remain faithful to their Christian profession they will avoid martyrdom, but it is easy to see how, with eschatological expectation still burning (cf. 1.2; 10.25, 37), the writer might entertain the possibility of escape from death, whatever the cause, for some or all of the community.

Fear of death could also and very naturally be accompanied by fear of imperial edicts against Christians, as may be suggested by the twin references in ch. 11 to the overcoming of such fear first on the part of Moses' parents and then by Moses himself (vv. 23, 27). Moses' parents hid him for three months because he seemed specially attractive; 'and they were not afraid of the king's edict'. The particular occasion when Moses himself left Egypt 'unafraid of the king's anger' may be debated as far as the exodus story is concerned, but the very phrasing of the statement in 11.27 may have been determined with an authorial eye on the circumstances of the addressees—especially if the verse is referring to Moses' hurried departure from Egypt when he fled in fear (Exod. 2.14) of the Pharaoh's wrath. 'If the writer is so intent on saying that Moses was activated by faith rather than by fear of the Pharaoh is it not because he wishes to raise the issue of fear of the king-emperor with his readers?'[8] Whether their problem was fear of Caesar or dread of some little local caesar, the 'Hebrews' were to draw strength from the story of Moses.

3. The Message

If the regular encouragements to take heart and to press on function like a refrain in *Hebrews* the 'hymn' itself could properly be described as a christological one, in which the writer sets out to demonstrate the uniqueness of Christ as divine Son and as heavenly priest, and the sufficiency of his self-offering to deal with the problem of human sinfulness. He believes that the Old Testament writings look forward to a new era to be inaugurated by someone capable of delivering what the religion of the older covenant of Moses could only prefigure. He is,

8. R.P. Gordon, 'Better Promises: Two Passages in Hebrews against the Background of the Old Testament Cultus', in W. Horbury (ed.), *Templum Amicitiae: Essays on the Second Temple Presented to Ernst Bammel* (JSNTSup, 48; Sheffield: JSOT Press, 1991), pp. 434-49 (436-37).

nevertheless, conscious of the possibility of the Christian adherent, in an era of non-fulfilment of eschatological hope and in the absence of more tangible cultic arrangements than Christianity provided, coming to conclusions about its inadequacy to deal with his or her fundamental spiritual needs. This is challenged already in the proem in 1.1-4 with its high Christology predicated upon the claim that God 'has spoken' finally and conclusively in the divine Son. The term 'son of God' was freely enough used in ancient times, as the discussion in Jn 10.31-39 illustrates, and it appears to be part of the author's endeavour in early *Hebrews* to show that the term 'son of God' can have more than one significance, and that even angels so denominated in Scripture do not compare with the unique divine Son acknowledged by Christian faith (e.g. 1.5). Sonship also features in the author's contrasting of Moses and Christ in 3.1-6, except that they are described as having the status of servant and son, respectively, in God's household. Of the remaining references to Christ as the 'Son of God', I have already noted that those in 6.6 and 10.29 are specially weighty, being intended to inculcate in the recipients some sense of the majesty of the one whom they or some of their number were tempted to disregard.

The author's conviction about the sufficiency of Christ is also in evidence when he deals with Christ's high-priestly role in chs. 9–10, where he speaks not only of 'good things to come' (10.1) but also of 'the good things that have come' (9.11). In the commentary on this latter text, as also at a number of other points, it is suggested that the author is addressing a problem of perceived 'cultic deprivation' on the part of the 'Hebrews'. The suggestion obviously works better if we assume that the letter was written to Jewish-Christians, but the possibilities do not end there. Even if the addressees were originally Gentile and familiar principally with Gentile temple cultuses, we should have to allow that the writer assumes on their behalf such an acquaintance with, and respect for, the religious institutions of Israel as to make them sensitive to 'cultic deprivation' in that particular context. The 'good things that have come' (cf. 9.11) noticeably revolve around the concept of Christ as his people's great high priest even more than his claim to the status of divine Son. This, as Lane has noted,[9] has strongly pastoral motivation, since it is in his role as high priest to his followers that Christ is engaged on their behalf, both in the punctiliar act of his self-offering and in his regular sustaining of them. When 5.8-10 says concessively that although

9.   Lane, *Hebrews 1–8*, p. cxliii.

Christ was a Son he learned obedience and was designated by God as a high priest the transition in the argument from Sonship to priesthood is well under way (cf. already 4.14). There are references thereafter to Christ as 'Son' but not as part of any extended discussion (cf. 6.6; 7.3, 28; 10.29).

The author also seems to be addressing the problem of cultic deprivation when he refers on several occasions to things that Christians 'have' in, or because of, Christ. In all but the last of the references to be cited the verb *echein* ('have') is used, whether as participle or finite verb, to express this idea. In Christ the 'Hebrews' have a 'great high priest' (4.14), and as those who have fled to take hold of God's proffered hope they have this hope as an anchor of the soul (6.19). In 8.1 it is again asserted that they have a high priest, now described as 'seated at the right hand of the throne of the Majesty in the heavens'. According to 10.19 they have confidence 'to enter the sanctuary'—by which is meant the objective right of access (see the commentary)—on the basis of Christ's self-offering, while in 10.34 they have something better and more durable than the temporal belongings lost because they had been victimized as Christians. Even 12.1, in saying that they have a great cloud of witnesses surrounding them as they run the race of Christian endurance, may be said to contribute to the theme. The final statement as to what the addressees 'have' calls for special attention because it not only claims that they 'have an altar' but also asserts that access to this altar is denied those who 'officiate in the tent' (13.10). Having made this much of the idea of possession, and even non-possession, the author makes a final assertion that explains the need for the others, namely that in this world Christians *do not have* a 'lasting city' (13.14). In the commentary I have also noted the possibility that the statement in 4.9 that there remains a sabbath rest for the people of God may speak to the question of what Christians have, inasmuch as it too makes an assertion about what is in store for those such as the 'Hebrews' who do not 'possess' the institution of sabbath but who may experience the realization of that to which the sabbath pointed. The section on sabbath rest in 3.7-4.11 is, strictly speaking, talking about 'sabbath rest' as assured to Christian faith rather than as fully entered upon here and now, for the reason that the writer wishes to remind the recipients of the moral challenge that confronts them. This is entirely appropriate to a section whose business is parenesis, admonishing and encouraging the 'Hebrews' to adhere to the faith and reap the rewards: 'Therefore, while the promise of entering his rest is still open, let us take care that none of you should seem to have failed to reach it' (4.1); 'Let us therefore make every effort to enter that rest, so that no one may fall through such disobedience as theirs' (4.11).

4. Communicating the Message

Just as the idea of divine speaking is important to the author of *Hebrews* so he himself wishes to come across as a speaker rather than a writer. The vocabulary of 'writing' is not much in evidence, and even in 13.22 where he says that he has 'written briefly' he calls his letter a 'word of exhortation', for which expression the synagogal address so described in Acts 13.15 provides the sole direct New Testament parallel. More typically he refers to himself as 'speaking': 'Even though we speak in this way, beloved' (6.9; cf. 2.5; 5.11; 9.5; 11.32). It is rather to be expected, then, that rhetorical features are introduced freely, and sufficiently to suggest acquaintance with the rhetorical conventions of the Graeco–Roman world. Even so, as the debate as to whether *Hebrews* represents deliberative or epideictic rhetoric shows, this author cannot so easily be pigeon-holed. Anaphora, hyperbaton, the rhetorical question, inclusio and the catch-word are among the devices that he summons up. These and other rhetorical conceits are introduced to help in the business of suasion, which is what rhetoric and *Hebrews* are all about, but they are not all and equally the special preserve of the orator.

The author has a liking for the first person plural, which he uses as if seeking to identify himself with his addressees as far as possible (cf. 2.1-4; 4.14-16). He does address them directly when referring to their circumstances and their previous experiences (cf. 6.9-12; 10.32-34), and when expressing his anxiety lest any of their number should lose their way (cf. 3.12; 12.15-16), yet even when he uses such direct second person address he can wind up with an optimistic first person expression of confidence: 'But we are not among those who shrink back and so are lost' (10.39); 'Therefore, since we are receiving a kingdom that cannot be shaken, let us give thanks' (12.28). Occasionally he addresses the 'Hebrews' as 'brothers' (NRSV 'brothers and sisters'; e.g. 3.1, 12), but no more than does Paul—to cite the obvious comparison—in his letters. Some have concluded from the style of the letter that it originated as a homily or was written down in the style of a homily, in which case the extant letter represents the homily-form with a personal postscript appended in 13.22-25 (though there are also personal references in earlier verses). Some of the homiletic features proposed, however, live happily well away from homilies, and it is probably wiser to allow that *Hebrews* contains homiletic features without itself being a proven homily. There is not, in any case, an abundance of evidence as to how homilies were constructed in the period when the letter was written.

The Bible of the writer of *Hebrews* was the Greek Septuagint version of the Old Testament, though this does not mean that his quotations always conform to extant Septuagintal readings, as Howard has well demonstrated.[10] The importance of the Old Testament in the development of the writer's thesis is paramount. It is arguable, indeed, that the whole letter is constructed around a series of Old Testament texts quoted and discussed at appropriate points throughout the letter. The main texts so treated are Ps. 8.4-6 (cf. 2.6-8); Ps. 95.7b-11 (cf. 3.7-11); Ps. 110.4 (cf. 5.6; 7.17, 21); Jer. 31.31-34 (cf. 8.8-12); Ps. 40.6-8 (cf. 10.5-7); Hab. 2.3-4 (cf. 10.37-38) and Prov. 3.11-12 (cf. 12.5-6). The importance of the Old Testament for the author is illustrated almost at the beginning of the letter when he presents his heptad of quotations in demonstration of the uniqueness of Christ's divine Sonship (1.5-13). Some of his exegetical procedures, such as his appeal to *a fortiori* argumentation (cf. 2.1-4), are part of the common currency, while his application of something akin to the *gezerah shavah* ('equal law') hermeneutical rule is more typical of rabbinic interpretation. This latter is in evidence in 4.3-5 where the author is able to develop his argument on the basis of the presence of a word for 'rest' in both Gen. 2.2 and Ps. 95.11. In this case two different, though synonymous, Hebrew roots are involved; the Septuagint, however, uses the same root in the two verses and so facilitates the comparison. On occasion the writer makes his point by exploiting the precise form of the Greek text known to him, even where, from a modern perspective, it is in obvious disagreement with the standard Hebrew version. At 10.37 he finds the Septuagint of Hab. 2.3 highly congenial as he talks about 'the coming one', which reading he has helped on its way with his addition of the definite article, while his argument in 12.5-11 depends somewhat on the variant Greek text of Prov. 3.12, which speaks of God's disciplining the children whom he receives and so allows the author to interpret this of God's disciplinary ways with Christian believers.

10. G. Howard, 'Hebrews and the Old Testament Quotations', *NovT* 10 (1968), pp. 208-216.

The author believes that he is living in the end times, and this possibly accounts for the minor switch from 'that generation' to 'this generation' in his quotation at 3.10 (*pace* NRSV). This is more obviously the case at 10.37 where a phrase from Isa. 26.20 ('in a very little while') is imported to increase the sense of imminence in what is basically a quotation from Hab. 2.3. In other cases where *Hebrews* differs from known biblical tradition we may suspect that the writer is influenced by post-biblical interpretation, as in the additional matter in his summary of Exod. 24.3-8 in 9.19, or that he is adapting his form of words to promote his pastoral aim, as in his reference to Christ's prayer to be saved from death in 5.7. His linking of Ps. 2.7 and 2 Sam. 7.14 as christological prooftexts in 1.5 can find a parallel of sorts in their inclusion in the Qumran messianic anthology 4Q174 1.10-19. At a couple of points his interweaving of text and interpretation reminds us of the *pesher* method used in the Qumran biblical commentaries. So at 2.9 he works his explanatory glosses in with elements of Ps. 8.5: 'But we see Jesus *made (for) a little (while) lower than angels* because of the suffering of death *crowned with glory and honour* so that by the grace of God he might taste death for everyone.' This very process of interweaving may account for a difficulty in the text, namely that the concluding clause 'so that by the grace of God...' comes after the reference to Christ's being crowned with glory and honour. The apparent hysteron proteron here may simply be a function of the exegetical method used. A similar, though not identical, exegetical procedure is involved at 3.12-13 where elements of Ps. 95.7-11 are repeated following the full quotation of the psalm section in the preceding verses.

5. Hebrews and Judaism

Hebrews is the only New Testament document to use the word 'better'—which it does on several occasions—in making comparisons between Christianity and Judaism, and to the disadvantage of the latter. The epistle is, in current parlance, 'supersessionist'. However, whereas it is a commonplace in the history of Christian exposition of the Old Testament to treat its narratives, institutions and characters 'typologically', as if they contained outline elements of New Testament doctrines that they prefigured, *Hebrews* is much more subtle and varied in its approach. At times the writer indulges in typology, but even in such a section as 3.7–4.11 much more is involved, and not least some hard pressing of the logic of Ps. 95.7-8 in a quite untypological way. His fundamental distinction between earthly and heavenly, as well as between past and present, also makes 'typology' a complex issue in *Hebrews*. At some other points he simply takes the Old Testament to be referring directly to Christ, as in some of his quotations in ch.1.

Often he writes in the contrastive mode, viewing the practices of the Israelite cultus and the hopes that it engendered as having been superseded by something of greater value and efficacy. If this can be included under the heading of typology[11] then it requires a separate subheading, not only for the sake of clarity as far as *Hebrews* is concerned but also for the benefit of those contemporary interpreters of the Old Testament who favour typologies of a *comparative* type, even though these reduce the Hebrew text to christological jejuneness and do scant justice to the variegatedness of the detail and the message of the original. Not surprisingly, the author's treatment of the figure of Moses inclines towards the contrastive mode. Moses, he allows, was a faithful servant of God, but, as already noted, his very servant status becomes the point of contrast with Christ the divine Son in 3.1-6. Moreover, Moses is subordinated to Christ in the sense that the order over which he presided is said to have prefigured the era of the Gospel (3.5). When Moses appears in the honours list of the faithful in ch. 11 it is not only as the leader of the children of Israel from slavery to freedom; the writer rather pointedly brings him into association with Christ in the striking assertion that he chose 'abuse suffered for the Christ' in preference to the treasures of Egypt (11.26).

Just as it is a feature of *Hebrews* that the new order inaugurated by Christ is seen as 'better' than what preceded it (e.g. 7.19, 22; 8.6; 9.23; 10.34; 11.40; 12.24), so the author is concerned to show up limits and deficiencies in the old order. This is specially evident in his treatment of the giving of the law and in his discussion of the Day of Atonement, in chs. 9-10. Thus in order to heighten the contrast between law and Gospel he represents the law-giving at Sinai as having come through the mediation of angels (2.2). This increased role for angels at Sinai is a feature of 'intertestamental' literature and is reflected in Acts 7.38 and Gal. 3.19, so that our author cannot be accused of innovative reductionism. On the other hand, when he returns to the subject in 12.25 he is apparently referring to God as he talks of 'the one who warned them on earth' (a reference to Moses is less likely). In 2.1-4 law is subordinated to Gospel in the course of an *a fortiori* argument based

---

11. So Lane, *Hebrews 1-8*, p. cxxiii.

on the participation of angels at Sinai and on the involvement of 'the Lord himself' in the first proclamation of the Christian message. In 12.25 it is the location of the divine speaker—communicating on earth when the law was given but speaking from heaven in the Gospel—that is regarded as decisive, though there are texts in the Old Testament that see 'Sinai speech' as communication from heaven (see Exod. 20.22; Deut. 4.36, where a form of 'bilocation' is in evidence: 'From heaven he made you hear his voice to discipline you. On earth he showed you his great fire, while you heard his words coming out of the fire.').[12] The reductionist intent of the author provides the simple explanation for this atomistic treatment of the giving of the law.

When discussing the significance of the Day of Atonement in relation to sin and its expiation our author also reveals reductionist tendencies as he limits the efficacy of the Day to dealing with sins of ignorance. Its ritual, he says, cannot affect the conscience of the worshipper, dealing only with 'food and drink and various baptisms' (9.9-10). The language of Leviticus 16, on the other hand, invests the Day of Atonement with more wide-ranging powers. The high priest is said to make atonement for the most holy place 'because of the uncleannesses of the people of Israel, and because of their transgressions, all their sins' (v. 16), and when he lays his hands on the head of the live goat 'for Azazel' he confesses over it 'all the iniquities of the people of Israel, and all their transgressions, all their sins' (v. 21). Finally, the purpose of these atonement rituals is 'to make atonement for the people of Israel once in the year for all their sins' (v. 34; cf. v. 30). It was certainly understood in the postbiblical period that the ritual of the Day of Atonement affected more than merely ritual matters: 'Repentance atones for minor transgressions against both positive and negative commands while for graver sins it suspends punishment until the Day of Atonement comes and effects atonement' (*m. Yom.* 8.8; cf. *b. Ker.* 7a). No doubt the writer of *Hebrews* would have defended his reductionism, and along the lines suggested in 10.3 where the old rituals are said to act as a reminder of sin every year. For him the desideratum was a sacrifice dealing in a once-and-for-all way with the problem of the human conscience, and seen in that light the Day of Atonement seemed to deal more in shadow than in substance.

At the same time, we can hardly over-emphasize the writer's high

---

12. Cf. I. Wilson, *Out of the Midst of the Fire: Divine Presence in Deuteronomy* (SBLDS, 151; Atlanta, GA: Scholars Press, 1995), pp. 66-73.

regard for the Old Testament writings as 'Scripture', and as testimony to Israel's authentic encounter with the divine. He believed that God had spoken to 'the fathers' (1.1), and he invested the laws of Sinai with as much authority as would any Jewish believer (2.1-2). Much of *Hebrews* is extended reflection on Old Testament texts, and the supersessionism that is a feature of the book is based on several passages from which the author deduces that the Christian Gospel as adumbrated in the Hebrew scriptures was part of the original plan of God for the world. His use of Pss 8.4-6; 40.6-8; 95.7b-11; 110.4; and Jer. 31.31-34 to show the extent of that plan makes, in almost every case, an original contribution to the New Testament's interpretation of the texts in question. From Ps. 110.4 he seeks to prove that the Old Testament itself knows a form of priesthood distinct from the Levitical order (7.1-28), from Jer. 31.31-34 that the prophet looked forward to a new covenant which by the generosity of its terms would eclipse its Mosaic predecessor (8.7-13), and from Ps. 40.6-8 that the doing of God's will is more acceptable to him than the offering of animal sacrifices (10.5-10). In this last case he could, indeed, have summoned other witnesses, both biblical and extra-biblical, to show that the insight was neither novel nor uniquely Christian, except insofar as he held that it was the perfect obedience and self-offering of Christ that made the system of animal sacrifices redundant. With Jer. 31.31-34 he had especially pliant material since this is a straight-forward prediction within a prophetic book—without specific messianic reference—of a major new religious and spiritual initiative such as answered to no obvious historical development to date. What all this implied for the author was that the Old Testament contains the seeds of its own supersession. His texts are not the usual ones that predicted, or that seemed to predict, the coming of a messiah to Israel. The Jewish messianic concept could be expressed in a non-supersessionist way, and he wanted to go further than mere messianism.

There is no point in trying to deny the charge that *Hebrews* is supersessionist. Yet 'charge' is neither a very significant nor a very appropriate word to use in a discussion like this. First we should note that the author's standpoint is that of someone arguing from within the faith continuum that he himself traces back to Abel in early Genesis. In a sense what he is offering is 'in-house' criticism, even if he has to conclude that the corollary of Christian faith is a movement outward from the 'camp' of Jewish religion (13.13). He was, after all, heir to a tradition that has the most strip-tearing of prophetic critiques of the people of Israel embedded in its scriptures. This has also to be borne in mind when other parts of the New Testament are being assessed for possible anti-Jewishness. Even the Fourth Gospel, often ill-regarded in this respect, has Jesus declare to a Samaritan woman that 'salvation is from the Jews' (Jn 4.22). Secondly, we should note that *Hebrews* does not attack Judaism by suggesting that the prophesied demise of the temple system would represent God's judgment upon it. He may have thought along those lines, but he noticeably does not express the thought in his reference to the imminent disappearance of what was 'obsolete and growing old' (8.13). It is Christian apostates whom he warns of the danger of being 'on the verge of being cursed' (6.8). If, as many hold, *Hebrews* dates from after the destruction of the temple in 70 CE the author's restraint in his criticisms of 'the old order' is the more significant.

One good reason for not being defensive on behalf of *Hebrews* in this matter of supersessionism is that *both* Judaism and Christianity are supersessionist in relation to the Old Testament, both having turned their backs on forms of worship that involve the satisfaction of the deity by means of animal sacrifices. As I have noted, the view had already been expressed within the Old Testament that animal sacrifices count for little with the creator of the earth (cf. Ps. 50.7-15). Nevertheless, there is no indication that there was any impetus towards abolition of the sacrificial cultus of the temple during the Second Commonwealth, notwithstanding the occasional repetition of the original insight by Philo and others who were at some intellectual, as well as physical, distance from the world of the Jerusalem temple or were in outright opposition to current practice there.[13] It was the destruction of the temple by the Romans that brought animal sacrifice to an end. *Hebrews*, it could fairly be claimed, is exemplary as a supersessionist text for the way in which it argues its case without rancour or abuse. If 13.9 is one of the texts that come nearest to being specific about the practical issues that worried the author as he thought of his friends the 'Hebrews', it comes across as a strikingly restrained expression of disagreement: 'it is well for the heart to be strengthened by grace, not by regulations about food, which have not benefited those who observe them'.

It would be regrettable if I were to round off this section without some comment on shared interests and insights as between Judaism and Christianity. A single example relating to the central issue of sin-cleans-

13. Cf. Philo, *Plant.* 126-69; *Spec. Leg.* 1.267-72; 1QS 9.4-5; 10.14.

ing will illustrate how even in diversity there is sharing of insight. In the commentary on 9.14 I note Jewish and Christian perspectives on 'works that lead to death' and the means by which reparation is made for them. We find that the division of sins into the two categories of Num. 15.22-31—sins of ignorance and high-handed offences—is constructive for both traditions, and that the challenge is to find an effective means of dealing with the high-handed category. In some Jewish sources repentance achieves the desired end, as is indicated in a saying associated with the name of Resh Lakish: 'Great is repentance, for deliberate sins are accounted as sins of ignorance' (*b. Yom.* 86b). A similar idea is expressed in the Targum to Hab. 3.1 where it is observed that the sins of the wicked can be treated like sins of inadvertence 'if they return to the law with a perfect heart'. What is so attractive about these statements is their conception of God as willing even to override his standards of justice in order to reinstate those who have wilfully disregarded his laws. *Hebrews* also regards repentance as essential to the transaction (cf. 6.1), but attributes the efficacy to Christ's sacrifice. Both approaches assume a large measure of divine mercy in circumstances where it is not deserved.

6. Date of Composition

The dating of New Testament books on the basis of purely internal evidence tends to be as difficult as it generally is with texts and translations from antiquity. In the case of *Hebrews* there are definite historical references, though none of them is sufficiently specific as to provide a clinching argument for the dating of the epistle. Even the epilogue in 13.22-25 contrives to be both specific and uninformative at the same time. The clear dependence of *1 Clem.* 36.2-5 gives a *terminus post quem* of about 120 CE, on current datings of 1 Clement, but most would have surmised that much without the help of Clement. It is clear that the author and his addressees had not encountered Christ during his public ministry, but had been instructed in the Gospel from 'those who heard him' (2.3). Nevertheless, that does not require that much time had passed before they themselves became Christians. Nor does the rebuke in 5.12 that the 'Hebrews' had been Christians long enough for them to have become teachers tell us very much about dating. The passage of a decade or two would satisfy both these statements as comfortably as would a longer period. The reference to an earlier phase of persecution affecting the addressees (see 10.32-34) is initially more promising, but would become significant only if more were known about the persecution. In 12.4 the 'Hebrews' are reminded that they had not yet 'resisted to the point of shedding your blood', which, if interpreted in a literal way, means that, whatever their earlier privations, these had not been crowned with martyrdom for any of their membership. Such persecution could have occurred almost anywhere, but the popularity of the conjectured Roman destination for the letter merits the observation that a *pre-*70 CE dating would require that this earlier phase of persecution took place in advance of the Neronian martyrdoms beginning in the mid-60s CE, or that *Hebrews* was written to a section of the Roman church that had just escaped the worst of the Neronian persecutions, while still having experienced, at some earlier point, hardship of the kind described in 10.32-34.

In the dating of Jewish and Christian documents from the first century CE the presence or absence of references to the watershed event of the destruction of Jerusalem and its temple in 70 CE can prove significant. On the face of it *Hebrews* might seem to offer a 'better hope' in this regard, since so much of its argumentation has to do with forms of worship that came to an end in 70 CE and that have never subsequently been reinstituted. In this connection the author's use of the present tense in description of Jewish cultic practices associated with the tabernacle (or tent of meeting) invariably comes in for comment, but often only to be dismissed in the light of clear instances in other writers of the present tense being used after 70 CE to describe already defunct rituals at the Jerusalem temple. Potentially more significant than this, however, is the claim that the Greek tenses are not fundamentally temporal, and that their 'temporality' has to be decided on the basis of other factors in the contexts in which they occur.[14] It has also been argued that the author's choice of the tabernacle and not the temple (whether first or second) as the basis for his contrasts between Judaism and Christianity means that he had no interest in the temple or in contemporary practice. This is not quite contradicted by the presence of postbiblical elements in his account of the tabernacle system. These are few and none too significant; nevertheless their inclusion warns against assuming too readily that the writer was not at all concerned with the Second Temple

14. See S.E. Porter, 'The Date of Composition of Hebrews and Use of the Present Tense-Form', in S.E. Porter, P. Joyce and D.E. Orton (eds.), *Crossing the Boundaries: Essays in Biblical Interpretation in Honour of Michael D. Goulder* (BIS, 8; Leiden: E.J. Brill, 1994), pp. 295-313.

and its rituals. If he chose to deal with the question of the contemporary Jewish cultus somewhat obliquely by means of a critique of the tabernacle and its worship we should not fault him for obliqueness when we might so readily have castigated him for anti-Jewishness if he had conducted his argument in some more direct manner.

The use in *Hebrews* of the present tense in description of the tabernacle system is therefore a fraught issue, and not much may be made of it. At the same time, we must avoid the danger of tying the author's hands to the extent that his text is made to sound odd and ill-judged rhetorically, as risks being the case at a couple of points in his letter if a post-70 CE date is insisted upon. In the two references that we are going to consider it is what the competing interpretations do to the text in respect of its sense and its rhetoric that interests us. In both references the passing up of what could have been a decisive argument is also involved, if indeed the Jerusalem temple had already been destroyed at the time of writing.

First, in 8.4 it is suggested that, in contrast with his recognition in the heavenly sphere as a priest 'in the succession of Melchizedek', Christ would not have been a priest on earth since there were already those whose task was to offer the sacrifices prescribed in the law of Moses. The verse as usually interpreted is referring to Christ in his heavenly session, and it therefore has a contemporary reference: Christ had been on earth, and the point of the statement derives from the author's belief that at the time of writing he was in a different realm. If so, to interpret the second half of the verse, referring to the activity of priests on earth, in a purely generalizing, timeless way is to mix the categories of the general and the specific within the one verse. The mere invocation of the 'general principles' explanation of the tenses does not solve all the difficulties and so, while acknowledging the superior insights of Harold Attridge into *Hebrews* generally, I am left a little dissatisfied by his footnote to this verse: 'The present tense of the participle, and of the verb in the next verse, implies nothing about the existence of the Levitical system in the author's day. Hebrews argues on the level of general principles founded on the timeless legislation of the Torah.'[15]

There is a further complication, and potentially an end to the discussion, if we feel bound to go along with Lane's translation of the

---

15. H.W. Attridge, *The Epistle to the Hebrews* (Hermeneia; Philadelphia: Fortress Press, 1989), p. 219 n. 36.

protatic clause with which 8.4 begins: 'So if he had been on earth (he would not be a priest)'.[16] Grammatically this is unexceptionable; Lane categorizes the full construction as 'a second-class conditional sentence that expresses an unreal (contrary-to-fact) or unfulfilled condition'.[17] Alford, however, had previously cited the subsequent present tenses in vv. 4-5 as grounds for translating by 'if he were',[18] the rendering represented in many English versions (e.g. AV, REB, NIV, NRSV). If the English pluperfect 'had been' were required the sense would not be good, since, of course, Christ *was* on earth during the period that is represented in *Hebrews* by the tabernacle, and for the comment to have meaning the scope of its reference would have to be confined to the period prior to the first century CE, which is just the kind of limitation that the writer is supposed to be avoiding in his regular use of the present tense in connection with Old Testament ritual.

The second reference that seems to involve the author of *Hebrews* in a self-denying ordinance—if we were to assume a post-70 CE dating—is 10.2, where he asks whether the sacrifices instituted under the Old Testament law would not have ceased to be offered if they were capable of perfecting those who offered them 'since the worshippers, cleansed once for all, would no longer have any consciousness of sin'. If they successfully dealt with the problem of sin, he suggests, they should have been discontinued at some point. If we were to assume for the sake of argument that the Roman destruction of Jerusalem had taken place at the time of writing this would be a strange turn of phrase for our author to use, even if the events of 70 CE do not answer to the kind of honourable retirement that he thinks would have been appropriate for an ultimately successful cultus. The wording may at the least be considered injudicious if the verse was actually written at a time when the offering of sacrifices in Jerusalem actually *had* ceased.

Since it seems likely to this writer that *Hebrews* is arguing that the Christian Gospel represents the fulfilment of expectations cherished within the ancestral faith of some at least of the addressees, the question

16. Lane, *Hebrews 1-8*, p. 199.
17. Lane, *Hebrews 1-8*, p. 201; cf. also Porter, 'The Date of Composition', p. 309.
18. 'not, "*had been*", though grammatically it might be so: the pres. part. *ontōn*, which follows, and *latreuousi*, continuing it, shew that this *ēn* is spoken of a continuing, not of a past hypothesis' (Alford, *The Epistle to the Hebrews*, p. 149 [commentary section]).

of supersessionism seems inevitably to arise (see above), in which case the absence of any clear reference to the destruction of the temple would be hard to understand if *Hebrews* is indeed a post-70 CE composition. This is the self-denying ordinance that the writer would have imposed upon himself, that would not be adequately explained by appeal to a 'first-principles-approach', and that is not required if the letter is dated before the destruction of the temple. Having said so much, however, I have to admit the slenderness of the internal evidence for the pre-70 CE composition of *Hebrews*. Contested explanations of a couple of verses such as have been discussed in this section are not much on which to build a theory of origins.

7. Inclusive Language

Since *Hebrews* several times refers to the recipients of the letter as *adelphoi* (cf. 3.1, 12; 10.19; 13.22), traditionally translated 'brethren' or 'brothers', and this term has been given a more inclusive sense in the most recent English versions, it will be useful to discuss the issue briefly. NIV generally represents *adelphoi* by 'brothers', while its inclusive language edition consistently uses 'brothers and sisters' in *Hebrews*, as commonly elsewhere. The preference in NRSV is for the inclusive 'brothers and sisters', normally with a footnote saying 'Gk *brothers*'. NRSV is not, however, completely consistent, and even in *Hebrews*, to go no further, strange things happen. At 10.19 *adelphoi* is represented by 'my friends', for no obvious reason. Also noteworthy is the treatment of *adelphoi hagioi* (lit. 'holy brothers') in 3.1, where NRSV chooses to join *hagioi* with the next phrase in the verse, thus producing 'Therefore, brothers and sisters, holy partners in a heavenly calling...' It would doubtless be wrong to assume that NRSV is so phrased as to avoid the expression 'holy brothers and sisters', but it is an unfortunate point at which to differ from the standard treatment of this verse, which, it may be noted, follows on particularly well from 2.11 ('For the one who *makes holy* [NRSV 'sanctifies'] and those who are *made holy* [NRSV 'are sanctified'] all have one origin. For this reason he is not ashamed to call them *adelphoi.*'). At Col. 1.2, which also closely links 'holy' with *adelphoi*, NRSV has 'saints and faithful brothers and sisters' (NIV 'holy and faithful brothers'), which at any rate maintains a certain type of consistency.

The reasons for treating *adelphoi* as inclusive can be simply stated. First, the Greek words for 'brother' and 'sister' are distinguished only by their case endings, both building on the *adelph*-base. It was much easier, therefore, for Greek-speakers to comprehend the two genders in the culturally dominant masculine form than it is in English, in which 'brother' and 'sister' have separate derivations. Secondly, we have situations in the New Testament where *adelphoi* is associated with the Greek *andres* in the expression 'men (and) brothers', and in most of which a predominantly male audience is indicated. The references are all in Acts, and they relate to the assembled group in the upper room in Jerusalem (1.16), the crowd addressed by Peter at Pentecost (2.29), the apostles themselves when addressed by the crowd in Jerusalem (2.37) or by synagogue leaders (13.15), the Sanhedrin (7.2; 23.1, 6), the synagogue congregation at Pisidian Antioch (13.26, 38), the apostles and elders at the Jerusalem council (15.7, 13), the mob that attacked Paul in Jerusalem (22.1), and Jewish leaders in Rome (28.17). Notwithstanding the occurrence in the pre-Pentecost context of Acts 1.15-26, where women also feature quite prominently, this is clearly not a typically Christian coinage; its associations are strongly Jewish, and its origins may be among Jewish Hellenistic synagogal circles.[19] In short, the expression *andres adelphoi* serves to throw into relief the epistolary use of *adelphoi* elsewhere in the New Testament. Thirdly, the situation in Hebrew is basically the same as in Greek: the words for 'brother' and 'sister' come from the same root, being *'āḫ* and *'āḫôt* respectively), and so the relevance of a text like Deut. 15.12 to the present discussion becomes apparent. This verse begins 'If your brother' and then adds by way of definition, 'whether a Hebrew man or a Hebrew woman', where 'man' and 'woman' are represented simply by the masculine and feminine forms of the gentilic 'Hebrew'. Here the inclusive nature of 'brother' is actually spelled out for us in a legal prescription.

It is not part of a translator's job to edit Scripture so as to make it conform to contemporary taste or to personal preference. On the other hand, where there is not an exact lexical fit between the source and the target language it is possible to misrepresent the original text by using literal (so-called) equivalents that do not, in fact, convey the original intention at all precisely. In the present case it might even be possible to conclude that the translation of *adelphoi* by 'brothers' is less accurate than the expansionist 'brothers and sisters' of recent versions. Even such a text as Jas 3.1 (NRSV 'Not many of you should become teachers, my

19. Cf. F.F. Bruce, *The Acts of the Apostles: Greek Text with Introduction and Commentary* (Grand Rapids: Eerdmans, 3rd edn, 1990), p. 108.

brothers and sisters'), which in view of its cultural and ecclesiastical setting might seem to demand a masculine equivalent for *adelphoi*, does not undermine the general point being made here. Some occurrences of a commonly used term like this will naturally tend, more than others, towards the masculine end of the spectrum, depending on the general sense and circumstances.

Hebrews 1: The Son and the Sons

Introductory Comment

This chapter amounts to a grand statement by the author on the subject of the divine Sonship of Christ. There is no epistolary greeting or any other attempt to phase the subject-matter in; the author proceeds straight to his theme. The chapter consists of an exordium, rich in christological assertion (vv. 1-4), and of a catena of editorially linked quotations from the Old Testament chosen to demonstrate that, though angels may be called 'sons of God' in the Hebrew scriptures, Christ's Sonship is of a different order (vv. 5-14). He has, indeed, obtained a 'more excellent name' than theirs, as already stated in the exordium (v. 4). This latter, in that it represents Christ not only as the divine Son but also, by impli-cation, as his people's high priest (v. 3), anticipates the two major structuring themes in chs. 1-10. In keeping with the author's use of language generally, it is an elegant composition—which is all the more notable given the anxieties that he harboured on behalf of those addressed.

God has spoken (1.1-4)

That God who spoke anciently to the people of Israel has spoken again, and uniquely, in Jesus of Nazareth is the basic contention of *Hebrews*. This claim is immediately surmounted by others of comparable gravity, but the implications of the divine speaking continue to exercise the writer, not only in the warning section that attaches to ch. 1 (see 2.1-4), but right through to the 'peroration' with which chs. 1-12 are con-cluded: 'See that you do not refuse him who is speaking' (12.25). Thus the main discourse of this exhortation-by-epistle (i.e. chs. 1-12; cf. 13.22) is framed by assertion and adjuration based on the fact of the divine speaking. If originally there was an epistolary greeting, such as might be expected of a letter that ends in the manner of 13.22-25, this has given way before the exordium. But there may never have been such an introduction, since the writer may have wished to highlight this idea of the divine address by omitting the usual form of greeting. If the intended effect was to add solemnity to his presentation of his case, he was also aware of the need to appeal to his addressees in a more down-to-earth manner (cf. 13.22). Within the exordium, v. 1 functions as a rhetorical introit in which the sizeable alliteration (*polumerōs-polutropōs-palai-patrasin-prophētais*) sustains the idea of the fragmentariness and variegatedness of the previous divine speech. Indeed, the most awesome speaking of all in ancient times, at Sinai, will come to be seen as but speech 'by angels' (2.2) and a warning 'on earth' which the writer will contrast with God's warning 'from heaven' in the Christian era (12.25). This view of the divine communication as fragmentary and varied in its expression does not alter the author's conviction that God did indeed speak in previous times. His frequent use of Scripture to support his argument bears this out, and no more clearly than in vv. 5-13 of this chapter. The mention of 'the fathers' does not, unfortunately, help in identifying the 'Hebrews' or their circumstances, since New Testament writers may as easily associate the patriarchs and other Old Testament characters with Gentile Christians as with Jews and Jewish converts to Christianity. So Paul even speaks of 'our fathers' in his letter to the predominantly Gentile church in Corinth (1 Cor. 10.1).

The expression 'in these last days' in v. 2 reflects a two-age view of history, dividing between the historical continuum of the centuries and the end-time, which latter the writer believes to have been inaugurated by Christ (cf. 1 Cor. 10.11: 'These things...were written down to instruct us, on whom the ends of the ages have come.'). By New Testament times the prophets mentioned in v. 1 were being seen more and more as foretellers of these 'last days' rather than as proclaimers of a moral and social message to their contemporaries. (So, for example, there are only two quotations from Amos in the New Testament, one [5.25-27] relating to misdirected Israelite worship in the wilderness [cf. Acts 7.42-43] and the other [9.11-12] to the inclusion of the Gentiles in God's salvific plan [cf. Acts 15.16-17].) However, this author's eschatology is as much of the imminent as of the realized variety, to judge from such references as 8.13; 10.25, 37. He says that God's word has finally come through 'a Son'—the word is anarthrous, but how best to represent this in English is a moot point, and there is something to be said for 'his Son' as in AV, NIV. The position of superiority occupied by this Son in relation to the prophets before him suggests comparisons with the Gospels parable in Mk 12.1-12 and parallels (note 'last of all', 'son', 'heir', vv. 6-7). 'Son' will remain an important christological title in *Hebrews* (cf. 1.5, 8; 3.6; 4.14; 5.5; 6.6; 7.3, 28), though not determinative of all that befalls the figure so designated (see on 5.8).

It is possible to find seven clauses descriptive of Christ in vv. 2b-4, beginning with two counterbalancing clauses in v. 2 that express, in reversed chronological order, the alpha-omega relationship of this Son to the created order: he is heir of all things, and it was through him that the worlds were made (cf. Col. 1.16, 'by him and for him'). Since the chain of prooftexts in vv. 5-13 begins with Ps. 2.7, the following verse in the psalm ('Ask of me, and I will make the nations your heritage') may have been in the writer's mind when he described Christ as the one whom God had appointed 'heir of all things'. The influence of Old Testament and of Hellenistic Jewish depictions of wisdom as God's companion or coadjutor at creation may be discerned in the reference to Christ as the one through whom God made the worlds (cf. Prov. 8.27; Wisd. 10.1; Ecclus 24.1-12). It may already have been traditional to describe the cosmic significance of Christ in terms drawn from the portrayal of wisdom in such texts. Pre-existence, though not necessarily 'eternal Sonship', is implied here; for the latter see 7.3.

With its participial clauses the hymnic-sounding v. 3 recalls the doxological participles of some Old Testament passages which celebrate the power and glory of God, especially as seen in creation (see Amos 4.13; 5.8-9; 9.5-6). Such passages are sometimes envisaged as hymnic in origin, and the same could apply to v. 3 (cf. the similar construction involving relative pronoun and participle at Phil. 2.6, which is part of a section that is often explained as hymnic in origin). The first two of these participial clauses associate the Son with God in respect of nature or essence ('who being...') and action ('and upholding...'). Underlying both statements is the conception of Christ as the divine wisdom (see Prov. 8.22-31; Wisd. 7.25-26). The word *apaugasma* translated 'reflection' in NRSV may as easily be rendered 'radiance', which implies a closer association with the source of the glory. The more passive idea of 'reflection' finds its counterpart—and, for some, its translational justification—in the second assertion, that the Son is the 'exact imprint' (NRSV, for *charaktēr*) of the divine being: a perfect correlation exists between the divine essence and its expression in Christ. Moreover, the creation which God brought into being by his powerful word (cf. 11.3)—and in finished form according to our author in 4.3—is sustained in the same way by the Son (cf. Col. 1.17). (A similar function is attributed to the Logos by Philo, e.g., *Migr. Abr.* 6.)

What completes v. 3 follows logically neither from the premise of the divine nature of the Son nor from the intermediate role of Wisdom or the Logos as expressions of divine essence or activity. But Christ's making purification for sins sums up the author's 'theology of the cross'—there are few direct references to the cross in *Hebrews*, though see 6.6; 12.2—and anticipates the later argument of the letter, notably in chs. 9–10. The purification of the conscience from dead works, and not merely of the flesh from ritual defilement, is given in 9.13-14 as the distinguishing feature of Christ's self-offering on his people's behalf. And since the so-called 'Levitical' priestly order does not provide a model that corresponds sufficiently to the author's conception of the priest-hood of Christ, the final statement of v. 3 draws already upon the idea of the 'Melchizedek priesthood', according to which one of David's con-nexion might, as a priestly prince, sit on the right hand of the divine majesty (cf. Ps. 110.1, 4; Heb. 5.6, 10; 6.20; 7.1-28). This 'sitting down' thus combines the idea of a priest who has fulfilled his ministrations (see 10.12) with that of a victorious figure given a place of honour in the divine presence pending the submission of his foes (10.13; Lk. 22.69). In this way Christ's superior status even above that of the angels is inferred (cf. v. 13). The expression 'the Majesty on high' at the end of v. 3 (cf. 'the Majesty in the heavens', 8.1) is not just a circumlocution or periphra-sis for 'God', which term the author has already used in his opening sentence (v. 1), but is intended to emphasize the exaltedness of Christ following his priestly work of making purification for sins.

This exaltation is important to the author for, if the designation 'Son (of God)' elevates Christ above his prophetic precursors (vv. 1-2), the title would not by itself distinguish him from the angelic hierarchy, of whom the term 'sons of God' is used in the Hebrew scriptures (e.g. Job 1.6; 2.1; 38.7). At the same time, the superior name given to Christ clearly is that of 'Son' (cf. v. 5). But common use of a term does not pre-clude other uses involving special status or relationship (cf. Jn 20.17). And so modern christological debate can learn from Hebrews 1 where the use of the term 'son (s) of God' in biblical and postbiblical Jewish texts is concerned. Strictly speaking, the comparison in v. 4b is between the better name and the angels themselves, except that 'than they' (AV) is to be understood *per* brachylogy as 'than theirs'. As elsewhere in *Hebrews*—with the single exception of the benediction in 13.20—the resurrection of Christ is not mentioned in the exordium, being absorbed into the author's preferred theme of his heavenly exaltation.

Greater than Angels (1.5-14)

Following upon the (possibly) seven statements about the divine Son in vv. 2-4 comes a heptad of biblical quotations chosen to demonstrate the superiority of the Son over angelic beings. While all three divisions of the Hebrew canon are represented in the catena, five of the quotations are taken from the Psalter which, on the evidence of *Hebrews* as a whole, occupies a special place in the author's thinking. Why the superiority of Christ over angels should be given such prominent attention is more easily asked than answered. It is clear that the *a fortiori* argument of 2.1-4 must play some part in the answer. Having argued in this section that Christ is superior to angels the author issues his first warning about spiritual lethargy in those verses; for if the laws of Sinai announced through angelic mediation carried sanctions for disobedience the 'Hebrews' could be certain that disregard of a message first declared by the Lord himself involved a greater risk. The suggestion of a tendency on the part of the addressees to pay undue respect to angels and the hypothesis of an unacceptable type of 'angel christology' labour under the difficulty that there is no head-on confrontation with one or other tendency in the letter. On the other hand, v. 14 has implications for angel worship when it makes the point that angels are meant to serve humans and not vice versa (cf. also on 13.2). Again, a 'low' Christology which focused on the humanity of Jesus of Nazareth—made 'a little lower than the angels', according to 2.7—might well have called forth the kind of argument that is developed in the remainder of ch. 1, as also the exegesis of Psalm 8 which, in 2.6-9, identifies Christ as the true referent of the psalm and traces the 'Christ event' from humiliation through to exaltation.

The series of quotations begins and ends with the same kind of question, thus producing the first major inclusio in the letter (vv. 5, 13). In v. 5 the two quotations are from Psalm 2 and 2 Samuel 7 respectively, and both originally have to do with the kingship ideology of ancient Israel, in which the newly crowned king entered by an adoptive decree (cf. Ps. 2.7) into a relationship of special privilege and nearness to God. Thus the original significance of 'today I have begotten you' has nothing to do with the 'only-begottenness' of the Son as represented in other christological and trinitarian formulations, as the very inclusion of the word 'today' would in any case suggest. The importance of earthing such Old Testament quotations in their primary contexts is even more evident in the case of 2 Sam. 7.14a, quoted in the second half of v. 5. In its original setting the quotation, which in a sense epitomizes the

Davidic dynastic oracle and its dependent ideology in the Old Testament, refers to David's son Solomon who succeeded him on the throne and who built the temple in Jerusalem, as is indicated in the preceding verse (2 Sam. 7.13). The quotation expresses, in its original context, the relationship that was supposed to exist between God and Solomon as the first of David's descendants to rule in Jerusalem. But the same text goes on to make the cautionary point: 'When he commits iniquity, I will punish him with a rod such as mortals use, with blows inflicted by human beings' (NRSV). And there is no obviously christo-logical reference or potential here.

These first two texts in the catena in fact illustrate a couple of important points as regards prophecy, fulfilment and prooftexting between the two Testaments. The first is that prooftexting is sometimes best seen as a kind of shorthand for the underlying institutions and ordinances—like prophecy, kingship, priesthood, sanctuary and sacri-fice—that set in motion the expectations that the Gospel claims to fulfil. Secondly, Ps. 2.7 is given a messianic interpretation in *Pss Sol.* 17.26, while Psalm 2 and 2 Samuel 7 feature with other texts in a Jewish mes-sianic anthology from Qumran (4Q174[4QFlor] 1.10-19)—a point spe-cially to be borne in mind when citations later in Hebrews 1 give the impression of arbitrariness born of Christian apologetic necessity. The New Testament writers are quite often applying an already interpreted Bible to their own interpretative ends. The point of v. 5, therefore, is that a unique Father-Son relationship exists between God and Christ. By contrast, the old Hebraic term 'sons of God', when applied to angels, finds no corresponding use of 'father', in either Testament, in descrip-tion of God in relation to angelic beings.

The third quotation (v. 6), while resembling a line in the Septuagintal version of Ps. 97.7 ('Worship him all his angels'), more probably provides the sole Pentateuchal reference in the series, representing part of Deut. 32.43 in its Septuagintal form. Yet even this Pentateuchal connection may be indirect since the closest parallel is with the version of Deut. 32.43 that appears in the Greek Bible as Ode 2.43 where, instead of 'sons of God', as in Deut. 32.43(LXX), the Greek has 'angels of God', a reading more congenial to our author's present purpose. (A Hebrew manuscript reflecting a text corresponding to the expanded Septuagintal version of Deut. 32.43 was among the early finds at Qumran. Even so, the author of *Hebrews* will have made use of a Greek rendering.) It is of some interest that, not for the only time in the New

Testament's use of the Old, a text which originally refers to the God of Israel is referred by a New Testament writer to Christ. The first impression created by the word-order in the Greek ('When again he brings the firstborn into the world'), that the parousia is in the author's mind, is rightly resisted in modern translations such as NRSV and NIV. 'Again' almost certainly functions as in v. 5 to introduce a further quotation supportive of the author's argument. It is therefore at the *incarnation* of the 'firstborn' that the angels are bidden to worship him, just as, in Jewish tradition, the angels were commanded to pay homage to Adam when he was created (cf. F.F. Bruce, *The Epistle to the Hebrews*, p. 16). The title 'firstborn' may have been inspired by Ps. 89.27 ('I will make him [*sc.* the Davidic king] the firstborn'; cf. Rev. 1.5), but, more importantly, it follows naturally from the designation of Christ as 'Son' and it makes the point that even the incarnate Christ was the worthy recipient of angels' praise—however the temporary subordination of 2.9 may relate to this. Whether the reference betrays awareness of the story of the angels in the Lukan nativity account is impossible to judge (cf. Lk. 2.8-14).

The view that 'world' here refers to the 'world to come', or heavenly world, finds some support in 2.5 where *oikoumenē* is also used, except that there the author uses the full expression 'the world to come' to indicate his meaning. If this explanation of 'world' could be sustained we should probably have to think of God presenting the exalted Christ to the universe, and in particular to the angels for their adoration. Angels, the fourth quotation (v. 7; see Ps. 104.4) observes, have as their proper role the service of God within the created order. (In v. 14 they are called 'spirits in the divine service' [NRSV].) In this instance the Septuagintal translator has possibly engaged in 'reverse predication', since the Hebrew original may be making a somewhat different point, as is suggested by the context in which the quotation appears: 'Who makes winds his messengers, flames of fire his ministers'. The Greek rendering of the verse is certainly more amenable to the point that *Hebrews* wants to make.

As the correlative particles at the beginning of vv. 7 and 8 suggest, the quotation from Psalm 104 in v. 7 is offset by the citations from Psalms 45 and 102 in vv. 8-9 and 10-12. Psalm 45, composed for an Israelite king at the time of his marriage, goes so far as to address him in v. 6 as 'God', as is especially clear in the Septuagintal rendering, which is not so patient of the face-saving alternatives that are sometimes imposed upon the

Hebrew text. 'Mighty god' as an appellation of a Davidic monarch in Isa. 9.6 shows that Ps. 45.6, understood in its natural sense, is not a theological solecism within the Old Testament. In the present passage the contrast is, at least in part, between the elemental and ephemeral (winds, fire) and the eternal throne of the one addressed as 'God'. The vocative 'O God' may also occur in v. 9 ('therefore, O God, your God has set you above your fellows', REB), though this is less certain. While the 'companions' who fail to compare with the anointed one may be identified with the 'partners (also *metochoi*) in a heavenly calling', namely Christian believers, of 3.1, it is difficult to exclude altogether the idea of the Son being exalted above the angelic beings who are conspicuously featured in the chapter. The companions in the original setting of the psalm will have been the contemporaries, kingly and common, of the king who is being addressed.

The penultimate prooftext is Ps. 102.25-27, quoted in vv. 10-12. This is straightforward address to God as creator of the heavens and the earth—eternally existent, and transcendent in relation to the material universe which will one day be done away with. It is 'high' Christology indeed when these same words are directed to the Son, but already the foundation has been laid in the exordium, in the ascribing of the creation and sustaining of the universe to him. Moreover, the regular translation of the Hebrew tetragrammaton by *kurios* ('Lord') in the Septuagint makes for an easier association in the New Testament between Christ as 'Lord' and God himself.

The seventh quotation is introduced in almost identical manner to the first: 'To which of the angels has he ever said?' (v. 13; cf. v. 5). This is the first time that Psalm 110 is quoted in the letter, though the mention of the heavenly session of Christ in the exordium (v. 3) contains already an allusion to the psalm. In v. 3 it is simply stated that Christ 'sat down', whereas here this is shown to have been at the invitation of God himself. Like Psalm 2, Psalm 110 contains address, in the form of a divine decree, to an Israelite monarch reigning in Jerusalem. The king thus addressed is assured of ultimate victory over all his enemies. Psalm 110 clearly played a major part in early Christian messianological statements, to judge from the various citations and allusions scattered through the New Testament (e.g. Mk 12.35-37; 14.62; Acts 2.34-35; 7.55-56; 1 Cor. 15.25). The recognition of Christ as 'Lord' facilitates the use of the Old Testament text, for Psalm 110 begins, 'The LORD said to my Lord', and the author of *Hebrews* treats the verse as a direct address to the messiah.

Here, as Lane notes, he 'cites Ps 110:1 as part of the colloquy between God and the Son that the church on earth, as it were, overhears' (*Hebrews 1-8*, p. 32). Since the psalm also addresses the divinely-approved ruler as a priest in the succession of the pre-Israelite priest-king Melchizedek (v. 4), it has a decisive influence upon the second main phase of the argument in *Hebrews*, in relation to the superiority of Christ's priesthood over the Aaronic priestly order. In contrast with this picture of exalted supremacy in v. 14, the angelic company is described as 'spirits in the divine service' who have been sent forth from the divine presence—compare Gabriel's missions expressed also by *apostellein* in Lk. 1.19, 26—to assist those who have the status of 'heirs' in the era of salvation. A subordinate role is associated with angels, therefore, not only in relation to the Son, but also as regards the human beneficiaries of his saving work on their behalf.

In the first part of his discourse, then, the author has moved from observation on the partial revelation through divine speaking in the era of the Hebrew prophets to an assertion about the supremacy and finality of Christ, and thence to a demonstration of his case based on a heptad of quotations taken from the Hebrew scriptures. Some of the texts cited more obviously have God as speaker than do others; nevertheless the prior emphasis upon divine speaking in the exordium, reinforced by the strategically placed questions introducing the first and last quotations in the series, helps to create an impression of God as speaker throughout (cf. 'he says', vv. 6, 7). Moreover, the God who remains eternally 'the same' (v. 12) is regarded as being as much the speaker in the one era as in the next, even if the mode of communication changes.

Hebrews 2: The Son and the Children

Introductory Comment

The contrast between Christ and angels developed in ch. 1 becomes the basis, in the first instance, of a short parenetic section—the first of several such in *Hebrews* (cf. 3.7-19, etc.)—in which the author argues that to receive the Christian message of salvation is to incur a particular responsibility. He reverts to prooftexting and to further development of the Christ-angel argument in vv. 5-18, explaining in particular why in an angel-conscious environment the Christian message is about Christ's involvement with the human family rather than with angelic hierarchies.

So Great a Salvation (2.1-4)

The series of prooftexts (see 1.5-13) is suspended at this point (cf. vv. 6-8) so that the author may insert the first of several admonitions to his readers against reneging on the faith that they have professed. The conjunction which begins the section builds, not on the statement about the role of angels in 1.14, but on the basic thesis of ch. 1, namely, the superiority of Christ as 'Son' in relation to angels. Still the writer includes himself with his readers as those to whom God has spoken (cf. 'to us', 1.2); the formal distinction between author and reader comes later (see 3.7-13), though the first person plural cohortative recurs throughout the letter (see 4.1, 14, etc.) as the writer strives to encourage his readers to remain in the Christian fold. The danger highlighted here is not that of their outright rejection of Christianity but of losing by neglect what had been promised them through the Gospel. So the writer makes a point based on the tradition of angelic mediation of the law to Moses on Mt Sinai. He argues, in *a fortiori* fashion, that, since the Mosaic law was hedged about with sanctions and penalties, and the agents by which that law was communicated were but angels, those who had received a message coming directly from 'the Lord'—an uncommon designation of Christ in *Hebrews*, though see 7.14; 13.20—were specially accountable.

This mediatorial function of angels at Sinai is not a feature of the biblical narrative (though see Deut. 33.2 for their presence at the giving of the law), but later tradition specifically accorded them such a role and it is reflected in other New Testament passages (see Acts 7.38, 53, 'the law as ordained by angels'; Gal. 3.19, 'ordained through angels by a mediator'). We have already noted (see on 1.1-4) the relegation of 'Sinai speech' to warning 'on earth' (contrast 12.25) in order to support a distinction of the type set out here. That the laws of Sinai were binding (v. 2) was seen in the penalties that were attached and that were to be implemented by a grateful Israel. Though, famously, the Ten Commandments do not have attaching penalty prescriptions, the general tenor of the Sinai legislation was of law *and* punishment. The occurrence of *parakoē* (v. 2), translated 'disobedience' in NRSV, is appropriate in a section dealing with speech and its reception, since etymologically the word connects with the root used in vv. 1 (lit. 'things heard') and 3 ('those who heard'). With 'every transgression' (*pasa parabasis*) it forms an alliteration such as the author sometimes favours (cf. on 1.1). The nature of the salvation that the 'Hebrews' are in danger of neglecting is not defined, but it becomes apparent as the letter progresses. Whether the expression 'so great a salvation' implies a contrast with any other 'salvation' is unclear. It is possible that the deliverance of the exodus, prelude to the encounter with God at Sinai, suggested itself to the writer's mind at this point. The Christian message of salvation is said to have been 'declared at first through the Lord' (v. 3), which sets up a simple contrast with the word 'declared through angels' (v. 2) and exploits further the Christ-angel antithesis outlined in ch. 1. There is also verbal correspondence in vv. 2 and 3 in relation to the angelic message that was 'valid' (*bebaios*, v. 2) and the message that was 'attested' (*ebebaiōthē*, v. 3) by those who heard Christ.

The writer includes himself among those who had not been witnesses of the original Christian proclamation but who had benefited from eyewitness testimony. There had therefore been a 'mediation' between the authenticating Lord and the 'us' of the author and his addressees, but any parallel with Sinai in this respect is treated as merely incidental, since what is held to be decisive is whether the divine-human communication was basically direct (v. 3) or only indirect (v. 2). As his readers evidently could testify, the message about Christ had come to them 'with a demonstration of the Spirit and of power' (1 Cor. 2.4), taking the form of the threefold 'signs, wonders and various miracles' (v. 4) to which appeal was no doubt frequently made in early Christian apologetic (Acts 2.22; cf. Rom. 15.19). The author naturally expected that this kind of apologetic would be especially effective in 'in-house' situations, among those who subscribed to such a tradition of the miraculous within nascent Christianity, or who might even themselves have claimed to be witnesses of the miraculous. The same kind of appeal, but with sharper edge, was made by Paul to his Galatian converts, whose situation bore more than a superficial resemblance to that of the first readers of *Hebrews*. He asks the Galatians whether they have forgotten the authenticating sign miracles that had attended the preaching of the Gospel by him and his associates (Gal. 3.5). Such appeals to experience would certainly have been counter-productive if there had not been something of significance upon which the appeal could be mounted. The references to the Lord, God and the Holy Spirit in vv. 3-4 do not measure up to a full-blown trinitarian formulation. Grammatically, the reference to the Spirit in v. 4 qualifies as an objective genitive—though too much can be made of syntactical asymmetry when making judgments of this kind in relation to biblical texts.

The 'Proper Man' (2.5-9)

The argument of 1.13-14 is now resumed: the Son has been given his place of honour at the right hand of God, and sovereignty, as is now indicated, over 'the world to come'. According to the Septuagintal version of Deut. 32.8 the boundaries of the nations were fixed 'according to the number of the angels of God', while the affairs of the nations are represented in the book of Daniel as the concern of 'angel princes' (10.20-21; 12.1). The author, however, is concerned not with the present world-order but with that which lies beyond it. His prooftext is Ps. 8.5-7 (LXX) which, in its Masoretic and Septuagintal versions, is headed, 'A Psalm of David', but which is introduced here by the vaguish 'Someone has testified somewhere saying'. This relaxed attitude to authorial bylines is found elsewhere in *Hebrews* (see 4.4) and is paralleled in, for example, Philo. It is more characteristic of the Hebrew scriptures, but it is specially appropriate to a letter whose author has apparently dispensed with the usual epistolary greeting at the beginning in order to make a point about the importance of the divine speaking in history and in Scripture.

In Psalm 8 the psalmist expresses wonderment that the majestic creator has vested so much in mere mortals, to whom, indeed, he has given sovereignty over the rest of creation. This, at any rate, is the special status accorded humanity in Israel's creation traditions (see especially Gen. 1.26-28). Real life might, however, mock the ideal, as in Job's apparent parody of Psalm 8 or of something very like it:

> What are human beings, that you make so much of them,
>> that you set your mind on them,
> visit them every morning,
>> test them every moment? (Job 7.17-18)

For Job in his sufferings, God's is an oppressive presence, and the attention of the deity a harrowing liability. By comparison, the author of *Hebrews* seriously understates the situation: 'As it is, we do not yet see everything in subjection to them [*sc.* humans]' (v. 8). Since 'all things', according to the psalmist, were subjected to human authority, there is a clear discrepancy between what is and what was meant to be. The resolution is offered in v. 9 in an expanded paraphrase of Ps. 8.5 which, with its interleaving of Old Testament lemma and actualizing comment, recalls the *pesher* method of some biblical commentaries found among the Qumran scrolls. The following literalish translation has the Old Testament lemma in italics: 'But we see Jesus *made (for) a little (while) lower than angels* because of the suffering of death *crowned with glory and honour* so that by the grace of God he might taste death for everyone.'

For 'human beings' we are now asked to understand Christ, who has become one of their number and the restorer of their lost glory. Here he is introduced simply as 'Jesus', the first in a series of such references where it is chiefly his solidarity with the human family that is in mind (cf. 3.1; 4.14; 6.20; 10.19; 12.2; 13.12). Happily, for the author of *Hebrews*, the Septuagintal version of Ps. 8.5 does not say that God made humans 'a little lower than God', as in the Hebrew original, but that he 'made [them] a little (or 'for a little while') lower than angels'—for the ancient translator balked at making any such comparison between God and humans. The clause sequence in the verse suggests that the crowning preceded the suffering of death, as the 'last [i.e. eschatological] Adam' (cf. 1 Cor. 15.45) exercised on earth the sovereign authority that humanity itself had forfeited. This could be what the author intended, but the splicing of lemma and commentary may have produced a syntactical arrangement that does not fully represent the intended sense of the passage, which could be that the crowning came in consequence of Christ's entering into death on humanity's behalf.

There is another possible approach to these verses, according to which the author of *Hebrews* identifies the 'man' and 'son of man' of Psalm 8 with Christ from the outset. Verses 8b-9 would then be explaining why Christ is not visibly sovereign over the created order in the present era. The arguments are finely balanced and the difference ultimately insubstantial, since, whichever way we take it, the author plainly regards Christ as fulfilling the terms of Psalm 8. Because the expression 'son of man' as it occurs in v. 6 does not conform specifically to usage in the Gospels where the definite article is almost invariably used with both nouns (*ho huios tou anthrōpou*)—Jn 5.27, the sole exception, is influenced by Dan. 7.13(LXX)—Lane concludes that the author did not interpret the psalm occurrence christologically (*Hebrews 1-8*, p. 47). However, since the expression appears only in its quotation form in v. 6 the wherewithal for such a judgment seems not to exist. The 'direct reference' approach is, of course, difficult to sustain on the basis of inclusive renderings such as NRSV's 'human beings' and 'mortals'. (NRSV excludes it in any case by translating v. 8b, 'we do not yet see everything in subjection *to them*'.)

Perfecting the Priest (2.10-18)

The author now addresses more directly the apparent contradiction that is at the heart of his Christology. For how can one who is higher than angels become so involved with humans as to identify with them at their weakest point? In fact, it was fitting for God, he says, to proceed as he did. As a gracious creator God was acting consistently with both his character and his ultimate goal when he provided a 'pioneer of salvation' who was able to fulfil his original purpose in creation. Moreover, it is God the source and efficient cause of *all things absolutely* (v. 10; 'all things' in v. 8 is more circumscribed) who has determined on this paradox. In leading human beings to heavenly glory he has chosen to make Christ the 'pioneer' of their salvation 'perfect' through his experience of suffering. This 'perfecting' is explained as his being equipped to function not only as eschatological deliverer but also as present saviour of those who travel the road from earthly suffering to glory. In vv. 17-18 this will be stated in explicitly high-priestly terms (cf. already v. 11). The use of the verb 'make perfect' in the present context is probably to be traced back to references to priestly installation in the Old Testament where the Septuagintal *teleioun* translates the Hebrew verb 'fill' in the idiomatic expression 'fill the hand (of a priest)', that is 'consecrate' (e. g. Exod. 29.9, 29). Later, using similar terminology, the writer will focus his addressees' attention on Jesus as the inspirational 'pioneer and perfecter' of faith (12.2). By saying that God is bringing many sons to glory, v. 10 is making the point that, whoever the precise referent in vv. 7a-8, the purpose of the glorified Christ's involvement with humanity was to bring them to glory as well. There is also irony in this suggestion of God bringing 'many sons' to glory, given the distinction between the divine Son and the angelic 'sons of God' that underlies the argument in chs. 1–2: God is creating yet more sons! (Again, inclusive renderings such as 'children' and 'sons and daughters' would limit the interpretative options here; cf. on vv. 5-9 above.)

In v. 11 Christ's identification with his people is seen in terms of his high-priestly activity on their behalf, on which point the writer will have considerably more to say in his letter. The 'one who sanctifies' is, no doubt, Christ. While there are Old Testament texts that speak of God as the one who sanctified his people (e. g. Lev. 20.8; 21.15, in the so-called 'Holiness Code' in Lev. 17-26), the association of the work of sanctification with Christ would follow well from the reference to his having been 'made perfect' in v. 10, and would find support in 13.12 where it is he who 'suffered outside the city gate' in order to 'sanctify the people'. NEB's targumizing of the first part of the verse assumes a generalizing statement rather than a specific assertion about the common origin of the Son and the 'sons': 'For a consecrating priest and those whom he consecrates are all of one stock.' The implication here is of the common origin of a shared humanity. (REB 'he who consecrates and those who are consecrated are all of one stock' noticeably retreats to a more literal rendering, but at the cost of one of the more interesting interpretative ventures in its predecessor.) NRSV represents the more usual interpretation of 'are all of one', referring the 'one' to God: 'For the one who sanctifies and those who are sanctified all have one Father' (where the epexegetical 'Father' answers to 'sons' [NRSV 'children'] in v. 10). Occasionally the 'one' has been identified with Adam as primal man or with Abraham as the progenitor of the Hebrew people, but these are very tentative strikes, notwithstanding the reference in 11.12 to innumerable descendants derived from Abraham the 'one person'. The measure of Christ's identifying himself with the human family is seen, moreover, in his acknowledgment as 'brothers' (NRSV 'brothers and sisters') of those who are the object of his saving activity. He is not ashamed to do so, and, if there was any unworthy tendency on the part of the readers to be ashamed of the faith that they had professed, there may be here an implicit rebuke of their much less excusable demurring (cf. 11.16). And just as v. 12 appears to have an eschatological reference, so there may be a hint in v. 11 of Christ's reciprocating acknowledgment at his coming of those who have not been ashamed of him (cf. Mk 8.38). The use of 'brother' (and 'sister'; cf. Rom. 16.1; Jas 2.15) as title and form of address among the early Christians (cf. Mt. 23.8; Jn 20.17; Acts 9.17) will have derived some of its attractiveness from the conception of individual believers as brothers and sisters of Christ, as in the present passage.

It is appropriate that the one who 'is not ashamed' should be represented as speaking in the first person in the three Old Testament quotations given in vv. 12-13. The excerpting of the first from Psalm 22 was natural in view of the messianic associations of the psalm in the early church (e.g. Mk 15.34; Jn 19.24). Psalm 22, which sets out as a personal lament, switches dramatically from expressions of dereliction in vv. 1-21a to a celebration of the psalmist's deliverance from his troubles in vv. 21b-31. (The intervention of a [now unscripted] priestly-prophetic 'oracle of salvation' between the two parts of the psalm is one possible explanation; cf. Ps. 60.6-8 in this respect.) The appropriateness of the citation of v. 22 derives not only from its mention of 'brothers' but also from the occurrence, in the Septuagintal rendering of the verse, of *ekklēsia* ('congregation'), which in the New Testament commonly has the specifically Christian denotation of 'church'. That the quotation marks the beginning of the hymnic section of the psalm may also be considered appropriate in view of the special post-Resurrection associations of the term 'brothers' in the Gospels tradition (see Mt. 28.10; Jn 20.17; contrast Jn 15.15). In the remaining two quotations, both evidently taken from Isa. 8.17-18—2 Sam. 22.3 and Isa. 12.2 are possible sources for the first, but less likely given that the writer had Isa. 8.18 in mind for the second—Christ is held to speak in the person of the prophet Isaiah, who declares his trust in God at a time when his contemporaries have rejected his message and forced him into 'retreat' (v. 17). In the meantime the prophet and 'the children whom the Lord has given me'—each with a symbolic name (cf. Isa. 7.3; 8.1-4)—will remain as signs to a recalcitrant populace (v. 18). The 'children' in this second quotation from Isaiah 8 obviously are meant to correspond to the 'sons' of v. 10 here. By his choice of quotations from Psalm 22 and Isaiah 8, therefore, the author of *Hebrews* makes two points: that the addressees are brothers and sisters of Christ who has emerged, psalmist-like, from his sufferings into the joy of deliverance, and that their proper attitude, as they await the fulfilment of their hopes, is one of Christ-like trust in God.

The fact that the 'children' of v. 13 were ordinary 'blood-and-flesh' human beings forms the basis of a statement in vv. 14-15 about what Christ's death achieved, and about its subsequent high-priestly—we might almost say 'pastoral'—effects in vv. 17-18. In the first place, Christ's fully ('likewise') participating in the human state enabled him to enter into the domain of death and deactivate the one who had held humans in a life-long grip of fear. The basic idea is reflected in the Gospel saying about the binding of the strong man and the plundering of his house (cf. Mk 3.27). In this soteriology it is assumed that the conquest of death must happen 'from our [sc. the human] side', which is not an obvious precondition for the subjecting of death to the divine power. However, since the author holds that it is human complicity in sin that lends death its terror (cf. 9.27), the incarnation of Christ becomes a necessary part of the scheme of salvation. Already the purpose of Christ's coming has been defined as the tasting of death for everyone (2.9). Now that the specific issue of the fear of death has been raised, it is possible to detect a pastoral concern on the writer's part. Those addressed had met persecution with fortitude in the early part of their Christian experience (see 10.32-34), but such is the emphasis within 11.1-40 on the defeating of death in whatever form it presents itself, and so clear are the implications in 12.1-11 ('you have not yet resisted to the point of shedding your blood', v. 4; 'Should we not be even more willing to be subject to the Father of spirits and live?', v. 9), that it seems likely that the continuance of these Christians in their faith depended to some extent on the resolution of this issue. 'Slavery' in v. 15 stands in contrast with the theme of sonship, and of God-given sovereignty (cf. vv. 6-8), rather as in Gal. 3.26–4.7, where also the Abrahamic connection is invoked (cf. v. 16 here). In Galatians, however, it is not the fear of death that enthrals humanity but 'the elemental principles (*stoicheia*) of the world' (4.3), however these may be defined.

So it is affirmed in v. 16 that it was mere humans in all their weakness that Christ came to help (lit. 'take hold of'). There may be an intended contrast between the angelic state that he by-passed and the particularity of 'the descendants of Abraham'—that is, Christ was not just born into the human race but specifically into the Jewish family. In this such a text as Isa. 41.8-10 may have been influential: 'But you, Israel, my servant, Jacob, whom I have chosen, the offspring of Abraham, my friend, whom I took hold of (LXX *antelabomēn*; cf. *epilambanetai* here in v. 16)...'

For some writers the reference to Abraham invokes the idea of Christian believers as his spiritual heirs, characterized by his kind of faith, though the relevant texts elsewhere in the New Testament differ in that they are specific on the point (cf. Rom. 4.16-17; Gal. 3.29). Verse 17 introduces the first specific reference to Christ as high priest of his people, and here as elsewhere (cf. already v. 11) this assumes his complete solidarity with those whom he came to benefit. Only so, it is argued, can he be truly 'merciful' and 'faithful' in relation to those whom he represents. 'Faithful' here is probably double-duty, however, in that it includes the idea of the faithful priest serving before God, most notably in the making of expiation for sins. Indeed, according to the soteriology of *Hebrews* the continuing task of sustaining those who suffer (v. 18) depends for its effectiveness upon the punctiliar offering of the 'sacrifice of atonement' at Golgotha (v. 17). The reference to 'the people' (v. 17) reflects Old Testament texts dealing with priestly ritual performed on behalf of the people of Israel (see on 13.12, and cf. 5.3; 7.27; 9.7). Here it implies continuity between the 'people of God' in the Old Testament and Christian believers such as are addressed in this letter (cf. 1 Pet. 2.10).

Hebrews 3.1–4.13: God's House/God's Rest

Introductory Comment

The goal of Christ's suffering is expressed in the previous section as his becoming a 'merciful and faithful high priest' in God's service and on behalf of his people (2.17). Some reconfiguring goes on in 3.1, but in talking about 'Jesus the apostle and high priest of our confession' the author holds on to these two attributes of the ideal high priest. It is indeed possible to see the larger section 3.1–5.10 as a reverse-order treatment of them. The faithfulness of Christ in the discharge of his duties is the focus of 3.1-6, while the contrast there developed between Christ and Moses, as respectively 'Son' and 'servant' in God's 'household', becomes the basis for an admonitory section that runs from 3.7 to 3.19 and that also casts its shadow over the hortatory matter in 4.1-13. (Since 4.14 corresponds to 3.1 as a possible inclusion it is arguable that the section should be defined so as to include 4.14. However, in view of the close connection between 4.14 and 4.15 the compromise of treating 4.14 as resumptive and transitional is preferable.) Thereafter the subject of the capacity of Christ as a 'merciful' high priest to sympathize with human weakness occupies 4.14–5.10. Coincidentally or otherwise, two neighbouring chapters in the book of Numbers form the background to this section: Numbers 12 attributes a privileged position to Moses that forms the basis of both comparison and contrast with Christ in 3.1-6, while the Numbers 14 account of the Israelites' 'rebellion' is the narrative counterpart to Ps. 95.7b-11, which structures the argument throughout 3.7–4.13.

God's House (3.1-6)

The verbal and thematic links with the preceding section are several, but a particular point is made of Christ's being *'faithful* to the one who appointed him' (v. 2; cf. 2.17). (Since there is no need to restrict the purview of *piston onta* ['being faithful'] to the past, as in NRSV and NIV, we should not assume that the writer has only the earthly life of Christ in mind.) This then leads into the contrast that the author wishes to make between Christ and Moses (vv. 2-6). First, however, we should note that the section begins and ends with enveloping references to the status of the recipients of the letter as associates with Christ in a heavenly calling (v. 1) and as members of his household bearing a responsibility to remain true to their calling (v. 6). In the opening address to them as 'holy brothers' (v. 1) two features of 2.11 are picked up—Christ's sanctifying of his people and his recognition of them as 'brothers'—and so the theologizing of the previous chapter is 'cashed in' for their immediate benefit. Again, Christ's participation (*meteschen*) in their humanity (2.14) has had the reciprocal effect of making them sharers (*metochoi*) in his heavenly calling (v. 1). Then the first imperative of the letter is issued—to consider Jesus the apostle and high priest whom they have confessed. In these two designations the whole action of Christ in relation to God and to humanity is encompassed. Though never actually called an 'apostle' elsewhere in the New Testament, Christ can be so described because he was sent by God to do his will (cf. 10.7-10). As high priest he is humanity's representative before God. But Moses, Israel's own law-giver, had been an 'apostle' (we might compare LXX *aposteilō,* used of God's sending of Moses to the Pharaoh in Exod. 3.10) and an intercessor *par excellence* (cf. Exod. 32.11-14; Jer. 15.1), and Num. 12.7-8 credits him with having been in a position of special intimacy with God and as 'entrusted' (LXX 'faithful' [*pistos*, v. 7b], as v. 2 here) with God's 'house'. In the Pentateuch he is also required to discharge priestly functions pending the establishment of a priesthood (e.g. Exod. 29.10-14), whence it was possible for the like of Philo in later times to regard him as having priestly, and even high-priestly, status (*Vit. Mos.* 2.66-186; *Praem. Poen.* 53, 56). The occurrence of *poiein* in the sense of 'appoint' is uncommon, but not unique, the verb being used in Mk 3.14 for the appointment of the twelve apostles and in 1 Sam. 12.6 (LXX; cf. MT) for the appointment of Moses and Aaron.

'House' then provides the author with a simple analogy: just as the builder of a house is greater than the house itself, so he recognizes Christ as greater than Moses (v. 3). (Verse 3 functions approximately as does 1.4 where a similar kind of contrast is being made.) It is best to take v. 4 as parenthetical (so NRSV) and as simply establishing that God is the builder of the 'house' in question (cf. v. 3) inasmuch as he is the builder of all that is (v. 4). It complicates the argument unnecessarily to introduce as an extra layer the suggestion that, as well as occupying a higher position than Moses, Christ is also involved with a greater 'house' (i.e. the whole created order) than was Moses. Some equivalence in function and status between God and Christ is assumed in vv. 3 and 4,

with the writer returning to the ideation of Christ as the divine Son in
v. 6. Verses 5 and 6, balanced by the correlative particles *men/de*, contrast Moses as 'servant' (*therapōn,* as in LXX Num. 12.7) and Christ as
'son' in a way that recalls the Christ-angel opposition in ch. 1 (see especially vv. 1-4, 14). This is not the only time in *Hebrews* that the role of
Moses as law-giver is played down (cf. 11.23-29). For the author, Moses
fulfilled his servant role by bearing witness to things that would later be
'spoken', by which, no doubt, he means the Gospel of the 'Christ-event'.

These things are not simply 'spoken about' but 'spoken', which agrees
with the emphasis in the letter upon the Christian message as a divine
speaking 'in these last days' (cf. on 1.1). The defining of Moses' role as
being 'for a testimony' (so AV) recalls the similar statement about John
the Baptist in Jn 1.7. Both cases involve the playing down of the importance of an individual whom others were reckoned to be venerating to
the detriment of their own Christian faith. Again, as he has already done
in 1.14, the author appears finally to elevate not only Christ but also the
body of Christian believers above the other party whom he has contrasted with Christ. Since the 'we' of v. 6 are deemed to be members of
God's household and Moses functioned as a servant (*therapōn*) in God's
house, the question of relative status not unnaturally arises. However,
the addressees' membership of the household is not taken for granted;
they by their persistence in faith are expected to provide the evidence of
membership (v. 6b). This element of conditionality leads into the second
'warning section' in the letter (cf. on 2.1-4), with the warning based this
time on appropriate material connected with the Moses tradition.

God's Rest (3.7-4.13)

Taking Ps. 95.7b-11 for his text, the author proceeds to warn the
'Hebrews' of the danger of their recapitulating the experience of the
Israelite exodus generation if they display a similar disinclination to keep
faith with 'the living God'. In this connection the framing verses from
the psalm excerpt (quoted in 3.7-11) are specially significant, each being
quoted or part-quoted twice (v. 7b at 3.15; 4.7, and v. 11 at 4.3, 5).
Somehow the appositeness of the parallel seems greater when the
addressees are regarded as converts from Judaism to Christianity, if only
because they would have identified more easily with the generation of
the biblical exodus tradition. If Paul's appeal to the experience of the
wilderness generation in 1 Cor. 10.1-11 is invoked to the contrary, the

mixed Jewish–Gentile composition of the church in Corinth and the apostle's perception that he must stress the relevance of the Old Testament narrative to his readers' situation (cf. vv. 6, 11) ought to be taken into account. Here the quotation of Ps. 95.7b-11 in vv. 7-11 is followed by hermeneutical application of the psalm text in vv. 12-19, in a section demarcated by occurrences of the verb *blepein* (NRSV 'take care', 'see') and the noun *apistia* (NRSV 'unbelieving [heart]', 'unbelief').

Psalm for 'Today' (3.7-11)

These verses introduce the 'second admonition' in *Hebrews* (= 3.7-19), in which the addressees are warned about the danger of failing to complete the spiritual journey upon which they had set out. The note of conditionality expressed in v. 6 is developed over the next several paragraphs, from 3.7 to 4.11, as the author draws lines of connection between the situation of his addressees and certain elements within Ps. 95.7b-11. As in 10.15-17, the biblical citation is regarded as the utterance of the Holy Spirit. Sometimes the present tense is used in the citation formula without having any special significance (cf. 1.6, 7; 5.6; 7.17; 8.8), but here and at 10.15 it has a particular contemporizing force. At 10.15 this is made clear by the simple addition of 'to us' ('the Holy Spirit also testifies to us'), while the usage here in 3.7 is illuminated by 4.1-2 where a direct comparison is made between those addressed and the exodus (or 'wilderness') generation to whom the quotation from Psalm 95 refers. The psalm consists of two distinct parts: a summons to worship God in the temple in vv. 1-7a, and an oracular utterance, which may have been delivered by a prophet-figure on such an occasion, in vv. 7b-11. The mention of the divine voice in v. 7b makes the citation especially appropriate in its new setting (see on 1.1).

Two other features of the quotation, in which it differs from both its Hebrew and Septuagintal forms, may be owing to the New Testament author's wish to make it apply more closely to the circumstances of those to whom he writes. First, according to v. 9 the 'fathers' saw God's actions over a period of 40 years, whereas the standard Hebrew text and the Septuagint alike say that God was angry with the exodus generation for 40 years. That the writer was aware of the latter reading, or at least interpretation, is clear from v. 17, but that still leaves a question about his quotation in v. 9. Is it possible that his insertion of *dio* ('Therefore') between 'forty years' and 'I was angry' was intended to set up a more hopeful comparison between the exodus generation who had witnessed

the mighty acts of God and the present generation who had been similarly privileged (cf. 2.4)? While it is impossible to show that Jewish
ideas about the significance of 'forty years' in relation to the end-time
have influenced the author, the elapse of approximately such a period
from the crucifixion of Christ to the time of writing—assuming a date of
composition just before 70 CE—could have been an unspoken consideration which those addressed would have needed little encouragement
to bring to the surface. If, on the other hand, *Hebrews* was written some
time after 70 CE the writer has not drawn an explicit parallel between
the wilderness generation and the last generation of the Second Temple
period, even though the significance of the 40-year comparison might
have seemed more compelling by then. The second possible instance of
modification of the biblical text for contemporizing purposes concerns
the minor alteration of 'that generation' (so LXX) to 'this generation' in
v. 10—*pace* modern versions like NRSV and NIV that do not observe the
distinction. The expression 'this generation' is relatively common in the
New Testament—in contrast with the unrepresented 'that generation'—
and conveys a sense of immediacy and directness that serves well the
purpose of an author writing 'in these last days' (1.2).

No Entry (3.12-19)

Whereas Psalm 95 speaks of a whole generation that fell short of their
expected goal, the author of *Hebrews* expresses his concern lest individuals in the community or communities with which he is concerned
may prove ungenuine. He is not just being tactful in limiting his concern
in this way, as 12.15 makes clear. The addressing of them as 'brothers'
(v. 12) is meant to reassure them as to his basic confidence in them (cf.
'beloved' in 6.9); at the same time, he equates a complaisant loss of faith
with defection from 'the *living* God', by which is meant the God of
Israel as much as the God of Christian profession (cf. Deut. 5.26; Josh.
3.10). The use of the term 'living God' would be ironical in this context
if the 'Hebrews' had originally converted from Judaism to Christianity,
for now the writer would be asserting that, far from returning to 'the
living God' worshipped by the generations of Israel, they would be turning away from him if they gave up on their Christianity. In vv. 12-13 key
words from the psalm quotation are woven into the author's exhortation
to avoid the fate of those described in the psalm. The italicizing of these
words in the following literalish rendering of vv. 12-13 will show how
this works and also the extent to which the commentary technique

recalls the *pesher* method already noted in connection with 2.6-9:

> Take care, brothers, lest there be in any of you an evil *heart* of unbe-
> lief, in turning away from the living God. But encourage one another
> *daily*, while it is called *'Today'*, lest any of you is *hardened* by the
> deceitfulness of sin.

In bidding them to 'exhort' (*parakaleite*) one another daily (v. 13), the
writer uses his own preferred term for what he himself is doing in his
letter—his 'word of exhortation (*paraklēseōs*)' (13.22). In the reference
to *daily* encouragement of one another there is almost certainly in his
mind, though it is not yet apparent in the text, the laggard tendency to
miss communal meetings that is addressed in 10.25 ('not neglecting to
meet together...but encouraging [*parakalountes*] one another'). The
parenthetical v. 14, which repeats the implicit warning of v. 6b, is trig-
gered by the reference to the deceitfulness of sin immediately preceding. Even the confidence expressed in the confessional-sounding 'we
have become' is conditionalized by the requirement that the confessor
hold fast to what was originally embraced at the time of conversion.
Verse 15, quoting again from Ps. 95.7-8, possibly rounds off the exhortation of vv. 12-13[14], but REB offers the attractive alternative of taking it
as protatic to v. 16: 'When scripture says, "Today...", who was it that
heard and yet rebelled?' There is, in any case, a series of questions in
vv. 16-18 that are based on the excerpt from Psalm 95 given in vv. 7-11.
The use of such questions was an effective way of making a point, according to ancient rhetorical canons.

The questions also have a broadly catechetical function, inviting comparison between the wilderness generation ('left Egypt'–'heard'–
'sinned'–'were disobedient') and those to whom they come as warning.
The Old Testament narrative background is Numbers 14, where sentence is passed on the exodus generation for their despairing response
to the report of the spies who had reconnoitred Canaan. Virtually the
whole generation that came out of Egypt is excluded from Canaan
(Num. 14.20-24), and it is a judgment that New Testament writers see fit
to highlight (cf. also 1 Cor. 10.1-5). Here the series of questions is meant
to elicit a recognition of what the tradition actually was saying about
these Israelites who had escaped Egypt only to die in the desert. In vv.
18 and 19 the transition from 'disobedient' to 'unbelief'—which, with
'see' (√ *blepein*), forms an inclusio to the section (cf. v. 12)—is aided by
assonance (*apeithēsasin–apistian*). In the original story in Numbers the
Israelites are faulted specifically for failure to believe God: 'And how

long will they refuse to believe in me, in spite of all the signs that I have done among them?' (Num. 14.11). They were 'unable to enter' (v. 19) in the sense that they tried and failed, according to Num. 14.39-45 which recounts how they 'presumed to go up to the heights of the hill country' and suffered a defeat by the Amalekites and Canaanites (vv. 44-45; cf. Deut. 1.41-45). The question of obedience and faith continues to be central to the argument in ch. 4 (vv. 2-3, 6, 11).

A Sabbath Rest Remains (4.1-11)

Chapter 3 ends with a comment on the debarring of the exodus generation from entering Canaan, which leads the author on to a consideration of the 'rest' denied them according to Ps. 95.11 as quoted in 3.11b ('They will not enter my rest'). That 4.1-11 is a discrete section within the larger unit is suggested by the presence of the initial and concluding cohortatives ('let us fear' [NRSV 'let us take care'], v. 1, and 'let us make every effort', v. 11) and, indeed, by the recapitulatory character of v. 11. The author expresses himself very carefully as he begins the section, adopting the first person plural in what amounts to a warning, and then disengaging himself from the potential source of the problem that causes him anxiety: 'Let us fear lest any of you...' The development of the theme of entering (or not entering) into 'rest' is facilitated by the parallels that he draws between the circumstances of the exodus generation and those of the 'Hebrews' themselves: the latter are also addressed in the promise of rest (v. 1), and both have been 'evangelized' (vv. 2, 6; cf. Gal. 3.8). The exodus generation had been 'evangelized' not just in the sense that they were heirs to ancient promises, but more particularly in that they had received good news in the report of the 'promised land' brought back by Caleb and Joshua—and indeed by the other spies, but for the enervating gloss that they put on what they had seen (cf. Num. 13.25-33). At the same time, the writer's concern is that what also applied to the Israelites negatively should not befall the addressees, hence his warning about 'falling short' (v. 1) or simply 'falling' (v. 11).

The good news announced to the Israelites is described in v. 2 as 'the word of hearing' (lit.), which develops further the theme of hearing and obeying introduced in ch. 3 on the basis of Psalm 95 (see 3.7-8, 15-16). According to the best attested reading, this good news did not benefit its hearers because they 'were not united by faith with those who listened' (so NRSV). This may be the correct reading, but such is the interpretative difficulty involved that Dean Henry Alford described the clause as 'almost a locus desperatus'. Even REB, which seldom puts down an opportunity for adventure, goes along with a weakly attested but more amenable alternative reading: 'for it was not combined with faith in those who heard it' (cf. NIV). If the writer is not thinking of Caleb and Joshua, the two exempted from the general judgment on the exodus generation (cf. Deut. 1.36, 38), the remaining possibility is that he is distinguishing between the exodus generation and those who in other circumstances did hear and believe the 'good news'. As far as *Hebrews* is concerned, these could include both Jewish and Christian believers, so that the author is not being quite so supersessionist as is usually assumed when the majority reading is commented upon. It is true that 11.39-40 states that the faithful of Old Testament times would not be made perfect 'apart from us (= Christians)', but to limit 'those who listened' to Christian believers is to lump together the exodus 'rebels' and the Old Testament faithful of ch. 11, which is scarcely the author's intention.

From v. 3 on the author begins to indicate what the 'rest' concept may mean within a Christian context. He allows that the 'Hebrews' have 'believed' and therefore qualify for the promised rest, and in 'we...enter' he uses the present tense as if to suggest an element of present experience of the rest, though he may actually be leaving open the question as to when the entering in takes place. To have said that those who believe '*have* entered' would have been to deal in the attractions of 'realized eschatology', but it would hardly have served his parenetic intention. In v. 10, indeed, he is able to associate the 'rest' with the eternal rest of the world to come. His statement that it is people of faith who enter the divine rest stands with his earlier conclusion that it was because of unbelief that the exodus generation failed to enter (3.19). In expounding the significance of 'rest'—now God's own rest, referred to in Gen. 2.2—he is helped by the fact that, although the underlying Hebrew words are different, the same Greek root is used to represent 'rest' in the Septuagint version at Ps. 95.11 and Gen. 2.2. Something akin to the rabbinic *gezerah shavah* ('equal law') method of interpretation— the illumination of one passage by another that has a word (or words) in common with it—is at work here. Our author notes God's determination that the exodus generation would not enter the 'rest' of Canaan, and yet he observes that, with the completion of his creative works 'from the foundation of the world', God had long since entered into his own rest which, by implication, was ever after available to others. Clearly, the idea of 'rest' is at the point of metamorphosing into a heavenly or spiritual reality as compared with the promised-land edition. The crucial point for the author is, at any rate, that until the Christian era there was a 'rest' unbestowed: Ps. 95.11 is repeated in vv. 3 and 5 because it is taken to mean not only that the intended recipients failed to accept the original offer in its then form, but also that there is a 'rest' that remains available to others coming after them.

This is stated resumptively in v. 6 which begins a second phase in the argument of vv. 1-11. In v. 7 a new day of opportunity, which is nothing less than an open-ended 'today', is recognized on the basis of Ps. 95.7. While the author would not have doubted that Joshua led the Israelites into the promised land, he argues in v. 8 that this cannot have exhausted the 'rest' that God intended for them, otherwise he would not have spoken at a later date in the way of Ps. 95.7. (No attempt is made to exploit the Joshua–Jesus analogy—both leaders of their peoples into promised inheritances—an analogy made the more plausible by the fact that these are Hebrew and Greek versions of the same name.) And so the ground has been prepared for the assertion in v. 9: 'a sabbath rest still remains for the people of God'. Sabbath observance had been a distinctive badge of Israel as the 'people of God' in Old Testament times and parlance, but the use of the rare form *sabbatismos* here may be intended to support a distinction between the institution of sabbath and the 'sabbath rest' into which God entered at the end of the Genesis creation week (Gen. 2.2-3; cf. below on v. 10). Verse 9 is notable on two further counts. First, it is likely that the addressees, or at least some of their number, saw themselves as having left the secure forms of Jewish worship, visible and palpable in its familiar manifestations, for the spiritualized and relatively cultless devotions of Christianity. They no longer had priesthood or altar or sacrifice, so that one of the points that the author seeks to establish in his letter is that they are not so disadvantaged as they may imagine (see especially 4.14; 8.1; 13.10). There may be the implication in this verse that 'sabbath rest' (*sabbatismos*), replacing traditional sabbath observance, was another of the redefined institutions of Judaism that was available to the addressees as Christians. Secondly, whatever their previous standing, the designation 'people of God' is now applied to them as much as to those of whom it was first used (cf. 1 Pet. 2.9-10).

The nature of the 'rest' that the writer has in mind is made clearer in v. 10 by way of straightforward comparison with God's 'rest' following his work of creation: so the faithful may look forward, earth's labours ended, to a participation in God's 'rest' (cf. Rev. 14.13). It remains, then, for the author to challenge the addressees to ensure that they attain to what God has made available to them (v. 11). If the rest to which they are to aspire is future they are not, of course, enjoined to seek death, but rather the worthiness to enjoy what God has prepared for them. While 'fall' in v. 11 could almost be paraphrased by 'fail', there is a very probable allusion to 'those who sinned, whose bodies fell in the wilderness', as the exodus generation is described in 3.17.

The Living Word (4.12-13)

These two verses belong closely with what immediately precedes, but the creation of a separate paragraph is defensible if *gar* (v. 12) is taken as a weak asseverative (NRSV 'indeed'). The advantage is that the verses can then more easily be taken as offering a reflection on all those elements in 3.7-4.11 that have to do with God's speaking to his people, and especially on Ps. 95.7b-11 as the 'word' around which the section has been constructed. The personification of the 'word of God' in v. 12 is such as almost to suggest identification with God himself. However, this would simply anticipate the development in v. 13 where God himself comes into view. As in 3.12, attention focuses on the heart as the seat of thoughts and intentions that may issue in outright defection from God (v. 12). Even these inner workings of the heart, says the writer, must feature in the account that every individual has to render to God (v. 13). For this latter idea the author uses *logos* ('word' in v. 12) in the sense of 'reckoning' or 'account'. He therefore comes near to saying that humans must give *logos* ('account') to the divine *logos.*

Hebrews 4.14-5.10: The Great High Priest

Introductory Comment

In 3.1 the writer had referred to Christ as both 'apostle' and 'high priest' and had proceeded in 3.2-6 to speak in a way more honed to the former than the latter. He now turns to the matter of the high priesthood, summarizing Christ's credentials in 4.14-15 and encouraging the 'Hebrews' to avail themselves of their heavenly high priest in 4.16. The question of eligibility is raised again in 5.1-10, in terms both of vocation and of personal fitness for the office. The section is important for the developing argument in *Hebrews* in that priesthood 'according to the order of Melchizedek' is specifically mentioned for the first time in the letter (5.6,10; cf. on 1.3).

The Throne of Grace (4.14-16)

The subject of the high-priestly role of Christ is first mentioned *expressis verbis* in 2.17-18 and will be expounded at length in chs. 7–10. Here the author, reflecting perspectives already represented in 2.17-18, concentrates on his suitability to act on behalf of weak and erring humanity. Verses 14 and 15 are very differently angled, but both are essential to the author's understanding of what legitimates Christ as his people's high priest. He has 'passed through the heavens', which at the least indicates a competence and a standing where it matters (see 6.19-20; 8.1-2; 9.11-12), and he has experienced the gamut of human suffering and testing, without which he could not function sympathetically towards his human dependants. In v. 14 the somewhat tautologous (though not unique; cf. 1 Macc. 13.42) use of 'great' in the expression 'great high priest' is in keeping with the general emphasis of the verse. Here too the simple name Jesus, which elsewhere the writer is happy to use on its own (cf. on 2.9), is augmented with the title 'Son of God' which has been much in the author's consciousness in earlier chapters. The attaching injunction to hold fast to 'our confession' may even contain a reminder that at conversion the addressees had confessed their belief that Jesus was 'the Son of God' (cf. Acts [8.37]; 9.20; 1 Jn 4.15; 5.5).

The litotes in v. 15 comes, no doubt, from the recognition that the claims of the previous verse could create an impression of distance and lofty impassibility in the minds of the addressees. As regards the specific point of Christ's capacity to sympathize with highly fallible human beings, it might be argued that the qualifying phrase 'yet without sin' weakens rather than strengthens the case. But that would be well on the way to subverting the soteriology of *Hebrews* (cf. 5.2-3; 10.11-12), and it is another testimony to the conviction of early Christianity on the sinlessness of Christ that this restrictive clause appears in such a context. Still, at this point the accent falls on the fact that the Christian high priest experienced testings in common with the rest of humanity, and in such a way as to be able to offer not only sympathy but strength to those seeking his help. Another exhortation, to come with boldness to the throne of grace, follows in v. 16. This 'boldness' (*parrēsia*) is the freedom and frankness of speech adopted by the great Abraham in his interviews with God (e.g. Gen. 15.2-3; cf. Philo, *Rer. Div. Her.* 5). According to 1.3, Christ, having made purification for sins, sat down 'at the right hand of the Majesty on high' (cf. also 8.1), but the throne with which his followers have to do is described here, for their comfort, as 'the throne of grace'. If the writer also has in mind the 'mercy seat' of the tabernacle and temple (cf. 9.5)—which the Old Testament associates with the divine throne (e.g. 1 Sam. 4.4)—this obtaining of mercy and grace is linked all the more specifically with Christ's high-priestly role. The use of the adjective *eukairos* in description of the help that may be obtained at this throne is paralleled nicely in a Greek inscription: *boētheito kata to eukairon* ('received timely help').

The Order of Melchizedek (5.1-10)

There is an introverted structure to this section in that vv. 1-3 are concerned with the character traits and the responsibilities of the typical Israelite high priest and v. 4 with the question of the authority by which a high priest came to exercise his office in the first place. Verses 5-6 then show the basis of Christ's claim to be a priest 'according to the order of Melchizedek' and vv. 7-9 (10) present his credentials in terms of the probative experiences that were his 'in the days of his flesh'. In v. 1 the author summarizes the duties of the Israelite high priest in respect of his cultic responsibilities. It is possible that, in talking about gifts and sacrifices for sins, he has the 'Day of Atonement' specially in mind, as explicitly in chs. 9–10. Verse 1 is, in any case, specially strong on the human dimension of the high-priestly function: the high priest is 'chosen from among mortals (*anthrōpōn*)', is appointed to act 'on behalf of mortals', and specifically to 'offer gifts and sacrifices for sins'.

There are passages in the Old Testament that outline the duties of priests and of high priests in particular, but v. 2a clearly derives its terms from the writer's view of Christ rather than from any Old Testament description of the high-priestly office. Even so, 'deal gently' (*metriopathein*) sounds like self-conscious understatement as compared with the active 'sympathizing' attributed to Christ in 4.15. What is commended as desirable in a high priest is an understanding of human weakness such that when infringements of the law come to his notice his response is measured and not destructive of the confidence of the ordinary worshipper. 'Ignorant (*agnoousin*) and wayward' is a hendiadys for 'straying through ignorance' and probably assumes the distinction made in Num. 15.22-31 between sins of ignorance (Heb. *šegāgâ*), for which reparation could be made, and high-handed sins, for which no sacrifice was prescribed. This distinction between the inadvertent and the high-handed structures the argument in Heb. 9.6-14 (note especially 9.7, 'for the sins committed unintentionally [*agnoēmatōn*] by the people'). The writer is interested to point out, partly in view of the contrastive use that he will make of it (cf. 7.27), that the priestly law of the Old Testament assumed the same fallibility in the high priest as in those on whose behalf he officiated. The fact was institutionalized in the ritual of the Day of Atonement (cf. Lev. 16.6). It followed, then, that no mere mortal should take upon himself the honour of becoming high priest (v. 4). The contrast between divine appointment and self-promotion is expressed in the occurrences of the verb 'take' (*lambanein*) in vv. 1 (*lambanomenos*, NRSV 'chosen') and 4 (*lambanei*, NRSV 'does [not] presume to take'). Since appointment to the high priesthood was according to family succession, the writer cites Aaron as standing at the head of the priestly line and the one who initially was appointed by God to serve as high priest (Exod. 28.1; cf. 29.29-30; Num. 20.23-29). It is assumed here that the hereditary principle co-existed with that of divine election, and no concession is made to the later history of the high priesthood when venality and politics determined appointments.

The *curriculum vitae* forming the basis of Christ's claim to high-priestly office is summarized in vv. 7-10, but the writer deals first with the matter of appointment in vv. 5-6. This, as I have already noted, gives the section 5.1-10 the appearance of a chiasmus. Whether the writer is implying anything about the 'chronology' of Christ's appointment as high priest—that is, by investing him with a priestly role in advance of his exaltation—cannot be so certainly said (see on 7.16-17). (The quotation of Ps. 2.7 [see below] already in 1.5 does not help in this regard since no chronological perspective is indicated in the earlier reference.) The proof that Christ did not arrogate high-priestly status to himself is found in two Old Testament texts that speak of divine decrees, the first of which has already been quoted by the author in order to substantiate Christ's claim to unique Sonship (Ps. 2.7; see 1.5). The author thus proceeds from the familiar (see also Mk 1.11; Acts 13.33; Rom. 1.4) to the less so, since his use of Ps. 110.4 in support of the concept of the eternal priesthood of Christ may well be an innovation on his part. The formal, decretal correspondence between the two texts will have helped to establish the admissibility of the second to the argument. Once admitted, Ps. 110.4 is not only quoted or alluded to hereafter (see 5.10; 6.20; 7.17, 21), but also sets the agenda for the discussion in 7.1-28.

In vv. 7-10 the question of Christ's fitness for high priesthood is addressed in terms of his human experience of suffering obedience. These verses form a lengthy sentence involving several participial clauses which, strictly speaking, is itself founded on a relative clause picking up the reference to Christ in v. 5. There is nothing strikingly hymnic about the section, though the introductory 'who' (NRSV 'Jesus') in v. 7, if taken independently of 'Christ' as its natural antecedent in v. 5, might suggest comparison with the hymnic-sounding Phil. 2.6-11 and 1 Tim. 3.16, both of which begin in the same way. The expression 'the days of his flesh' in v. 7 denotes Christ's earthly life (cf. NIV), but in a way that emphasizes his truly human nature. In this verse the author evinces a brief interest in the traditions about the incarnate Christ, though in terms that are not directly reflective of the Gospel narratives and that are sometimes attributed to a variant form of, for example, the Gethsemane tradition. However, I have noted already how the author can 'mix his colours' in the sense that the detail of his descriptions may sometimes be indebted to contemporary circumstances or needs with which he is specially concerned (see, for example, on 5.2). This may apply particularly to the reference to prayer 'to him who was able to save him from death'. This expression obviously functions not just in description of God—and scarcely as a 'traditional circumlocution for God' in this passage, as Lane would have it (*Hebrews 1-8*, p. 120)—but also as an indication of the content of the prayers and petitions offered to God. And, as I have already noted in connection with 2.15, the 'fear of death' appears to have been a serious preoccupation for the author because it was very much so for his friends the 'Hebrews'. When he takes up this point in a major way in ch. 11 he will emphasize that death in whatever aspect one may care to name it is overcome by Christian faith. This seems to be very relevant here at 5.7, for the likelihood is that the author has Gethsemane in mind, despite the reservations sometimes expressed on the point. The prayers in Gethsemane for deliverance from the cup of suffering and death are, then, answered in the way of ch. 11 where the heroes of faith, even when they had to submit to death, defied it in their still speaking (v. 4) or by their confident expectations and utterances before death (vv. 13, 21-22)—to say nothing of the instances of death avoided, cheated and overcome that the old biblical narratives them- selves supply (cf. vv. 5, 19, 33-34). When ch. 11 with its multi-per- spectival approach to death and the defiance of it is taken into account such a question as whether *ek thanatou* here means 'from imminent death' or 'out of actual death' becomes less urgent.

The difference between ordinary ideas of 'sonship' and the divine Son- ship of Christ is evident in the use of the concessive conjunction 'although' in v. 8. The experience of learning obedience is part of enlightened childhood training, as the author himself observes in 12.5- 11—where, indeed, an element of disciplinary suffering is regarded as natural to the process. Our author, however, makes the point that, *despite* his Sonship, Christ experienced the pain of obedience: 'son though he was, he learned obedience through his sufferings' (REB). He is therefore thinking in terms of that unique category of Sonship that forms the basis of his argument in 1.5-9. The assonance in *emathen/epathen* ('learned'/'suffered'), a familiar pairing in ancient Greek writings, rein- forces the association between learning and suffering. The people on whose behalf Christ functions as high priest are here represented in 'all who obey him' (NRSV, for *tois hupakouousin autōi*), which phrase corresponds to the reference in v. 8 to the perfect obedience (*hupakoēn*) rendered by Christ himself. 'Saved' as he himself was (cf. *sōzein*, v. 7), he becomes the author of eternal salvation to his people (v. 9). Verse 10 brings the section to a formal conclusion with the specific statement that Christ was appointed *by God*, and with the occurrence of *hiereus* in LXX Ps. 109(110).4 filled out in *archiereus* ('high priest'). The word 'order' (*taxis*) is, of course, used in a strictly limited sense in connection with Melchizedek since one of the most important features of the 'order of Melchizedek' is its independence of the succession principle (cf. 7.23-24).

Hebrews 5.11–6.8: Obstacles to Progress

Introductory Comment

At this point, says the author, he would have preferred to continue with an exposition of Christ's priesthood 'according to the order of Melchizedek'. This, however, he delays until 7.1 because he has doubts about the addressees' capacity to take in what he has to say. He has much to pass on to them; how much of it is actually included in *Hebrews* it is impossible to judge. At 9.5 he implies that he could have gone into a more detailed discussion of the furniture in the Israelite tent of meeting, but he forbears. His remark in 13.22 that he has written but a short letter (*dia bracheōn*, 'briefly') suggests that perhaps a sense of urgency, or just the fear of overstaying his welcome, has made him choose brevity as a matter of policy. The section 5.11–6.8 divides fairly straightforwardly into two main parts, the first (5.11–6.3) stating the need for the monitory digression, but also the overriding need to 'go on toward perfection' (6.1), while the second (6.4-8) delivers a blunt warning about apostasy.

From Milk to Maturity (5.11–6.3)

Within 5.11-14 the discussion moves between two poles represented in *nōthroi* ('sluggish'; NRSV 'dull [in understanding]', v. 11) and *gegumnasmena* ('trained', v. 14). The only other occurrence of *nōthroi* in the New Testament is at 6.12 where the writer prescribes diligence (cf. v. 11) as the antidote to moral sluggishness. What is envisaged in the present passage is a kind of spiritual fitness programme—which includes dietary advice (vv. 12-14)—so that those who are sluggish *in their hearing* (v. 11; NRSV 'dull in understanding') may have *their faculties* trained to distinguish between good and evil (v. 14). In blaming his communication problem on the sluggishness of his addressees the author noticeably puts the emphasis on reader perspicacity rather than the perspicuity of his text! Reserving his more emollient comments for later (see 6.9-12), he chides his friends for having failed to make progress despite having had adequate time since their conversion ('because of the time' [lit.], v. 12). The short genitival chain, 'the rudiments of the first principles of the oracles of God' (RV), does not

concede much in its estimation of their grasp of basic Christian teaching
(v. 12).

This leads into a contrast, developed elsewhere in the New Testament
(see 1 Cor. 3.1-2) and paralleled in Hellenistic writers, between milk and
solid food as representing the simpler and more advanced levels of
Christian instruction. At the end of v. 12 'You need' (NRSV, NIV) translates *gegonate chreian echontes* without acknowledging the possibility
that the construction is meant to suggest reversion to a prior state (perhaps implied in AV's 'are become such as have need of'). The contrast
between infants and mature adults in vv. 13-14 easily follows, with the
key terms more closely positioned and more obviously counterbalanced
in the Greek text than in most English translations. The 'word of righteousness' of v. 13 has been variously defined by writers on *Hebrews*. It
probably relates to the capacity for discrimination between good and
evil mentioned in v. 14, and, if so, presumably as the means by which
the spiritual senses are trained and the capacity for such discrimination
awakened in the trainee. When the subject of Melchizedek is finally taken
up in ch. 7 his name is explained as meaning 'king of righteousness'
(v. 2), but it is unlikely that the 'word of righteousness' in 5.13 alludes to
the great Melchizedek theme that the writer would rather be developing
at this point. Verse 14 with its abbreviated version of an athletics metaphor anticipates the more developed use of the same metaphor in 12.1-
2, 12-13 where a related point is made about perseverance in the Christian life. There is also alliteration in the verse, in the words used for
'good' (*kalou*) and 'evil' (*kakou*). The Septuagintal renderings of the
expression 'good and evil' in the Old Testament (e.g. Gen. 2.17; 3.5, 22)
do not produce this fairly easy alliteration.

The infancy-maturity polarity continues into 6.1-3 as the author
indicates his intention of moving on to more advanced levels of teaching
represented here by the term *teleiotēs* (NRSV 'perfection', NIV, NRSVn.
'maturity'). It clearly is his hope that this will be more than a mere lit-
erary exercise, and that the result for the 'Hebrews' will be an enhanced
appreciation of Christian doctrine. Although the *telei-* root has already
occurred in the letter (cf. 2.10; 5.9) its use is more frequent, and more
varied, from this point on (7.11, 19, 28; 9.9, 11; 10.1, 14; 11.40; 12.23).
'Therefore' (*dio*, 6.1) frequently excites comment as creating a *non
sequitur* in relation to the immediately preceding assertions about the
addressees' immaturity and unsuitability for more advanced instruction.
But having castigated them for regressing to the point of needing baby

food again the author declines to revisit the basic teaching that had already been passed on to them. He intends to press on with the work of education as he develops his theme of the Melchizedek priesthood of Christ. The cohortative 'let us go on' (v. 1) is also a form of self-address relating to his own immediate intention, as v. 3 ('And we will do this') indicates. This merging of horizons functions to unite temporarily author and audience in a common goal.

What the author wishes to avoid is repetition of 'the word of the beginning of Christ' (lit.), variously rendered 'the basic teaching about Christ' (NRSV; cf. NIV), 'the rudiments of Christianity' (REB), or 'the initial message of Christ' (Attridge, comparing 2.3). Most probably the expression encompasses the foundational teachings that the writer goes on to list in vv. 1-2. As is invariably noted, the list is remarkable for the way in which it could command the assent of both Jews and Christians. Six credenda are listed, and, if the early reading *didachēn* (accusative) is to be preferred to the more widely-attested *didachēs* (genitive) in v. 2, they are divided into two and four by their association with the terms 'foundation' and 'teaching' respectively. They also clearly form three pairs: repentance and faith, ritual washings and the laying on of hands, resurrection and judgment. Nothing explicitly christological is included in the list (contrast, for example, 1 Tim. 3.16), though it is possible to link each of the items listed with some aspect of the high-priestly Christology developed in chs. 7–10 (Lane, *Hebrews 1-8*, p. 140).

The highlighting at this point of such continuities between Judaism and Christianity in an epistle that makes much of the *dis*continuities between the two is noteworthy. Thus a more characteristically 'Christianized' formulation of the first pair of credenda is found in Acts 20.21: 'repentance toward God and faith toward our Lord Jesus', while *baptismōn* in v. 2, by virtue of deriving from *baptismos* rather than *baptisma*, may more naturally be interpreted of ritual washings than specifically of Christian baptism (cf. 9.10). The expression 'dead works' (v. 1) is paraphrased by 'acts that lead to death' in NIV, and correctly so, as will become apparent in the discussion of ch. 9 where the proper understanding of the expression is important for the exegesis of the early part of that chapter. The conclusion to v. 3 ('if God permits') is scarcely confinable to the author's intention of continuing with the rest of his letter, but suggests that he has in his sights the goal of mature understanding of the doctrine of Christ on the part of himself and the 'Hebrews'—a veritable 'going on to perfection'. Reflection on the 'impossibility' that he is about to introduce in v. 4 may well have contributed to this note of caution.

The First Impossibility (6.4-8)

Verses 4-8 follow statement (vv. 4-6) with analogy (vv. 7-8), in pursuance of the single main point that it is possible so to disavow a profession of Christian faith as never to be able to return to it. There are five aorist participles in vv. 4-6, and the first four emphasize the extent of the encounter with the divine that can be experienced even by those who subsequently 'fall away'. The writer uses the plural throughout, suggesting that the danger of which he warns concerns more than some merely hypothetical individual. 'Enlightenment' is described as a once and for all experience (*hapax*, v. 4), which is by the same reckoning impossible to renew. Later the author will refer to the 'Hebrews' as having been 'enlightened' at conversion (10.32). There is no indication that at this stage 'enlightenment' referred to baptism, as it did subsequently (cf. the Syriac Peshitta's 'have gone down into baptism'). The remaining expressions in vv. 4-5 could describe people whose experience of Christianity fell short of outright commitment (see the standard commentaries for discussion). The matching features in the case of Simon Magus are often cited in this regard (cf. Acts 8.9-24). This may provide the elements for a sufficient explanation of the present very difficult passage; nevertheless there are sufficient texts of similar hue elsewhere in the New Testament as to dissuade a commentator from trying to remove their theological sting, and therewith their moral challenge. When it comes to the solemn conclusion in v. 6 there is no mention of who or what might otherwise be the agent of repentance. Is the author discreetly avoiding the direct assertion that this is an impossibility even for God? (If so, we might compare Paul's choice of words in Rom. 9.22-23 where God prepares the objects of his mercy for glory, whereas the objects of his wrath are represented in a passive construction as having been 'fitted for destruction'.)

Whether *anastaurountas* (v. 6) should be translated 'crucifying again' (NRSV; cf. NIV) or simply 'crucifying' (so Attridge) is debated. Since there are occurrences of the verb in this compound form apparently without any sense of repetition involved, it may be that the function of the prefix is simply to emphasize the connection between attitudinal crucifying (*anastaurountas*) of Christ and the impossibility of renewal (*anakainizein*) to repentance. At the same time, the kind of apostasy

envisaged might well have been regarded by the author as a recru-
cifixion of Christ, who is here described as 'Son of God' probably not so
much in recollection of a title important in the earlier discussion (e.g.
1.2; 4.14) as in order to stress the seriousness of apostatizing from him
(cf. 10.29, 'who have spurned the Son of God'). The reflexive *heautois*
with *anastaurountas* may function as a dative of disadvantage (cf. NIV
'to their loss'), but NRSV 'on their own' (i.e. an ethical dative) thinks of
the apostates as simply ratifying the original act of crucifixion. This is
not regarded as the full extent of their wrongdoing, seeing that they
subject this Son of God 'to public disgrace' (cf. NIV for *paradeigma-
tizontas*)—an expression made all the more meaningful if their renounc-
ing of Christianity were to involve a public display of their renunciation.
The use of present participles in 'are crucifying [again]' and 'are subjecting [him] to public disgrace' indicates that the original act of falling
away (*parapesontas*) has been confirmed in a sustained rejection of
Christ himself.

In vv. 7-8 the author turns from a theological and not ordinarily
verifiable statement (vv. 4-6) to an observable feature of the natural
world that illustrates the possibility of the right attendant conditions
failing to produce a beneficial result. But first, and somewhat in antici-
pation of the more cordial tone of vv. 9-12, he describes the 'desirable
norm' in v. 7. It is the land that receives a generous supply of rain *and
that produces a crop* that partakes (*metalambanei*) of blessing; which
statement recalls the participatory language of vv. 4-5. Verse 8, on the
other hand, describes the state of the apostate, using, in relation to unproductive ground, the double-duty *adokimos*, which usually describes
the kind of individuals that inspired this particular figure of speech (see
Rom. 1.28; 1 Cor. 9.27; 2 Cor. 13.5-7; 2 Tim. 3.8; Tit. 1.16). The language of the verse is evocative of the 'fall narrative' in Genesis 3, in the
mention of the thorns and thistles and the reference to a curse (cf. Gen.
3.17-18)—though the 'curse' is in obvious contrast with 'blessing' in v. 7
here. *kataras engus* (lit. 'near a curse') has a temporal force comparable
with *engus aphanismou* ('near disappearing') in 8.13.

Hebrews 6.9-20: Inheriting the Promises

Introductory Comment

This section sees more normal communication restored after the castigation of 5.11-14 and the oblique warning of 6.4-8. The occurrences of 'sluggish' in 5.11 (NRSV 'dull [in understanding]') and 6.12 could be cited as an inclusion favouring the linking of vv. 9-12 with the preceding section. Nevertheless, 6.9-20 represents a tonal unit. Verses 9-10 are very much in the nature of a *captatio benevolentiae* as the writer seeks to re-engage the sympathy of his addressees. But even his expression of confidence in them comes with a parenetic appendix in vv. 11-12. Then, building on the theme of hope, promise and fulfilment, in vv. 13-20 he takes the Genesis tradition of the promise to Abraham as the paradigm for God's faithful dealings with the 'heirs of the promise' in later times. These verses incorporate a number of legal terms (e.g. *antilogias*, 'dispute', v. 16; *emesiteusen*, 'guaranteed', v. 17) that serve well the author's purpose of convincing the 'Hebrews' of the trustworthiness of the message to which they had committed themselves. By the end of the section he is ready to return to the subject of Melchizedek and his order of priesthood.

Show the Same Diligence (6.9-12)

For the only time in the epistle the addressees are called 'dear friends' (v. 9), as the writer significantly changes his tone in comparison with the previous section. He more or less apologizes for having to write as he has done ('Even though we speak in this way'), and he expresses his confidence that theirs is a better case than the hypothetical one that he has just outlined. 'Better' being a favoured term in *Hebrews* because of the contrasts made between Judaism and Christianity (e.g. 7.19, 22; 8.6), the word could have had a kind of *sensus plenior* for the author in the present context, but this may be to court the danger of over-exegesis. For the moment he speaks of their 'salvation' as if it hinged upon their own moral effort. The use of the present participle (*diakonountes*) as well as the aorist (*diakonēsantes*) in v. 10 concedes that they are displaying the primary Christian virtue of love within their community. 'Work' and 'love'—are they 'things that belong to salvation' (v. 9)?—probably correspond to the crop that features in the analogy in v. 7 as being evidence of God's blessing upon the community. This 'work' is viewed positively and is strongly contrastive with the 'dead works' of v. 1.

In the litotes in v. 10 ('not...unjust') the writer associates his hopes for the 'Hebrews' with the character of God himself, implying that God's own justice would be compromised were he not to take note of their good works. This also is in their favour: that their acts of goodness have been done 'for his sake' ('in his name' [lit.]; cf. Mt. 10.41-42), and so it becomes a matter of personal honour for God not to forget what has been done 'for his sake'. NIV, 'the love you have shown him', equating the name with the person, makes the point that these acts have been rendered primarily to God, even though his people were the immediate beneficiaries of them (cf. Mt. 25.40, 45). Now it is not that some new, additional exaction is to be asked of them (vv. 11-12); the author wants them to make progress by continuing as they have been doing. The familiar triad of love-hope-faith is represented in vv. 10-12, each of the elements being linked with suitably pragmatic companion terms ('work', 'diligence', 'patience') lest the author's point be dissipated in mere abstractions.

Finally, the reminder of the danger of becoming slothful (v. 12) echoes the original warning in 5.11, at the beginning of the parenetic section just concluded. At the same time, v. 12 is transitional in that the reference to the inheriting of God's promises leads into a reflection on God's ways with Abraham and with the inheritors of the promises generally. These latter are often taken to be the faithful of the Old Testament era, and the mention of Abraham immediately following (v. 13) supports the identification. Nevertheless, the 'heirs of the promise' mentioned in v. 17 are closely linked with the 'we' of v. 18, so that it may be unwise to define too closely in v. 12 where the present participle *klēronomountōn* can certainly accommodate a contemporary perspective. The idea of imitation, found mainly in the Pauline writings in the New Testament (e.g. 1 Cor. 4.16; 1 Thess. 1.6), is compatible with either a past or a past-present interpretation. In 13.7 the 'Hebrews' are encouraged to 'imitate' the faith of a generation of leaders whom they had known in the recent past.

The Second Impossibility (6.13-20)

This section, which treats of a second major impossibility (v. 18; cf. v. 4) in the area of divine–human relationships, neatly dovetails with the adjoining passages, continuing the theme of the promises from v. 12 and finally returning discussion to the subject of the Melchizedek priesthood of Christ (see 5.11; 7.1). The figure of Abraham himself is, of course, a bridging factor because of his involvement in Genesis 14 where Melchizedek makes his brief appearance (vv. 18-20). So from contemplating the possibility of making shipwreck of one's faith (vv. 1-8), and having expressed a more confident expectation about those to whom he writes (vv. 9-12), the author moves on to talk of the strong confidence that God's commitment to his people, formalized in both a promise and an oath, should engender.

The example of Abraham was already in the writer's mind when he introduced the idea of imitation in v. 12. If the addressees were Jewish converts to Christianity then he would doubtless have been happy for them to consider themselves as living proof of the fulfilment of the promise to Abraham. The participle underlying 'made a promise' (NRSV, v. 13) may be a coincident aorist (cf. Acts 19.2), implying that both the promise and oath are covered by Gen. 22.15-18. However, the first mention of the promise comes at the outset of the Abraham story in Gen. 12.2-3, while promise and oath are coalesced in the later reference. If the promise and oath were regarded as having been introduced separately the point about Abraham's having to 'endure patiently' before receiving the fulfilment of the promise (v. 15) would be well served. At any rate, Gen. 22.17 is part-quoted in v. 14 to emphasize that God's swearing by himself circumvented the normal rules of oath-making, such was his desire to demonstrate his commitment to his promise. (A very striking instance of the same, but represented in symbolical fashion, comes in the ceremony of the covenant in Gen. 15.12-21 where the firepot passing between the pieces of the covenant animals represents God taking the covenant obligations upon himself.) By one method of reckoning Abraham did *not* receive the promise (11.13, 39), but it is the short-term fulfilment in the birth of Isaac that is probably in view here.

It is not so likely that Genesis 22 is still in the author's mind in v. 15, as if the restoration of Isaac after his binding on the altar corresponds to Abraham's obtaining of the divine promise (cf. Gen. 22.10-14). At best such an 'obtaining' would be figurative. However, when the recovery of Isaac from the altar is given a figurative significance in 11.19—as a kind of resurrection from the dead—the writer indicates explicitly that he is treating the story symbolically. Rather, the patient endurance evinced by Abraham in the circumstances of Genesis 22 is regarded as typical of the man to whom the promise had originally been made and for whom it was eventually fulfilled. The analogy of ordinary human oath-swearing is taken up in v. 16 and applied in v. 17, where the advantage of an oath over a promise is spelled out: with the former there is no question of retraction or of avoidance of obligation with impunity. So God is depicted as moving in some eagerness to supplement his promise with an oath, in order to put the nature of his undertaking beyond question—this now not just for the benefit of a patriarch but for the 'heirs of the promise', by which the writer means also himself and his contemporaries (cf. 'we' in v. 18). In v. 17 the author is commenting on the nature of the 'transaction' in Genesis 22. It is unlikely that he is thinking of a new element—such as the oath sworn to the priest in the order of Melchizedek in Ps. 110.4—being introduced for the benefit of latter-day 'heirs of the promise'. The two 'unchangeable things' (v. 18) are God's promissory word and his oath, as they originally featured in the Abraham story.

Verses 18-19 combine a couple of figures in a way that has inspired a variety of responses in the literature on *Hebrews*. The author describes himself and his friends as having 'fled for refuge', which has often been interpreted in the light of the provision for sanctuary-seekers in the so-called 'cities of refuge' in ancient Israel (e.g. Deut. 19.1-13). Others, influenced by the reference to the anchor in v. 19, think of the Christian convert as seeking safe haven in Christ. It is more likely, however, that the Old Testament references to the custom of seeking sanctuary by taking hold of the horns of the altar at the tabernacle or temple have suggested the figure here. Such a provision for the accidental homicide is probably implied in Exod. 21.14 ('But if someone wilfully attacks and kills another by treachery, you shall take the killer from my altar for execution'), and narrative illustration is provided in the cases of Adonijah and Joab, both of whom fled to the sanctuary and grasped the horns of the altar, thereby invoking divine protection from the vengeance of King Solomon (1 Kgs 1.50; 2.28). When, therefore, Amos announces that the horns of the altar of Bethel will be cut off and thrown to the ground (3.14), he evidently is talking not only of the physical destruction of the altar but also of the removal of the Israelites' last hope of sanctuary and supplication. God, our author implies, has provided a 'hopeful' source of sanctuary to which both author and addressees have betaken themselves for protection. This hope is firm and secure, like an anchor for the soul, and—in a surrealist extension of the metaphor so recently taken up—it is said to enter the inner shrine where Christ himself has gone (vv. 19-20). Possibly the author had in mind the unhappy associations of seeking sanctuary at the altar in the Old Testament narratives: something better than the 'security' from which a man might be forcibly removed at the word of a king, as in the case of Joab, was obviously desirable. And so the 'extended' metaphor comes into play, for the hope of the altar horns as he envisages it reaches beyond the court of the tabernacle and temple, entering right into the inner sanctuary behind the curtain (*eis to esōteron tou katapetasmatos*), proof against all hostile interference.

This leads easily into the reference (v. 20) to Jesus as priest in the Melchizedek tradition—picking up 5.10 in good *Wiederaufnahme* fashion after the lengthy warning digression, beginning at 5.11, on the dangers of falling away. 'Forerunner' (NRSV) presumably does not take any of its colour from the idea of fleeing for refuge (v. 18), but hints at the privileged status enjoyed by the suppliant for whom Christ acts as herald and representative. The idea that the earthly Jesus had entered into the inner shrine of the heavenly sanctuary would have been bold enough; to claim that he stood at the head of a great number of mere earthlings similarly entitled was to go far beyond what was symbolized in the furnishings and rituals associated with the Israelite tabernacle and temple.

Hebrews 7: Another Priesthood

Introductory Comment

This chapter expands on the importance of Melchizedek on the basis of the two Old Testament passages in which he briefly features. Verses 1-10 dwell exegetically (or eisegetically!) on Gen. 14.18-20, while vv. 11-28 revolve around the idea of the priestly order associated with Melchizedek in Ps. 110.4. The author's awareness of postbiblical enlargements upon the figure of Melchizedek can safely be assumed to have contributed to his discussion of him. At the same time, he seeks to relate what he wants to say about Melchizedek to aspects of the biblical text. According to the Old Testament Melchizedek was both a king and a priest and so exercised a form of sacral kingship that for the most part was regarded as inappropriate for Israelite rulers. Not much is made of Melchizedek's royal status in this chapter (*pace* v. 2), though when the author comments that 'it is evident that our Lord was descended from Judah' (v. 14) he may have noted the royalist potential in this association of Christ the high priest 'according to the order of Melchizedek' with that tribe in Israel from which came the Davidic dynasty.

Melchizedek of Salem (7.1-3)

These three verses make up one long sentence beginning 'This Melchizedek' and ending 'remains a priest forever'. The first part of the sentence, down to 'one-tenth of everything' in v. 2, is basically a summary of Gen. 14.18-20, though the use of *kopē* for 'defeat' in v. 1 is influenced by the Septuagintal version of Gen. 14.17, which describes Abraham's return after defeating the confederate kings and his accosting by the king of Sodom. Some features of the Genesis passage are passed over, but the giving of a tithe by Abraham to Melchizedek is highlighted in v. 2 and the significance of the act will be brought out in the next section.

The name and title in v. 1 ('Melchizedek king of Salem'), and in that order, will be invested with special meaning in v. 2. Melchizedek is called simply a priest in keeping with the strict terms of Gen. 14.18 and Ps. 110.4. Since Christ is called a 'high priest' in the order of Melchizedek (cf. 5.10; 6.20) and the author of *Hebrews* certainly does not wish to play down Melchizedek's importance ('See how great he is!',

v. 4) it is probable that Melchizedek himself was assumed to have been a high priest (cf. v. 15). (For other instances of 'priest' possibly denoting 'chief [or 'high'] priest' in the Old Testament see Exod. 3.1; 1 Sam. 1.9.) His name consists of two elements, here explained as meaning 'king of righteousness'. On a similar level, the place-name Salem is explained, as commonly in the period, on the basis of the Hebrew *šālôm* ('peace'). It is implied that the order 'righteousness'>'peace' is significant, though we are left to infer what the significance of the terms occurring in this order might be. Peace is described as the 'effect' of righteousness in Isa. 32.17, in a chapter with a broadly messianic interest ('A king will reign in righteousness, and princes will rule with justice', v. 1); perhaps some such association is implied here.

That no genealogical or any other such information is given for Melchizedek in Genesis 14 is made the basis for an interpretative, rabbinic-type conceit in v. 3. (Contrariwise, possession of proper genealogical title was essential to the exercise of priesthood in the world of the Old Testament; cf. Ezra 2.61-62.) It is likely that this very imaginative explanation of Melchizedek's missing pedigree derives in the first instance from the writer's conception of Christ as 'Son of God': because he conceives of Christ the 'Son of God' as 'having neither beginning of days nor end of life'—this is expressed in neat chiastic form in the Greek—the strange presentation of Melchizedek can suggest itself. Thus, for all the talk of Christ's having become a priest 'according to the order of Melchizedek', the reverse order of precedence is implied in the assertion that it is Melchizedek who is 'made like the Son of God'. At the same time, there is clear evidence of speculation in the intertestamental period and beyond about the figure of Melchizedek, for example in the fragmentary Dead Sea text 11Q13 (11QMelch) which assigns him a quasi-messianic role and, less obviously, supramundane existence, according to some scholars. So far in *Hebrews* the divine sonship of Christ has been portrayed as setting him apart from angels and from Moses, but this would be the first and only time that the eternality of this sonship is affirmed. For the moment, however, it is the exposition of the significance of Melchizedek that engages the writer's attention, and the climax of the long period beginning in v. 1 comes in the assertion that 'this Melchizedek' (v. 1) 'remains a priest forever'. The point is not, then, one of theological abstraction, but one of great practical significance for those addressees ready to hear about Christ's perpetual priesthood on their behalf.

Melchizedek and Abraham (7.4-10)

The references to Melchizedek in Genesis 14 and Psalm 110 do not suggest a major character in the Israelite religious consciousness, though, as we have seen, that did not prevent him from becoming the focus for learned speculation in later times. The writer of *Hebrews*, wishing to bring out the significance of Christ's priesthood 'according to the order of Melchizedek', therefore feels the need to establish more clearly the credentials of this most shadowy of Old Testament characters: 'See how great he is!' (v. 4). Abraham *the patriarch* recognized his greatness by offering him a tenth of the spoils that he brought back with him after his pursuit of the confederate kings (Gen. 14.20). The special status of Melchizedek is evident in two respects, according to vv. 5-6. First, he needs no formal legal entitlement to take tithes from the great patriarch. Our author acknowledges that the Levites received tithes from the people of Israel, but he is careful to establish the limits of their authority. In so doing they were beholden to *commandment* and *law* (v. 5; see Num. 18.21-32). The fact that they were receiving their tithes from fellow-Israelites, who were also descendants of Abraham, put their perquisite in the category of a special concession, for Hebrew law was in other respects very restrictive in what it permitted an Israelite to take from another Israelite, especially if the second party were likely to be disadvantaged. By contrast, Melchizedek does not derive his authority from membership of the Levitical connexion—he 'does not belong to their ancestry'—and yet he is authorized to receive a tithe from the great Abraham himself (v. 6).

The second sign of Melchizedek's greatness is the fact that he pronounced a blessing on Abraham (v. 6b), and this in accordance with a principle that the writer seems possibly to coin for the occasion, namely, that 'the inferior is blessed by the superior' (v. 7). (Since the principle is not always acknowledged in practice in the Old Testament, the universalizing addition of 'always' in NEB and REB is ill-advised.) The reference to blessing has added point because the Levite connexion had as part of their duty the blessing of the people of Israel (Deut. 10.8). That Melchizedek blessed Abraham *who had the promises* (v. 6) is taken as further evidence of his greatness, for this is Abraham *en grande tenue* as the recipient of promises that would affect the generations descended from him. A verbal contrast between the Levites and Melchizedek is also apparent in that the Levites are said to have had a command (*entolēn echousin*, v. 5), whereas Melchizedek blessed, and so declared his superiority to, Abraham who had God's promises (*ton echonta tas epangelias*, v. 6).

A more direct contrast between Melchizedek and the Levites is exegetically available to the author, moreover, in view of his explanation of the 'silences' of Gen. 14.18-20 already in v. 3. The Levites, being but mortal, compare ill with one 'having neither beginning of days nor end of life', of whom it is said circumspectly in v. 8 that he 'lives'. This latter statement may reflect awareness of the postbiblical speculation about Melchizedek's identity. It is certainly an understatement in comparison with v. 3, but perhaps because there it was easier for the characterization of Melchizedek to be coloured by the author's understanding of Christ as 'Son of God'. Then, in almost playful vein ('One might even say', v. 9), this section is concluded with the suggestion that the subservience of the Levitical priestly order to Melchizedek is also evidenced in the meeting between Abraham and the priest-king of Salem in the sense that Levi himself, in the person of Abraham his ancestor, could be said to have paid tithes to Melchizedek (vv. 9-10). Here the writer comes close to coining another hermeneutical principle whereby to prise unsuspected meaning from the biblical text (cf. v. 7).

New Priesthood—New Law (7.11-19)

The argument now builds on Ps. 110.4 with its decree of perpetual priesthood for a member of the Davidic dynasty. That such a conferment should be announced already within the lifetime of the Levitical priesthood is taken as indication that that priestly system was deficient. When later it is said of Christ that by his offering of a single sacrifice for sins he 'perfected for all time' those who are being made holy (10.14) the author gives some indication of what he means here by 'perfection'. For the time being the idea of perfection and the goal of an effective cultus are represented in the last verse of our section: 'the introduction of a better hope, through which we approach God' (v. 19). That 'law' ultimately as much as, and perhaps more than, priesthood is the writer's target is apparent from v. 12 (cf. vv. 16, 18-19). The people of Israel had received the Levitical priesthood concomitantly with the law. Indeed a common interpretation of *ep' autēs nenomothetētai* (v. 11) is that the law was established on the foundation of that priesthood (though see Lane, *Hebrews 1-8*, pp. 173-74, for the translation of the whole clause in v. 11 by 'for the people received regulations *concerning* the Levitical priesthood'). Such is the synergism of priesthood and law that the removal of the one must involve the abolition of the other, and to underline the point the same root (*metatithēmi–metathesis*) is used for both operations. Some idea of the radicality of this step may be gained from the fact that *metathesis*, as in NRSV 'a *change* in the law' here in v. 12, is used in 12.27 in relation to the end-time convulsions out of which the new eternal order emerges.

In v. 13 'these things' seems to imply the presentation of Christ *sub specie* Melchizedek in the chapter so far; strictly speaking the expression refers to the authorial inferences drawn from Gen. 14.18-20 in vv. 1-10 and from the decree of Ps. 110.4 that already informs the discussion (cf. 6.20; 7.3, 11) and that will soon be quoted again (v. 17). Verses 13-14 add to the argument of vv. 11-12 the observation that, when the new priestly figure appeared, his tribal affiliation, which was Judahite rather than Levitical, confirmed that the Aaronite priesthood was being superseded, for Israelite law gave no entitlement to non-Levites to serve at the altar. In v. 13 the word-play in *meteschēken* ('belonged to') and *proseschēken* ('served') emphasizes that the consequence of *belonging* to the tribe of Judah was that it was not possible to *serve* in a priestly capacity in Israel. The tradition of Christ's Judahite descent, evidently a feature of early Christian preaching (cf. Rom. 1.3; 2 Tim. 2.8) as well as of the Gospels themselves, is obviously well-established for the author. So much may possibly also be implied in the occurrence of *anatetalken* (NRSV 'was descended') in v. 14, if it is meant to recall the prophecy in Num. 24.17 of the (presumably Judahite) ruler ('star') who would 'arise (LXX *anatelei*) out of Jacob'. (The corresponding noun-form *anatolē* ['shoot'] is used in Jer. 23.5 of the expected Davidic ruler [NRSV 'Branch'; cf. LXX Zech. 6.12].) As the writer observes, there is nothing in the Pentateuchal legislation connecting the tribe of Judah with priesthood. Moses, who is taken to be the author of the Pentateuch, says nothing on the subject in the legal sections, and makes no mention of priesthood in his blessing on Judah in Deut. 33.7.

The beginning of v. 15 bears slight formal correspondence to v. 14, but it is elliptical by comparison, since what is 'even more clear' is not quite so clear, and hence the assisting 'And what we have said (is even more clear)' in NIV. The point of vv. 15-16 is, in any case, that the indestructible life of Christ, evidenced in his resurrection and exaltation, shows him to be truly a priest 'according to the likeness (*kata tēn homoiotēta*) of Melchizedek'. This last expression may be intended as a synonym for 'according to the order (*kata tēn taxin*) of Melchizedek', but with the emphasis more on Melchizedek as example than as hierarch. If the expression is synonymous with 'according to the order of Melchizedek' then the latter has been evacuated of any sense of succession and simply emphasizes the similarities between Melchizedek and Christ, notably in respect of perpetuity of office. However, the expression 'the order of Aaron' in v. 11 is not so easily treated in this way, unless it is regarded as purely analogous with 'the order of Melchizedek'. There is in any case an element of reversal here as compared with v. 3 where it is Melchizedek who is said to have been 'made like (NRSV 'resembling') the Son of God'.

In v. 16 deprecating reference is made to law and commandment (*nomon entolēs*, NRSV 'a legal requirement') as the basis of Levitical entitlement to office (cf. on v. 5). Moreover, the command is described as 'fleshly (*sarkinēs*)' because it had to do merely with 'physical descent' (so NRSV, paraphrasing), and also because 'fleshly' implies transience and may be contrasted unfavourably with 'the power of [Christ's] indestructible life'. In vv. 16 and 17 the 'power of an indestructible life' and the appointment to the Melchizedek priesthood are linked in such a way as to suggest that the resurrection-exaltation of Christ is the point at which his exercise of priesthood began (cf. on 5.5-6). His indestructibility, it is noted in v. 17, is indicated in the prooftext of Ps. 110.4, for the one addressed there is declared to be 'a priest *forever*'. This phase of the argument is regarded as settled by vv. 18-19 where bold statement ('the law made nothing perfect', v. 19) answers per inclusio to the hypothetical condition of v. 11 ('if perfection had been attainable'). The commandment in question in v. 18 is that by which the Levitical tribe was authorized to exercise the priesthood in Israel, and it is pronounced 'weak and ineffectual'—with the help of an effective enough alliteration (*asthenes/anōpheles*)—because it belonged to that larger system of law that could not bring about 'perfection' for those relying on it. This description of the commandment resonates with the Pauline characterization of 'the law' in Rom. 8.3 as 'weak through the flesh', whatever the other perspectival differences between the two texts. But our section concludes with a reference to the 'better hope' (v. 19) that supersedes (cf. *epeisagōgē* [NRSV 'introduction'], where the preposition *epi* may suggest the idea of introduction 'over and in addition to') 'law' in that it is able to make the seeker after God fit for the divine presence (cf. 6.18-20; 10.19-22).

Permanent Priesthood (7.20-28)

Another feature of Ps. 110.4 is brought into prominence in order to demonstrate the uniqueness of Christ's priesthood 'according to the order of Melchizedek': it was founded upon a divine oath. There are framing references to this oath in vv. 20 and 28. Thus for the second time in the epistle a clinching argument is made of the swearing of a divine oath (see 6.13, 17); the previous invoking of the idea in ch. 6 may have facilitated its reappearance here.

The litotes in 'not without' in v. 20 (*ou chōris*) almost has the effect of making the Aaronic priesthood sound anomalous in not having an oath confirmatory of the status of its anointed priests, though see also 4.15 and 6.10 for other instances of litotes as a stylistic feature in *Hebrews*. (NRSV 'This was confirmed with an oath' drops the litotes, but cf. NIV 'And it was not without an oath!') Verses 20-22 are constructed on two correlative clauses, beginning 'and to the extent that' (*kai kath hoson*, v. 20) and 'by so much' (*kata tosouto*, v. 22), though modern English versions have not felt obliged to indicate this (cf., however, AV, ASV). (See 1.4 for a similar construction, with the correlative terms in the reverse order as compared with 7.20, 22.) In the Greek, moreover, the name 'Jesus' is given prominence by being the last word in the sentence (v. 22). Within this framework there is a nicely balanced parenthesis constructed on *hoi men* (v. 20) and *ho de* (v. 21), contrasting the Aaronic priests and Christ in relation to divine oaths and the basis of priesthood. (Texts such as Exod. 29.9 and 1 Sam. 2.30 make no mention of an oath when referring to the bestowal of priesthood upon the house of Aaron.) And because oath and covenant are so closely linked in ancient covenant- and treaty-making the topic of the 'better covenant' can make its appearance in *Hebrews* for the first time, in v. 22. Jesus is said to be the 'guarantor' (*enguos*) of this covenant, by which it is implied that he ensures its continuance, supplying what is necessary to fulfil its terms.

Verses 23-24 reproduce the *hoi men/ho de* contrast of vv. 20 and 21. The fact that the Aaronite priests were mere mortals is noted in v. 8, and more is now made of the point as they are compared, to their disadvantage, with Christ. Verse 23 ('Now there have been many of those priests', NIV) picks up the phrasing of v. 20 (*hiereis gegonotes > gegonotes hiereis*) and observes that there were many of those 'oath-less' priests for the simple reason that they were subject to death like the ordinary mortals that they were. That Christ's priesthood continues on a permanent basis produces the major conclusion of v. 25: he is able perpetually to save those who, in accordance with the better hope of v. 19, seek to avail themselves of their newly-gained access to God. The difference between NRSV 'for all time' and NIV 'completely', in translation of *eis to panteles*, is not great, though the temporal emphasis of the former makes the contrast with the insecure tenure of the Aaronite priests of v. 23 the more visible. However, the only other occurrence of the expression is in Lk. 13.11 where it is used in connection with the crippled woman who was *completely* (*eis to panteles*) incapable of straightening up. As in Heb. 7.25, the verb *dunamai* ('be able') is in close attendance, which encourages a preference here for translating by 'is completely able'. The good offices of Christ are said to be effective for those who approach (*tous proserchomenous*) God through him, which contrasts with the writer's verdict in 10.1 on the sacrificial system of the law that could not make perfect *tous proserchomenous* ('those who draw near to worship', NIV). Specifically, the enduring nature of the life of Christ, emphasized at several points in the chapter already (vv. 3, 8, 16, 24), enables him to fulfil in perpetuity the priestly function of making intercession on behalf of his people.

The idea of Christ's unique competence as intercessor is developed in vv. 26-28, in what amounts to a job description that is followed up in 8.1 with the statement 'we do have such a high priest'. Previously the writer has said that it was fitting (*eprepen*) that Christ should achieve perfect competence in his role as pioneer of salvation through his experience of human suffering (2.10). What now fits him to be high priest to his people is his distinctness from them: 'holy, blameless, undefiled, separated from sinners, and exalted above the heavens' (v. 26). 'Exalted above the heavens' suggests that he is beyond the locus of human sinning and in the realm where perfect intercession can be made. The weakness of the Israelite high priests, referred to simply as 'the high priests' in v. 27, is again seen in the fact that before they could act on behalf of the general populace they had to make expiation for their own wrongdoing (cf. 5.3). In this respect they were not 'separated from sinners' (v. 26). The argument of the section requires that *touto* ('this') in v. 27 should mean 'this latter', referring only to the necessity of Christ's offering a sacrifice on behalf of his people. *Hebrews* consistently holds to the doctrine of the indefectibility of Christ (cf. 4.15; 9.14, and the comment on 12.3).

Verse 28 concludes this phase of the discussion by setting out two pairs of contrasting elements, first in the law-oath opposition and then in the contrast between the Aaronite priests and Christ. The Old Testament institution of priesthood depended upon mere humans (*anthrōpous*) beset with human weakness (*astheneian*; cf. 5.2, 'beset with weakness') for its continuation, whereas the supersessionary oath is concerned with the divine Son (introduced anarthrously as in 1.2) 'made perfect forever'. This oath of installation, it is noted, came 'after the law' (v. 28), as if to say that the mere chronology indicates the inferiority of the earlier and the superiority of what follows it. This is a kind of argument that is familiar in *Hebrews* (cf. 7.11; 8.7, 13); it is the principle of 'abolishing the first in order to establish the second' (see 10.9). When dealing with related questions Paul can as easily appeal to chronological priority as indicating superiority, except that in such a case it is law that comes second (see Rom. 4.10-11; Gal. 3.17).

Hebrews 8: The New Covenant

Introductory Comment

If 7.26-27 sets out a kind of high-priestly job description, this chapter begins with the assertion that Christ meets the specifications (though Christ is not mentioned by name until 9.11). One such was that the high priest should be 'exalted above the heavens' (7.26), and the first verses of the chapter bring this into the centre of the discussion. The fact that Christ did not belong to the Jewish priestly connexion is not considered a disadvantage in view of his higher sphere of operation, the validity of which derives from the new covenant dispensation already predicted in the Hebrew scriptures, in Jeremiah 31. In fact, virtually half of this short chapter consists of a quotation from the Jeremianic section on the new covenant (vv. 8-12; cf. Jer. 31.31-34). The chapter prepares the way for the discussion of Christ's sacrifice in 9.1-10.18 by presenting his high-priestly credentials and thus his capacity to deal with the problem of human sinfulness. Covenants—regarded as the basis of God's relationship with his people—stand or fall according to their ability to deal with this same problem (vv. 10-12; cf. 9.15; 10.16-18).

We Have Such a High Priest (8.1-6)

It is appropriate to summarize the 'main point' (v. 1, NRSV) of the previous argument, seeing that the writer is about to embark upon a major discussion of the priestly mediation of Christ in chs. 9-10. The expression 'such a high priest' (v. 1) echoes 7.26, and the whole clause assures the reader that what has been described as necessary in the preceding verses (7.26-27) has become available in Christ. The assertion 'we have' is characteristic of *Hebrews* (6.19; 13.10; cf. 4.14; 10.19; 12.1) and is meant to counter the perception of some of the addressees that Christianity might better be defined vis-à-vis Judaism in terms of manifest cultic impoverishment. In its language v. 1 marks a return to 1.3 with its deferential, and characteristically Jewish, allusion to God ('sat down at the right hand of *the Majesty on high*'). The addition of the reference to the divine throne here in 8.1 recalls the 'throne of grace' in 4.16, where also the throne of God is understood to have become a source of mercy because the Christian high priest is in attendance there.

The assumption behind v. 2 is that the Jewish sanctuaries were the earthly counterparts of the real and permanent shrine of God in heaven. Seen in this light, the Mosaic tabernacle was only a 'sketch and shadow' of the heavenly archetype (v. 5). 'Sanctuary' and 'true tent' seem to imply a bicameral layout for the heavenly prototype, since the use of *hagia* for the inner sanctuary would be paralleled at several points in chs. 9 and 10 (e.g. 9.12; 10.19, both in relation to the heavenly sanctuary); but it is possible that the sanctuary and tent are to be regarded as co-extensive and therefore reflecting a unicameral heavenly sanctuary, as becomes the case in 10.19-20 with the tearing of the curtain and the opening up of the 'new and living way' into the divine presence. The mention of 'the true tent which the Lord pitched' (lit.) finds a purely verbal parallel in the Septuagint's rendering of a line in Num. 24.6 where the standard Hebrew text talks about 'aloes' planted by the Lord and the Greek, representing a couple of small textual variants, introduces the idea of the Lord pitching 'tents'. The point of the statement is that God's pitching of the (true) tabernacle removes any suggestion of impermanence such as would naturally be associated with an earthly tent or 'tabernacle'. The 'mortal' who did set up the taber-nacle is identified in v. 5 as Moses. It is also implicit in v. 2, though not so important for the author's immediate purpose, that God does not dwell in temples made by human hands (cf. Acts 17.24; Isa. 66.1). In 9.24 the author states that Christ did not enter 'a sanctuary made by human hands' but went into heaven itself.

At the same time, it is suggested in v. 3 that talk of Christ as a high priest would be meaningless if he did not have something to offer as a sacrifice. The argument at this point is expressed as a kind of logical necessity (cf. 7.12), and the definition of high-priestly function is again in terms of the offering of gifts and sacrifices, as in 5.1. To the extent that a distinction may be made between present and aorist subjunctives in the Greek of the New Testament, the use of the aorist with 'offer' may suggest a single act of offering, which would be in keeping with explicit statements about Christ's offering of himself in sacrifice in, for example, 7.27 and 10.12. (Conversely, the present subjunctive with the same verb represents repeated action in 9.25.) Strictly speaking, the requirement that Christ should have 'something to offer' has already been addressed in 7.27 where it is said that he 'offered himself', but, in terms of the developing argument, the way in which he *as offerer* justifies his title of high priest does not become fully apparent until 9.11-14, following discussion of the old and new covenants (8.6-13) and of the ancient sanctuary and its regulations for worship (9.1-10).

Christ's high priesthood, however, is not exercised on a this-worldly basis (v. 4). The significance of his non-Levitical, Judahite descent has already been noted in 7.13-17, where the supersession of the Levitical priesthood is seen as the proper inference to be drawn from the introduction of Christ as a priest according to the order of Melchizedek. Here the concern is, rather, to exclude by the same consideration the earthly realm as the sphere of Christ's high-priestly activity. If he were on earth, says the writer, he would not even be a member of the priestly connexion ('a priest'). A unity in biblical revelation is assumed: the operation of one system of priesthood *according to the law* is inconsonant with the operation of another. (It is not clear that 'law' has a negative connotation here, as it has in 7.16, 18-19, 28.) While it might also be inferred from the use of the present participle (NRSV 'there are priests') in v. 4 that the Jerusalem temple and priesthood were still functioning at the time of writing, consideration of the grammar and syntax will not necessarily lead to this conclusion. The verse is discussed in the Introduction ('Date of Composition').

In this section and hereafter it is the Old Testament tabernacle or 'tent of meeting', and not the temple, that is brought into contrast with the Christian 'new order'. The author may have intended to sound less confrontational by thus adopting a slightly oblique approach to the verbal dismantling of the Jewish cultic system which, after all, he regarded as having originally been God-given. At the same time, since none of his readers could have been in any doubt about his intention (cf. 8.13; 13.9-16), the tabernacle may simply have appealed to him as more amenable to his purpose, either because of its closer association with the tradition of the Mosaic covenant, or because it represented more vividly the temporariness and provisionality of the old order, or because he wanted to deal in first principles, setting out arguments that held good irrespective of the state or standing of the Herodian temple. These possibilities are not, of course, mutually exclusive.

In v. 5 the earthly sanctuary is now characterized per hendiadys as a 'sketch and shadow' of a heavenly prototype. In the Old Testament the location of the divine presence is associated with both heaven and earth, and sometimes—by dint of bilocation or a kind of 'superposition'—with both at the same time (e.g. Pss 20.2, 6; 80.1-2, 14). Here the reference to the tabernacle recalls the instruction given to Moses in Exod. 25.40 to construct it 'according to the pattern' (*kata ton tupon*) shown to him at Sinai (cf. Exod. 25.9; 26.30; 27.8; and compare, with reference to the Solomonic temple, 1 Chron. 28.19). The inclusion of the word 'everything' in the quotation from Exodus underlines the fact that in all respects the tabernacle was derivative from, and subordinate to, the heavenly exemplar. There is very slight textual support for the inclusion of the word in LXX Exod. 25.40, but it could as easily have been introduced by our author himself.

The idea of a temple plan being revealed to a divinely commissioned builder has ancient near eastern parallels that may go back as far as Gudea the king of Sumerian Lagash in the late third millennium BCE (what precisely Gudea saw in his dream is discussed in Hurowitz, pp. 33-57). To the extent that *Hebrews* envisages an actual heavenly sanctuary with a terrestrial counterpart the comparison could be said to lean towards Platonic idealism, but the concept of a heavenly temple is so clearly present in the Old Testament that the author's dependence upon non-biblical categories would require further demonstration. In Col. 2.17 a contrast is drawn in respect of certain religious observances between shadow and substance without necessarily involving Platonic influence. This concept of heavenly prototype and earthly counterpart noticeably is not applied by the author to the constitution or governance of the Christian church—as if Christian life and worship should be determined according to a rigorous patternism rather than guided by general principles of behaviour. As in general, so in this respect the writer would have wished to *contrast* the system of worship represented by the tabernacle and the newer Christian order (cf. 13.9-16).

Since the 'ministry' (cf. v. 2) of the tabernacle was founded upon a covenant, the writer proceeds to strengthen his argument by appeal to the prophetic expectation of a new covenant that would by the sheer generosity of its terms render its predecessor redundant (v. 6). And just as Moses was the mediator of the first covenant (cf. Gal. 3.19, and see *Ass. Mos.* 1.14; 3.12), so Christ is said to be the mediator of this new covenant (cf. 9.15; 12.24). The terms expressive of superiority ('more excellent' [*diaphorōteras*] and 'better' [*kreittonos*]), as also the use of the correlative *hosōi* (lit. 'by so much'), recall 1.4 and its statement on the relative status of Christ and the angels. Covenant and promise are near synonyms in a context like this (cf. Eph. 2.12), but the conditional nature of the promises attaching to the Mosaic covenant tradition (see Exod. 23.22; 24.3, 7) is regarded by the writer as the Achilles' heel of the old system, as becomes apparent from the long quotation in vv. 8-12.

The Covenant Terms (8.7-13)

The strength of the argument at this point consists in the fact that it is the Hebrew scriptures themselves that envisage the replacement of the Sinaitic covenant by something more radical and more effective. It is appropriate, then, that vv. 8-12, in repeating a modified form of the Septuagintal version of Jer. 31(LXX 38).31-34, represent the longest Old Testament quotation in *Hebrews*. Moreover, the repetition of vv. 33-34 at 10.16-17 means that the whole section dealing with Christ's priesthood and self-offering is framed by the Jeremianic passage. It is inferred from the Jeremianic reference to a new covenant that the old one was faulty in some way (v. 7), though the writer may well have shared the Pauline estimation of the law as 'holy' (Rom. 7.12) and yet 'weakened by the flesh' (Rom. 8.3) because of the human subjects with whom it had to operate. Such a distinction is suggested by v. 8 where God is said to find fault with 'them' (masculine), by which the people of Israel, and not the covenant or its promises, are meant. At the same time, the provisional and ultimately inadequate character of the original institution is argued in chs. 9 and 10 (see 9.9-10; 10.1). That 'the days' (v. 8) of Jer. 31.31 had now come would not have been doubted by a writer who could claim in the first sentence of his letter that the Christian era belonged in the 'last days' (1.2).

The new covenant envisaged in Jeremiah 31 is first described here in negative terms (v. 9) and then positively (vv. 10-12). First the addressees are reminded that the Sinaitic covenant was established at the time of the Israelites' exodus from Egypt, when God 'took them by the hand' (v. 9). At that point they had pledged their obedience to the terms of the covenant (Exod. 24.7), but they had failed to live up to their undertaking and so God 'had no concern for (*ēmelēsa*) them'. The discrepancy between the standard Hebrew text and the Septuagint at Jer. 31.32 has been discussed extensively but inconclusively. The Hebrew *b'lty* almost certainly implies marriage relationship ('though I was their husband', NRSV), which would suit very well the covenant context there, given the depiction of marriage in covenant terms in other Old Testament passages (see Prov. 2.17; Hos. 2.16-20; Mal. 2.14). The Septuagint rendering is difficult to square with the Hebrew, possibly because it involves a measure of exegetical activity. Since *amelein* occurs in LXX Jer. 4.17 in description of Jerusalem's disregard of (MT rebellion against) God, an element of *quid pro quo* may have been introduced (intertextually!) in 31.32. There are other passages where human rejection of God is reciprocated by God's rejection of those concerned (cf. 1 Sam. 15.23, 26; Hos. 4.6).

Some of the features of the Jeremianic 'new covenant' would have supplied agreeable matter had the author been minded to incorporate them in his argument, but he is concerned principally with the problem of sin and its removal from the conscience of those who seek freedom from it. In this respect, the final assurance that iniquities would be graciously dealt with and sins remembered no more is crucial (v. 12), for the perceived ineffectiveness of the old covenant lay in its inability to operate at this level (cf. 9.9-10). The very positioning of the assurance of mercy and forgiveness (v. 12) after the statement about the writing of God's laws on the heart (v. 10) will easily have been interpreted as implying the possibility of renewal for those who, even while in covenant relationship with God, still fell short of his standards. The text thus has something to say on the question of post-baptismal sin that so vexed some Christians in the early history of the church, and perhaps most famously Tertullian (*On Modesty* 20), who based his argument on another passage in *Hebrews* (6.4-8) which speaks of the impossibility of renewal to repentance.

The main point of the excerpt, but surely not the sole point to be drawn from such an extended quotation, is repeated in v. 13 (cf. v. 7): the mere use of the word 'new' implies the superannuation of the old. What follows may be taken as a general principle—'anything that is becoming obsolete and growing old will shortly disappear' (REB)—but it would be a strangely disinterested comment by an otherwise interested party if it were not also a comment on the imminent fate of the Jerusalem cultus. Again, as with v. 4, the possibility cannot be excluded that the temple was still standing at the time of writing. The phrase *to palaioumenon* (NRSV 'what is obsolete') could be translated 'what is becoming obsolete', with perhaps a more self-conscious reference to impending events in Palestine. Similarly, the Greek *aphanismou* in the expression 'will soon disappear' (so NRSV, NIV) could as easily be translated by 'destruction' (cf. LXX Deut. 7.2), and the whole clause by 'will soon be destroyed' (lit. '[is] near destruction').

Hebrews 9: Purifying the Conscience

Introductory Comment

In the short section 9.1-10 two aspects of the cultic order attaching to the 'old covenant' are summarized, namely, the regulations for worship and the layout and contents of the 'earthly sanctuary'. The order in which these two matters are discussed is the reverse of that given in v. 1. The framing occurrences of 'regulations' (*dikaiōmata*) in vv. 1 and 10 help to delimit the section and characterize its subject-matter. Thereafter, in vv. 11-28 the author seeks to demonstrate how precisely Christ as fulfilment of the older order goes beyond the externalities mentioned in v. 10. Crucially, the cleansing of the conscience of the individual Christian believer creates the conditions in which he or she may worship the living God (vv. 11-14). In strictly biblical and juridical terms, for this to be possible the requirements of the old covenant to which Israel had been bound at Sinai had to be met, and so in vv. 15-22 the idea of the supersession of the Sinaitic covenant by its Christian counterpart is developed. Then, in the third movement within the section, Christ's capacity as officiating high priest to operate within the higher, heavenly realm becomes the basis of the writer's doctrine of finality in relation to Christ's sacrificial death (vv. 23-28).

The Tent of Meeting (9.1-5)

The Exodus narrative sequence of covenant-making (ch. 24) and then the construction of the tent of meeting (chs. 25-31; 35-40) is itself suggestive of the close connection between covenant and cultus that is made here (v. 1). The chapter begins elliptically with the statement that 'the first' had regulations and an earthly sanctuary. It is clearly the 'first' covenant that is meant. In that case the use of the imperfect tense in *had* ('had [*eiche*] regulations for worship') need not imply that Judaism had lost its sanctuary by the time of writing. Thereafter the two compartments of the tent of meeting are each described as a 'tent', with the first called here *hagia*, which term elsewhere in *Hebrews* refers to the inner shrine or to the heavenly sanctuary (cf. 9.8, 12, 24, 25; 10.19). The term used in v. 3 for the inner compartment is 'holy of holies' (*hagia hagiōn*), which is a Hebraism (e.g. Exod. 26.33-34).

The listing of the furnishings in the two compartments (vv. 2-5) assumes no detailed knowledge on the part of the addressees but at the same time presents one or two problems for the interpreter. Chief among these is the allocation of the altar of incense—for this is what must be intended by *thumiatērion*—to the most holy place (v. 4). There are, however, Old Testament references that associate this altar with the inner sanctum and its furnishings. In Exod. 30.6 its positioning is given as 'in front of the curtain that is above the ark of the covenant, in front of the mercy seat that is over the covenant', while according to Exod. 40.5 it was to be installed 'before the ark of the covenant'. (It may also be significant that the altar of incense is not mentioned in the MT or the Septuagint of Exod. 25.23-40, in the instructions for the furnishings of the outer 'tent', but is given separate treatment in 30.1-10. LXX Exod. 38 [MT 37] also fails to mention this altar [contrast MT 37.25-28] [Gooding, pp. 66-69]. The Samaritan Pentateuch, on the other hand, has the first account of the altar of incense [= Exod. 30.1-10] between vv. 35 and 36 of Exod. 26 [Von Gall, pp. 172-73].) Again, 1 Kgs 6.22, in its account of the building of the temple, talks of 'the [whole] altar that belonged to the inner sanctuary', with which we may especially compare the use of *echousa* (lit. 'having') in v. 4 here (NIV 'which had'; NRSV, less sensitively, 'In it stood'). The association of the altar of incense with the annual ritual of atonement (see Exod. 30.10), soon to become important as the argument of ch. 9 develops, may also be a relevant consideration. Thus the special relationship between this altar and the adytum may have inspired varying interpretations of its location in relation to the ark of the covenant. The idea of a heavenly prototype of the tabernacle (and temple) featuring an altar of incense (cf. Isa. 6.6; Rev. 8.3 ['the golden altar that is before the throne']) may also have contributed to this development.

Similarly, the statement that the ark of the covenant was the repository for the jar of manna and for Aaron's rod goes beyond the Old Testament references to their being laid up 'before the covenant' (see Exod. 16.33-34; Num. 17.10-11). Their inclusion at all in this list at least serves to underline the transient character of the tabernacle, which is associated primarily with Israel's wilderness traditions. The interests of brevity (cf. 13.22) foreclosed discussion of the possible significance of the several items listed in vv. 2-5. No doubt the writer could have supplied the omission, and many have done so on his behalf, but, by declining to expand as he could have, he implies something about the relative unimportance of such preoccupation compared with the agenda that unfolds in chs. 9–10. The main purpose of vv. 1-5, then, is scene-setting in preparation for the cultic activity, whether by Jewish priests or the Christian high priest, reviewed in these two chapters.

Limited Atonement (9.6-10)

The ritual activities associated with the two compartments in the tabernacle are summarized and contrasted in vv. 6 and 7. The outer room (lit. 'first tent') was the scene of regular (daily) activity by the priesthood—represented in v. 6 by the ordinary term 'priests' in order to strengthen the contrast with v. 7—but entrance to the inner compartment was on a different basis and restricted to the annual fast of the Day of Atonement, when the high priest was required to perform a blood ritual centred on the ark of the covenant. The contrast is carefully set out in the two correlative statements of vv. 6 and 7: the first tent—continually—the priests/the second (tent)—once a year—only the high priest.

A point has already been made of the fact that the Israelite priests had faults of their own to address before ever they could act on behalf of the ordinary worshippers (see 5.3). With a degree of circumspection not considered necessary at 7.27 the writer says that the high priest presented his offering 'on behalf of himself', whereas the sins of the nation are explicitly mentioned in connection with the national sin offering. In 5.3 the word 'sin' is used in connection with the sacrifices presented by the high priest, although the context also speaks of those who are 'ignorant and wayward' (5.2). Now, in an apparently reductionist statement on the scope of the high-priestly ministrations on the Day of Atonement, the 'sins' are characterized as 'sins of ignorance' (*agnoēmatōn*), whereas Leviticus 16 says that the high priest makes atonement for the Holy of Holies 'because of the uncleannesses of the people of Israel, and because of their transgressions, all their sins' (v. 16), and that he confesses over the head of the live goat 'all the iniquities of the people of Israel and all their transgressions' (v. 21), with the result that Israel are cleansed from all their sins (v. 30). It is important, at any rate, that *agnoēma* is here given its more usual sense of 'sin of ignorance' and is not generalized to 'sin', as a mere alternative to *hamartia*, since it is basic to the argument of the passage that it was only sins of ignorance that were covered under the old system, in contrast with the more serious offences that were the focus of Christ's high-priestly activity (see below on v. 14).

In v. 8 the writer suggests that the Holy Spirit is demonstrating through the mere existence of the earthly shrine and its restricted access the absence of a more direct means of approach to the divine presence. The 'first tent' could in theory denote the tabernacle as a whole but may more probably have the same significance as in v. 6 where it refers to the outer compartment or 'holy place'. The writer is then saying that the very existence of an outer compartment symbolized the restriction of access to God that characterized the original earthly sanctuary. In saying that the Holy Spirit 'shows' that the way into the Holy of Holies had not yet been opened up the writer is evidently thinking of the Spirit as author of the biblical text (cf. 3.7): he 'shows' (*dēlountos*) this in the written account of the tabernacle and its arrangements in Exodus-Leviticus (perhaps compare Heb. 12.27 where a phrase from a biblical quotation 'shows' [*dēloi*] a particular truth that the writer thereupon spells out). Moreover, the limitations of the tabernacle ritual are regarded as symptomatic of that whole period, right up to the author's time, when the same basic system was in operation (v. 9). (AV, on the other hand, has 'the time *then* present', which makes for a statement more specifically about the tabernacle era.) 'This' at the beginning of v. 9 could refer to the tabernacle ritual described in vv. 6-7(8), but it is more natural, and probably more in keeping with the author's style, to find the antecedent in 'the first tent' at the end of v. 8. The point is the same in the end.

The crux of the matter was that the ceremonial law could not deal with the bedrock problem of a human conscience suffering under the awareness of defects more fundamental than any breach of ritual requirements (cf. 9.14; 10.2, 22). So the word 'conscience' in v. 9 is given prominence: 'that cannot *in respect of conscience* perfect the worshipper'. The inadequacy of the ceremonial law is underlined in the root-reprise whereby '(cannot) perfect the worshipper' (*teleiōsai ton latreuonta*) recalls the reference in v. 6 to the priests who carry out their ritual duties (*tas latreias epitelountes*) in the tabernacle. The one is within the officiants' competence, but the other is beyond their jurisdiction. What comes within the jurisdiction of the Israelite priests is summed up in v. 10 as matters relating to food and drink and sundry ritual washings, here viewed as merely interim observances awaiting the time of reformation (*diorthōsis*, a *hapax legomenon* in the New Testament). The assonance in 'food' (*brōmasin*) and 'drink' (*pomasin*) contributes to a sense of their insignificance as compared with what the author regards as the main issue. 'Food and drink and various baptisms' would fairly sum up that part of Leviticus immediately preceding ch. 16 and the subject of the Day of Atonement that is never far from the author's mind in Heb. 9-10. The main topics in Lev. 11-15 are food laws (ch. 11) and ritual purification (chs. 12–15).

Eternal Redemption (9.11-14)

Verses 11-12 make two basic points, namely that Christ officiates in a 'tent' more elevated than any earthly sanctuary made by human hands, and that his presence there is on the basis not of mere animal sacrifice but of his own self-offering. The focus is on the exalted sphere of Christ's high-priestly activity, but an important insight into the author's thinking is offered in the qualifying phrase 'the good things that have come' (AV 'good things to come') (v. 11). Whereas in 10.1 the writer speaks of 'the good things to come', here the preferred reading is 'the good things that have come' (i.e. *genomenōn* rather than *mellontōn*), which seems to agree more readily with the reference to Christ's having already come as high priest, and which may be regarded as answering to the 'time of reformation' of v. 10. The future orientation of the expression in 10.1 makes sense there as representing the perspective of the Old Testament adherent of the law, with the basic authorial standpoint remaining essentially as here. At the same time, the explicit force of *genomenōn* here in 9.11 was not to be missed by a constituency that may have been more conscious of cultic deprivation than of spiritual gain as a result of their having embraced Christianity. The 'good things' of the Christian era have come about, then, because Christ has entered into the heavenly Holy of Holies (which is what *ta hagia* must mean in v. 12), thus demonstrating his competence to deal not only with the superficies of ceremonial purity but also with the basic problem of humanity's estrangement from God. While it is possible to translate *paragenomenos* (NRSV, NIV 'came') in v. 11 by 'having arrived' (i.e. 'on the heavenly scene'; so Attridge) the participle may as easily refer to the supervention of Christ as the new and transforming element in the story of humanity's relationship to God (for the general sense of 'arriving on the scene' see Mt. 3.1; Lk. 12.51).

If heaven is Christ's sphere of ministry, says v. 12, then it was not animal sacrifice such as featured on the Day of Atonement (cf. 'the blood of goats and calves') that secured his access there. Moreover, his entry into that higher realm indicates that the goal of 'eternal redemption' has been achieved. This redemption was obtained when Christ died at Golgotha, rather than in a complex of actions starting at Golgotha and including his self-presentation in heaven. Thus he is said to enter the heavenly sanctuary 'through his own blood'. A more loaded rendering of the preposition *dia* in v. 12, as in NRSV 'he entered...*with* his own blood', tends towards the second view, though NRSV at least represents a toning down as compared with its RSV forbear ('*taking* not the blood of goats and calves but his own blood'). Again, NIV 'having obtained eternal redemption' is probably better than the discovery by NRSV of a coincident aorist in *heuramenos* ('he entered once for all into the Holy Place...thus obtaining eternal redemption'), and certainly so if the appeal to the coincident aorist is meant to combine with the doubtful rendering of *dia* just noted. That he entered 'by his own blood' carries a definite implication about the sacrificial nature of Christ's death, grounded in the conviction that humanity's alienation from God is basically a moral issue and that this too involves its own kind of reparation to God. For the author, Christ had incontrovertibly been raised to glory, and manifestly had not yet emerged from the heavenly sanctuary. Thus even the passage of time between his departure and return would have given weight to the claim that he had entered the heavenly sanctuary 'once for all'; his second appearance would not be in sacrificial submission but in delivering power (see v. 28). The view that *ephapax* ('once for all') in v. 12 is meant to contrast with the 'double entrance' of the high priest into the Israelite Holy of Holies on the Day of Atonement, when he presented first his own offering and then the national offering (see Lev. 16.11-14, 15), may find collateral in 7.27, but the reference there is not limited to the annual Atonement ritual (cf. 'day after day'), and a more general statement about the finality of Christ's sacrifice is to be expected here (cf. 10.10, where also *ephapax* is used).

While a minimalist view is taken of tabernacle rituals earlier in the chapter (vv. 9-10), the limited efficacy conceded there is again acknowledged in vv. 13-14 in the interests of an *a fortiori* argument about the far-reaching consequences of Christ's sacrifice. (It is possible that 'the blood of goats and bulls' is a generalizing reference to the Israelite sacrificial system, but the Day of Atonement is probably still uppermost in the writer's mind.) The ritual of the 'red heifer' of Numbers 19 is also introduced, whether as featuring in some postbiblical version of the Day of Atonement (cf. *m. Par.* 3.1) or, perhaps, as affording another prime example of an Israelite cleansing rite, in this case associated with the ritual cleansing of people who had touched a corpse or had merely been in close proximity to one (Num. 19.11, 13, 14, 16). That the red heifer is designated as a sin offering (or 'purification offering') in Num. 19.9, 17 may also have contributed to its association here with the sin offerings of the Day of Atonement (cf. Lev. 16.3, 5, 6, 9, 11, 15, 25, 27). By contrast, says our author, Christ's blood purifies the human conscience stained with 'dead works', and so as to render the individual fit to serve the living God (v. 14; cf. v. 9). Again there is emphasis on the difference of sphere in which Christ operates, now by stating that his sacrifice was made 'through the eternal Spirit', that is, through the medium appropriate to the realm where God most truly is (cf. 1 Cor. 2.11). It is this extra 'dimension' to what Christ did that encourages the large claims that the author makes in connection with his death. There is also the difference that whereas the red heifer of Numbers 19 was to be physically 'without blemish' (v. 2), Christ offered himself to God as one morally 'without blemish' (*amōmos* [v. 14] as in LXX Num. 19.2).

The expression 'dead works', as in v. 14 (cf. 6.1), has been variously explained. At the least it describes the spiritually dead and unproductive life that fails to comply with God's standards. But it is likely that these works are described as 'dead' because they lead to death (so NIV), in which case we should recall Num. 15.22-31 and the two categories of sin discussed there, namely sins of ignorance for which sacrifices were prescribed (vv. 22-29; cf. v. 7 above) and 'high-handed' sins which carried the death penalty (vv. 30-31). When, therefore, *Hebrews* claims that Christ's death atones for 'works that lead to death' the contrast with the Jewish ritual law is fully visible. The distinction between 'inadvertent' and 'high-handed' as in Numbers 15 is no longer relevant. The present writer has noted elsewhere (Gordon, pp. 445-46) how that postbiblical Judaism attributed to the concept of repentance (cf. Heb. 6.1) the same power to dissolve this distinction, as in the saying associated with Resh Lakish in *b. Yom.* 86b: 'Great is repentance, for deliberate sins are accounted as sins of ignorance.' The expansion of Hab. 3.1 in the Targum to the verse expresses the same idea:

> The prayer that Habakkuk the prophet prayed when it was revealed to him concerning the extension that is given to the wicked, that if they return to the law with a perfect heart they will be forgiven, and all their sins that they have committed before him will be like sins of inadvertence.

So, according to the author of *Hebrews*, the human conscience may be cleansed from the moral defilement that disqualifies the individual from worshipful access to God (cf. 10.22). Sacrifices that were merely animal and physical were ineffectual in this regard, but he maintains that Christ's sacrifice offered through the eternal Spirit, in the realm of the divine, can equip his addressees and himself for worship of 'the living God'.

Will and Testament (9.15-22)

The terms of the Mosaic covenant—which draws the Mosaic legislation in general after it—did not, of course, provide for the reinstatement of the high-handed offender in the way of v. 14. If what has been said there is to have any validity, therefore, a new order constituted in a different covenantal arrangement is required. And so it is argued, principally in vv. 15-17, that Christ has met the claims of the first covenant against its earthly covenant partners by means of his death. This does not mean that the author views Christ's death simply as a retrospective tailpiece to the Mosaic covenant; on the contrary, the clear implication of v. 18 is that the new covenant is based on sacrificial death ('not even the first covenant was inaugurated without blood'), and with this the words of institution in the New Testament accounts of the Lord's Supper are in agreement ('This cup is the new covenant in my blood', 1 Cor. 11.25; 'This cup that is poured out for you is the new covenant in my blood', Lk. 22.20). Most importantly for our author, Christ in his death has fulfilled the commonplace requirement of the Old Testament law that largely accounts for the discussion in these verses: 'without the shedding [on which see below] of blood there is no forgiveness of sins' (v. 22).

The benefits of the new covenant are said to be for 'those who are called' (*keklēmenoi*, v. 15), described elsewhere in the letter as 'those who are to inherit salvation' (1.14), 'partners in a heavenly calling' (3.1) and 'heirs of the promise' (6.17). The language of 'call' sounds restrictive, but only superficially so. In the first place, the idea of divine calling is meant to confirm in the addressees the conviction that though they are outside the Jewish fold they are truly 'heirs of the promise'. In this connection, the use of the perfect passive participle in *keklēmenoi* where the New Testament normally uses the verbal adjective *klētoi* does nothing to weaken the sense of security deriving from the divine initiative. Secondly, the 'called' in the new order embrace both Jews and Gentiles, and the covenant concept is therefore opened up to a much wider circle than hitherto ('including us whom he has called, not from the Jews only but also from the Gentiles', Rom. 9.24). This v. 15, indeed, caps the argument and claims of the preceding verses in saying that even the *parabaseis* ('transgressions') committed during the period of the first covenant are now dealt with by Christ's death (cf. Rom. 3.25-26). This is Christian covenantal imperialism, to be sure, but necessarily so for the author, who is concerned with the theology of real redemption from real sin.

In vv. 16 and 17 the argument is based, according to a common view, on another meaning of *diathēkē*, which not only was the word used to translate the Hebrew *bᵉrît* ('covenant') in the Greek Old Testament but also was the regular Greek term for 'testament', as in the English expression 'last will and testament'. There is probably a similar play on the meanings of *diathēkē* in Gal. 3.15, 17. According to this view, it is only by observing this distinction that we can interpret vv. 16 and 17 satisfactorily, since the death of the 'testator' (AV, REB) is required for the implementation of a will whereas the enforcement of covenant agreements does not involve the death of contracting parties. Moreover, if this variation in the use of the Greek word is admitted, vv. 16 and 17 would follow more directly on from the reference to the eternal inheritance of v. 15 (with which indeed that verse ends, though this may not be apparent from English translations that restructure the Greek syntax in the interests of English idiom and comprehension).

However, this explanation has been challenged on the grounds that the activation of wills in the Greco-Roman world did not depend upon the death of contracting parties, and that inheritance could as easily take place before death as afterwards. Moreover, the phrase *epi nekrois* (v. 17) which is translated 'at death' in NRSV (NIV 'only when somebody has died') may be better rendered 'on the basis of dead (things)', in which case it could refer to the covenantal victims (sometimes loosely called 'sacrifices' by modern writers) that were killed in the ratification ceremonies for covenants and treaties in antiquity (cf. Gen. 15.7-21; Jer. 34.18). There is a good parallel to *epi nekrois* in the expression *epi thusiais* ('on the basis of sacrifices'), occurring in a covenantal context in LXX Ps 49(50).5. Even this explanation of *diathēkē* is not without difficulty, however, in that v. 16b refers unmistakably to the death of the ratifier of the will/covenant as being essential for its implementation. To sustain the covenant explanation, therefore, it is necessary to interpret this as the symbolical death of the ratifier as represented in the killing of the covenant victim. And that requires a lot of reading between the lines in v. 16b, and even more so in verse 17b which emphasizes that a will/covenant cannot come into force so long as the ratifier is alive. But whichever explanation we choose, Exodus 24—which gives the account of the ratification of the Mosaic covenant—involves a blood ritual, and so the author can claim in vv. 18-22 here that the principle 'not without blood' has been consistently observed from the time of the 'first' (by which is meant the Mosaic) covenant.

There are details in the summary of Exod. 24.3-8 given in v. 19 that are not found in the Old Testament passage, such as the inclusion of goats' blood in the aspersion ritual (though 'and goats', omitted by a number of texts, may be an addition influenced by vv. 12-13) and the mention of water, scarlet wool and hyssop, which may represent an intentional fusing with other Old Testament rituals, especially that of the 'red heifer' (cf. on v. 13; see also Num. 19.6, 9, 17-18). More surprising is the apparent replacement of the 'altar' of Exod. 24.6 by 'scroll', since in the original narrative the point of including the altar in the blood ritual was presumably to symbolize the new covenantal partnership between God, as represented by his altar (v. 6), and his people (v. 8). That the order scroll-people parallels the altar-people sequence in Exod. 24.6, 8 tends to support the conclusion that 'scroll' replaces 'altar' here. The 'scroll' or book in question is, of course, the 'book of the covenant' that contained the ordinances laid upon Israel at Sinai. If it is indeed replacing the mention of the altar and is not just another datum additional to the Exodus account, it may also represent the divine part in the proceedings, though it still leaves us without an explanation as to why the substitution was made in the first place. We can, at the same time, imagine that our author was quite willing to reproduce a text or tradition that depicted the scroll of the covenant, with its legal 'ordinances' (cf. Exod. 24.3), as having been subjected to a purification rite. The three occurrences of 'every'/'all' in v. 19 are noteworthy (cf. also vv. 21-22). Attridge comments well on the 'repeated insistence on the comprehensiveness of the proceeding' as 'striking' and as suggesting 'the foundational importance of the event'.

The quotation in v. 20 differs in small details from the Septuagintal version of Exod. 24.8. On the one hand, the element of commandment in the Mosaic covenant is emphasized in *eneteilato* (lit. 'commanded') for the LXX *dietheto* ('established', 'made'), while the initial *touto* ('This') for LXX *Idou* ('Behold'), which latter is a literal translation of the

Hebrew *hinnēh*, helps to set up a verbal parallel between the Exodus verse and part of the 'words of institution' in their Markan form (compare *touto estin to haima mou tēs diathēkēs* in Mk 14.24 with *touto to haima tēs diathēkēs* here). For that matter, says the writer, similar rites were applied to the rest of the cultic paraphernalia of ancient Israel (v. 21), in keeping with a general principle evident in the Old Testament, namely that purification usually involves blood ritual (v. 22). In so saying he goes beyond the biblical tradition, since there is no reference to the comprehensive purification of the tabernacle in a blood ritual (though Josephus refers to such a purification, *Ant.* 3.206). The forgiveness of sins, with which v. 22 and the section end, transcends these ritual matters and brings us back to the main issue, which is to show how Christ deals with the problem of sin and forgiveness. Already the answer has been given—'a death has occurred' (v. 15)—and in that sense v. 22 looks back as well as forward into the remainder of the chapter. 'Forgiveness' is used here absolutely, which is very unusual, but the element of vagueness may be deliberate in view of the previous insistence on the inadequacy of animal sacrifices to bring about purification in the moral realm (see vv. 9-10). What is meant is that such cleansing as was possible 'under law' required the *haimatekchusia* of sacrificial blood. There is no prior occurrence of *haimatekchusia* which, strictly speaking, refers, not to the shedding of blood, but to its being poured out at the altar (e.g. Lev. 4.7, 18).

Christ 'Appearing' (9.23-28)

From consideration of covenant inauguration by blood ritual the argument of the previous section had proceeded to the necessity of a general cleansing of the sanctuary and its utensils (vv. 21-22). The closing statement of v. 22 is more than enough to suggest that this necessity arose because of the contaminant effect of human use of these sacred objects whose acceptability for divine service was only possible after their subjection to a purification rite. The already developed contrast between worship on the earthly and heavenly planes largely accounts for the terms in which v. 23 makes its point. Again the earthly sanctuary and its furnishings are regarded as terrestrial counterparts to a heavenly prototype (cf. 8.5). But while the idea that the heavens are not clean in God's sight will have been familiar to the writer (cf. Job 15.15), this probably contributes little to the argument here, even though the verb 'purified' (*katharizesthai*) functions grammatically for the second part of the verse as much as for the first. The point that the author wants to establish is that Christ's actions as high priest had to do, not with a tabernacle or temple merely of the present world order, but with the realm of the divine and the eternal, and that Christ himself was fully qualified and equipped so to act (v. 24). That he appears before God 'on our behalf', that is, on behalf of people who are morally flawed and 'defiled', does, on the other hand, give a certain point to the statement in v. 23 that the heavenly sanctuary needed to be purified with something better than animal sacrifices.

The mention of the heavenly sanctuary leads the author to expand in vv. 25-28 on the idea of the finality of Christ's sacrifice (cf. v. 12). And whereas the Day of Atonement was the sole occasion in the year when the Israelite high priest was authorized to enter the Holy of Holies (see v. 7), in the present context it is the regular repetition over centuries of these otherwise rare events that features in the argument. The high priest obviously had to enter with blood that was 'not his own' (*allotriōi*, v. 25; with which contrast 'by the sacrifice of himself', v. 26). Significantly, as far as eucharistic theology is concerned, the writer does not countenance any idea of the repetition of Christ's sacrifice *in heaven or on earth* (vv. 25-26). If repetition of his sacrifice were required, then, it is argued, his physical death would have been required on each such occasion. Moreover, the requirement would extend not just to the time of the Israelite priesthood, but to the whole of human history, since it is a question of moral and spiritual cleansing rather than of ritual purification. As it is, the coming of Christ is located at 'the end of the ages (*sic*)', which goes beyond the use of the expression 'these last days' of 1.2 in that the Christ-event is seen more specifically as the culmination of the ages. So much for the sufficiency of Christ's self-offering; but its 'once-for-all-ness' is also to be seen as a consequence of Christ's humanity, since it is the norm for humans to die once and then face judgment. This reference to post-mortem judgment as the normal expectation of humans renders even more remote the idea of repeated physical dying on the part of Christ.

The comparison with ordinary mortals is made with the help of the correlatives *kath hoson* and *houtōs* at the beginning of vv. 27 and 28. In the second half of v. 28, however, the comparison appears to be left behind as another one is suggested by the ritual of the Day of Atonement. The picture of Christ appearing a second time, not now sin-bearing as at the time of his crucifixion but bringing salvation for his people, is probably inspired by the idea of the Jewish high priest emerging from the sanctuary after carrying out the ritual peculiar to the Day of Atonement, to the relief and pleasure of the waiting worshippers. (It would be surprising if the writer could use the language of v. 28 without himself thinking of the Day of Atonement, which has already surfaced and resurfaced within the chapter.) Just as the high priest came out from the sanctuary having made atonement for himself and the people of Israel, so, says v. 28, Christ will return 'without sin' (*chōris hamartias*), seeing that he has settled that issue once and for all. But the section ends on a hortatory note, for, if it is those who are eagerly waiting for the heavenly high priest who experience his salvation, then the author would again remind his addressees of the necessity of endurance that is laid upon them.

Hebrews 10.1-18: One Sacrifice for Sins

Introductory Comment

Verses 1-4 repeat the familiar assertion that the sacrifices of the Israelite cultus could not deal effectively with the problem of sin, while vv. 5-10 build on an insight already expressed in Psalm 40, according to which animal sacrifices are nothing in God's sight as compared with the obedience of the speaker in the psalm. Other Old Testament texts make the same point, notably in the prophetic books, but Psalm 40 held the additional attraction that it included first-person speech that could be interpreted as a messianic utterance. In vv. 11-18, in the final phase of the argument about the uniqueness of Christ's self-offering, the recurrent priestly rituals of the tabernacle, now on a daily basis as distinct from the annual enactment of the Atonement ritual (cf. v. 3), are contrasted with the one act by which Christ dealt with the problem of sin (vv. 11-14). Moreover, the passage in Jeremiah 31 about the new covenant is found to have anticipated the end of the sacrificial cultus in virtue of the generous terms decreed in the covenant (vv. 15-18).

Annual Reminders (10.1-4)

Since, according to 7.11, the Old Testament system of law was founded on the Levitical priesthood the failure of the latter, which the writer sought to demonstrate in ch. 9, would have implications for the whole superstructure. The entire system of Jewish law is here judged to be in the category of 'shadow' (cf. Col. 2.17), now overtaken by the substance of the things to which it had pointed forward. *eikona,* which is in contrast with *skian* ('shadow', v. 1), is fairly translated '(true) form' by NRSV, and, together with *pragmatōn* (lit. 'things'; NRSV 'realities'), conveys a sense of substance as compared with the shadow of the previously unrealized 'good things' in the era of Old Testament law. There is not necessarily a tension between the author's earlier reference to 'the good things that have come' in 9.11 and 'the good things to come' here in v. 1, since the perspective reflected here is that of the people of Old Testament times. For this reason NRSV 'the good things to come' is preferable to NIV 'the good things that are coming', since the latter is committed to a future perspective even from the standpoint of *Hebrews.*

There is more than a suggestion of futility in the expressions used in v. 1 to summarize the ritual of the Day of Atonement: the same sacrifices— continually—year after year. Moreover, the weakness of the law is seen in its inability to bring the worshipper to 'perfection', that is, to the perfect worship of God in which the inhibition of sin and guilt is no longer present. While the immediate discussion focuses on Christ's sacrifice of obedience, the question of those who 'approach (God)', in a Christian context, will be addressed in v. 22.

In v. 2 the writer can indulge in a rhetorical question since, even if his addressees were not to share his christological presuppositions, he can be confident about the logical force of his argument. The purifying of conscience remains the issue (cf. 9.9), and if that could be achieved under the law by means of a cleansing 'once for all' (*hapax*)—the term recalls Christ's once-for-all sacrifice (9.12, 26, 28)—the worshipper should no longer feel the need to offer animal sacrifices to God. What brought the Jewish sacrificial system to an end was, of course, the destruction of the Jerusalem temple in 70 CE. We cannot be certain that the question 'Would they not have ceased being offered?' implies the continuance of the sacrificial system at the time of writing, but it could very naturally be taken that way. Even if this falls short of being a decisive argument, its possible significance should be respected in discussions of the dating of *Hebrews*.

Far from banishing sin from the consciousness of the community, the ritual of the Day of Atonement, as v. 3 points out, involved the calling of sins to remembrance: the high priest confessed over the head of the 'scapegoat' all the sins of the people of Israel (cf. Lev. 16.21). Again there is an element of reductionism here (cf. on 9.9-10), for the Day of Atonement was also concerned with the 'making of atonement', as the name suggests (cf. Lev. 16.30). But by characterizing it in this way the writer implies a contrast with the provisions of the new covenant, according to which sins are erased from the divine memory (cf. vv. 17-18; 8.12). *anamnēsis* ('reminder') is also the word that occurs in the accounts of the institution of the Lord's Supper ('Do this in remembrance of me', Lk. 22.19; 1 Cor. 11.24-25), and that commonly is invested with ideas of 'making present and effective', in the interests of a theology of the eucharist that is difficult to sustain on this basis. The idea of the making of sin 'present and effective' (or any such thing) certainly would have little to contribute to the understanding of the present text. As v. 4 implies, the great defect of the older system was that the 'reminder' of sins on the Day of Atonement was not accompanied by an effective means of dealing with them.

'To Do Your Will' (10.5-10)

The conviction that animal sacrifices were ineffectual as regards sin and its forgiveness was not original with Christianity, as the text goes on to show with its quotation from Psalm 40. The Old Testament has already been cited for its intimations of a different era in regard to the knowledge and worship of God, notably in 8.8-12 where verses from Jeremiah 31 are cited at some length to show that a new order was in prospect and has now arrived. Psalm 40, attributed in its superscription 'to David' (in whatever sense that expression should be taken), is regarded by the author as in part or in whole the utterance of Christ, speaking by the spirit of prophecy, as he comes (*eiserchomenos* [v. 5], no doubt inspired by *hēkō* ['I come'] in v. 7) into the world (cf. 1.6). Already in 2.12-13 we have had first person utterances of a psalmist and a prophet interpreted as christological speech. The point of the quotation from this psalm is that God seeks inward obedience on the part of his people rather than the presentation of animal sacrifices. A similar idea is expressed in Ps. 51.16-17 where, most understandably, the psalmist recognizes that his serious transgression needs more than animal offerings to reinstate him with God (cf. Ps. 50.7-15). In Psalm 40 the familiar regime of burnt offering and sin offering is contrasted with the interiorized obedience of the psalmist and his pleasure in doing God's will, and God's approval of the second rather than the first is acknowledged. In this case the insight comes from the psalmist's sense of elation at having experienced God's deliverance, and from the grateful recognition that something more than mere cultic performance is appropriate to the circumstances.

While it is true that such Old Testament passages tend to relativize rather than to deny altogether the importance of the institution of sacrifice—Psalm 51, for example, has an appendix in which the acceptable offering of sacrifices, given the right conditions, is envisaged (vv. 18-19)—the instinct towards more spiritual conceptions of worship is clearly present. Worship, for that matter, is but one of a number of major subjects on which the Old Testament is visibly in dialogue with itself. This dialectical approach is also evident in statements on such matters as after-life, kingship, conceptions of divine presence, and the definition of 'Israel', which makes it all the more important that pronouncements on 'the Old Testament view' of a given subject rest not on individual texts or passages but on a rounded appreciation of the sum of the evidence. And the same may apply in the New Testament, for example in the area of eschatology.

In v. 5 our author reproduces the Septuagintal rendering of the clause 'ears you have dug (lit.) for me' (Ps. 40. 6) by 'a body you have prepared for me' (LXX Ps. 39.7). There is a certain graphic similarity between the Greek ΩΤΙΑ ('ears') and ΣΩΜΑ ('body'), and the case for internal corruption in the Septuagint would be stronger still if the possibility of dittography of the Σ at the end of the word now immediately preceding ΣΩΜΑ were allowed. Nevertheless, the Septuagintal reading is often explained as a paraphrase of the Hebrew, and this may be the case. The psalm itself, in recounting the psalmist's declaration, 'Then I said, "Behold, I come" ' (v. 7), clearly appealed to the writer as a statement by Christ at the time of his incarnation, and the Septuagintal reading 'a body you have prepared for me' obviously comported very well with this interpretation. Thus the author, whose principal interest in ch. 9 had been Christ's heavenly entrance and session, now looks back to the time of his incarnation. But it is also the case that a more literal rendering of the Hebrew would have suited the writer's emphasis upon willing obedience as superior to the offering of uncomprehending animals in sacrifice (cf. Isa. 50.5, 'The Lord God has opened my ear'). The omission, indeed, of 'I delight' (LXX 'I have decided') from the quotation of Ps. 40.8 (LXX 39.9) in v. 7 makes the purpose of the incarnation, if anything, more specifically the fulfilling of God's will. Originally the psalm will have referred to the psalmist's obligation to keep the law of God, in whatever written form it was available to him. A reference to the law of the king in Deut. 17.14-20 cannot be ruled out in view of the psalm's association with the 'Davidic' collection.

Verses 8 and 9 see prefigured in Psalm 40 the supersession of animal sacrifices by Christ's willing obedience: the former, representative of the Levitical system of law, are replaced by the latter. By grouping together the several categories of sacrifice mentioned in the verses that he quotes and then repeating the two (negated) verbs that express disapprobation, the writer gives his verdict on the whole gamut of Old Testament sacrifices. Verse 10 then combines the two ideas contrasted in the excerpt from Ps. 40(39) by asserting that the fulfilment of the *will* of God through the offering of the *body* of Christ means sanctification for his people. Here 'by which will' (lit.) may be quite elliptical, meaning

Christ's fulfilment of the will of God: his obedience has made possible the sanctifying of his followers. On the other hand, the writer may be wishing to say simply that the Christian's sanctification comes about in accordance with God's will. If so, the verse indicates that the offering of Christ's body is essential to the implementation of that divine will, and the meaning is not vastly different. The Gethsemane prayer of Christ answers to both possibilities, expressing with unique intensity the idea of his having come to fulfil God's will in the giving of himself (cf. Lk. 22.42). There is a verbal parallel in 1 Thess. 4.3 ('For this is the will of God, your sanctification'), but the meaning there is that it is God's desire that his people should live their lives according to the dictates of holiness, as becomes clear in the verses that follow. This being 'made holy' here in v. 10, stated as an accomplished fact ('we have been made holy' [NIV]), is noticeably grounded in the once-for-all action of Christ and not in any attempt at self-sanctification on the part of the Christian believer. This time the finality of Christ's sacrifice is emphasized by the positioning of *ephapax* last in the sentence.

Sitting, Waiting (10.11-14)

Verses 11 (*pas men hiereus*) and 12 (*houtos de*) are markedly contrastive. There is emphasis on the fact that the lot of the Israelite priest was to *stand* as he served daily in the sanctuary, whereas Christ offered himself as sacrifice and then *sat down* 'at the right hand of God'. Again there is laboured emphasis on the endless routine of the daily sacrifices ('day after day...again and again the same sacrifices', v. 11). By contrast, Christ is said in v. 12 to have offered one sacrifice *eis to diēnekes*, which repeats the term used in v. 1, except that, whereas there it described the continual offering of sacrifices, here it expresses the idea of the continual efficacy of the one offering of Christ. There is not so much to be said for the suggestion that *eis to diēnekes* relates to Christ's act of sitting down rather than to the sacrifice that he offered. The positioning of this temporal adverb at the end of the clause in which it belongs is paralleled in v. 1, and also in the case of *ephapax* ('once for all') at the end of v. 10. While perfect consistency between one section and another as regards the use of figurative speech should not be expected, it remains a fair question whether a writer who has so recently talked of the second 'appearing' of Christ as high priest in 9.28 would now declare that he had 'sat down for ever'. The proof of the completeness of this offering is evident, then, in the fact that 'this priest' (NIV for *houtos* [lit. 'this (one)']; AV 'this man') sat down 'at the right hand of God'. We are now back with Psalm 110, which has so influenced the central chapters of *Hebrews* and whose opening verse accounts for the 'waiting theme' in v. 13 here. Not only are Christians 'eagerly waiting' for Christ (cf. *tois auton apekdechomenois* in 9.28), but Christ himself is described here as waiting (*ekdechomenos*) the full visible expression of his victory—for now there is some recognition of the warrior motif in Psalm 110 as also being appropriate in relation to Christ's action within human history. The author may well have wished his addressees to note, moreover, that the issue of the delayed parousia (cf. vv. 36-39) was already addressed in the ancient psalm. 'Until' implies an interval between Christ's installation at God's right hand and the subjugation of his enemies (cf. 1 Cor. 15.25, 'For he must reign until he has put all his enemies under his feet'). The question of judgment will be taken up later in the chapter (see vv. 26-31).

In the meantime Christ's people are 'being made holy' (v. 14, NIV). The use of the present participle here contrasts with the occurrence of the perfect in v. 10, the issue now being the process by which the Christian's moral state is brought into line with his or her God-given status in Christ. But there is no suggestion of contingency in this choice of the present participle, because those who are undergoing the process are said to have been made perfect (*teteleiōken*, 'he has perfected'). The perfection in question is that of being made fit for the presence and the worship of God. This the writer has already declared to be unattainable on the basis of the law: 'There is, on the one hand, the abrogation of an earlier commandment because it was weak and ineffectual (for the law made nothing perfect); there is, on the other hand, the introduction of a better hope, through which we approach God' (7.18-19; cf. 7.11; 10.1). In earlier references to perfection it has been Christ as 'pioneer of salvation' (2.10) and as high priest (5.9; 7.28) who has been 'made perfect', in the sense of becoming qualified to act as high priest on behalf of his people. The 'perfect corollary' of this is their free access to the divine presence.

Remembering No More (10.15-18)

The author seeks to clinch the foregoing argument by citing two verses from Jeremiah 31, the chapter of the 'new covenant' from which extensive quotation was made in 8.8-12. Recognized as the author of Scripture (cf. 3.7), the Holy Spirit is said to 'testify' concerning the new reality of

v. 14. This testimony is, moreover, 'to us', which, even more than saying that the ancient scriptures were 'written for our instruction' (Rom. 15.4), recognizes that the author and his addressees personally have a stake in the covenant promises of Jeremiah 31. The citation of Jer. 31.33-34 here differs in several points of detail from the form quoted in 8.10, 12. Most significant, perhaps, is the replacement of 'with the house of Israel' (so 8.10) by 'with them', which derestricts the text now that the implications of the 'new covenant' have been worked through in chs. 9–10.

The occurrence of *meta gar to eirēkenai* ('for after saying') in v. 15 suggests that the quotation from Jeremiah is meant to be divided into two parts, with the second in some sense capping the first. The procedure commonly adopted in translations, and supported by some later manuscripts of *Hebrews*, is to make the break between vv. 16 and 17, with the insertion of something like 'he also adds' (NRSV) or 'Then he adds' (NIV) as introduction to v. 17. The writer is, then, highlighting the concluding statement that God will banish from his memory the sins committed by his people; and so the contrast with the annual remembering of sins occasioned by the Day of Atonement (cf. v. 3) is strengthened. The expression 'their sins and their lawless deeds' corresponds more closely to the Hebrew text at Jer. 31.34 than does the quotation of the same verse in 8.12, where only 'sins' are mentioned; the longer text expresses an appropriate comprehensiveness which the writer will have wanted to suggest at this point. Others regard the formulaic 'the Lord says' in v. 16 as introducing the second part of the quotation ('For after saying...the Lord says'), in which case both the implanting of the divine laws in human hearts and also the comprehensive forgiving of sins are highlighted as being the evidence, or product, of Christ's perfecting of his people. After his lengthy quotation from Jeremiah 31 in 8.8-12 the author emphasized the word 'new' and pronounced summarily on the imminent closure of the era of the 'old covenant'; here the word 'forgiveness' (v. 18), not actually present in his quotation but represented in verb-form in the Hebrew text of Jer. 31.34 ('for *I will forgive* their iniquity, and remember their sin no more'), is equally conclusive: the covenantal undertaking actually to forgive sins removes the rationale for the cultic presentation of animal sacrifices.

Hebrews 10.19-39: Entering and Enduring

Introductory Comment

The basis of Christ's heavenly priesthood having been outlined, the author encourages his addressees to avail themselves of the access to the divine presence that Christ has made possible for them (vv. 19-25). However, he is concerned to point out to them that even Christ's sacrifice and high-priestly intercessions will not avail for them should they reject 'the knowledge of the truth' that they had once ostensibly embraced (vv. 26-31). Finally, he reverts to exhortation as he reminds them of the privations that they had previously borne because they had fixed their hopes on the fulfilment of God's promises announced in the Gospel (vv. 32-39). The section acts as a bridge between the long exposition of the priestly self-offering of Christ in 8.1-10.18 and the panegyric on faith in ch. 11, and in this the articular function of 10.39 is especially clear ('But we are not among those who shrink back and so are lost, but among those who have faith and so are saved').

Confidence to Enter (10.19-25)

As previously in the letter, a statement of doctrine is followed by exhortation to respond in an appropriate manner. The note of personal appeal is strengthened by the use of *adelphoi* (NIV 'brothers'; NRSV 'my friends'; cf. 3.1, 12; 13.22; Rom. 12.1 [also beginning a practical exhortation, following on an extended doctrinal statement], and see the Introduction). A close formal comparison is provided by 4.14: 'Since, then, we have (*echontes oun*) a great high priest…let us hold fast to our confession.' The 'confidence to enter' (*parrēsian eis tēn eisodon*) here in v. 19 may be included among those 'compensatory' privileges that the author wishes to draw to the attention of the 'Hebrews' (see on 4.9; 8.1). 'Confidence to enter' implies in this context not just the subjective feeling but the objective right of access to God's own presence. Such 'confidence' was not a characteristic of the cultic worship of the Old Testament (cf. 9.7-10 and see on v. 20 below). Up to this point the preoccupation has been with Christ's entry into the heavenly sanctuary, though there have been intimations of the opening up of access for his followers, for example in 4.16, in the exhortation to approach the throne of grace 'with boldness'. Now the possibility of the Christian believer's direct access to God's presence is assumed as fact. Already 'confidence' has been presented as a necessary element of Christian discipleship (3.6), and as the appropriate attitude of the suppliant at the heavenly throne of grace (4.16). Verse 19 can state the theological basis for this confidence—the sacrificial blood of Jesus—in the light of the preceding argument, in a way that the earlier references could not. Moreover, we should not be surprised to find that the Christian's entry into the divine presence 'by (*en*) the blood of Jesus' is put on the same basis as Christ's own entry 'through (*dia*) his own blood' (9.12), since it was as forerunner and high priest that he entered the heavenly sanctuary.

The means of approach is described in v. 20 as a 'new and living way'. It is as if Christ's 'entry' has become an 'entrance' and then the very way of approach for his people. This way may be described as 'living' because of the indissoluble life of Christ who pioneered it (7.16, 25), and it may be contrasted with the 'works that lead to death' in 6.1; 9.14. However, a more meaningful contrast can be made with the means of approach to God as represented in Pentateuchal law. The high-priestly robe of the ephod had bells attached to its hem so that the bells would be heard when the high priest entered the Holy Place and came out, 'so that he may not die' (Exod. 28.35); similarly, the generality of the priesthood had to wear appropriate attire when they were engaged in altar service, 'or they will bring guilt on themselves and die' (Exod. 28.43). Similar warnings are issued in the context of the deaths of Nadab and Abihu (Lev. 10.6, 7, 9) and in connection with the entry of high priests into the Holy of Holies (Lev. 16.2). What is described here, on the other hand, is a 'new and living way' in the sense that those who approach God on this basis do so 'with confidence', and not in fear of their lives.

This 'way' Christ has 'opened' or 'dedicated' (*enekainisen*) for his followers. The verb has already been used for the inauguration of the Mosaic covenant in 9.18, and it is also used for the dedication of the Solomonic temple in LXX 1 Kgs 8.63 (cf. the 'Feast of Dedication' [*enkainia*] in Jn 10.22, referring to the rededication of the Second Temple after the Seleucid desecration of it). While 'curtain' (*katapetasma[tos]*) could refer to either the outer (entrance) screen or the inner curtain of the tabernacle, the commoner usage and the sense of the passage strongly support the latter (cf. 'the second curtain' of 9.3). The epexegetical *tout estin tēs sarkos autou* has been much discussed. It is probably simplest and best to recognize 'curtain' and 'flesh' as being in apposition. Just as entry to the sanctuary is said to be 'by the blood of Jesus' in v. 19, so here it is 'through his flesh'. It is unclear whether 'through the curtain' implies its being torn, as in the Synoptic tradition about the tearing of the temple curtain at the time of the crucifixion (Mt. 27.51; Mk 15.38; Lk. 23.45). The use of *dia* ('through') does not necessarily imply entry through a *torn* curtain (cf. 9.11; Jn 10.1). On the other hand, the Old Testament talks of ' (entering) within the curtain' when ritual entrance is in question, and the Septuagintal prepositional phrase for this is *esōteron tou katapetasmatos* (cf. Exod. 26.33; Lev. 16.2, 12, 15), reflected in Heb. 6.19 in the statement about hope entering *eis to esōteron tou katapetasmatos*. Thus there is a case for thinking either that the Synoptic tradition was known to the author, or that he, independently, saw the possible significance of a symbolically torn curtain along similar lines. If the idea of a torn curtain is present in the text, then we may also have to reckon with the possibility that the phrase ' (through) his flesh' implies that the way of access to God was opened up in consequence of a 'rending' of Christ's flesh when he offered himself in sacrifice on the cross.

Syntactically v. 21 belongs to the construction beginning with the participle *echontes* in v. 19, to which participle, indeed, it supplies another object ('a great priest'). The long sentence starting with v. 19 continues to the end of v. 22. Already similar content and phrasing in 4.14 have formed the basis of a summons to endure, and of an invitation to approach the divine throne (4.16). The 'house of God' over which the 'great priest' presides is not the heavenly sanctuary, but the people of God conceived as a sanctuary, as in 3.6. In the spirit of 9.1-6 (see especially v. 6), the author has thus outlined the basic 'cultic' provision for the worship of God by Christian believers. Verse 22, in turn, introduces the first element of a threefold exhortation in vv. 22, 23 and 24-25. In the first of these the author sets out his equivalent of the older ritual requirements for standing in the divine presence (v. 22). The first of these, a true heart, has straightforward Old Testament antecedents, as the psalmic entrance liturgies testify ('and speak the truth from their heart', Ps. 15.2; 'those who have clean hands and pure hearts', Ps. 24.4). This is conjoined with 'the full assurance of faith', as if the resolute exercise of faith is essential to the maintaining of a true heart. Faith is, in any event, a prerequisite for the one who would come near (*ton proserchomenon;* cf. *proserchōmetha* here) to God, according to 11.6. The subject of faith is confined mainly to ch. 11 and its adjoining verses within *Hebrews* (cf. 10.38, 39; 12.2 [though see 4.2; 6.1, 12; 13.7]). *plērophoria* ('full assurance') also occurs in 6.11, where it is associated with hope, in an exhortation to maintain hope to the end. All three members of the traditional Christian triad of faith, hope and love feature in this section (vv. 22, 23, 24).

The remainder of v. 22, consisting of two descriptive participial clauses, shows how the Christian worshipper has been made fit—two perfect passive participles are used in *rerantismenoi* ('sprinkled') and *lelousmenoi* ('washed')—for the divine presence. According to 9.14 it is the blood of Christ that cleanses the conscience 'from dead works'. While the writer undoubtedly would want to maintain that perspective on Christ's self-offering, the mention of sprinkling and the reference to water in the adjacent clause strongly suggest that he has in mind the red heifer ritual of Num. 19.9-22, which prescribes the aspersion of purificatory water for a person who comes in contact with a dead body. The previous reference to the red heifer ritual has drawn attention to its ineffectiveness in dealing with the problem of the human conscience (see 9.13-14; cf. 9.19), but the ritual is now spiritualized in service of the claim that Christ's sacrificial death effects a complete cleansing of the conscience. Such a spiritualization of ritual sprinkling is already present in the Old Testament, in Ezek. 36.25-26 where God promises cleansing through sprinkling for his people, and the bestowal of a new heart and a new spirit (cf. Jn 3.5; Titus 3.4-5). Ezekiel's sprinkling is not specifically linked with the purificatory water of Numbers 19, but may well have been influenced by awareness of the red heifer ritual. There are few other references to sprinkling with water in the Old Testament (cf. Num. 8.7). The Targum to Ezek. 36.25 makes specific mention of the 'water of purification' and the 'ashes of a heifer': 'I will forgive your sins as if they were purified with water of purification and with the ashes of a heifer for a sin-offering' (cf. *Targ. Zech.* 13.1).

Again, just as the Israelite priests were washed with water before entering upon office (Exod. 29.4), so the writer notes that Christians have had their bodies 'washed with pure water'. Or, if some other Old Testament precedent is in view, the author may have been thinking of the high priest's bathing before embarking on the ritual of the Day of Atonement (Lev. 16.4). Or, in view of the probable allusion to the red heifer ritual in the preceding clause, we should note that those involved in the burning of the carcass of the heifer had to wash themselves afterwards (Num. 19.7-8). This washing of the body may also have an inward, spiritual significance in the way of Jn 13.10 ('One who has bathed does not need to wash, except for the feet, but is entirely clean. And you are clean, though not all of you.'). A spiritual cleansing once and for all, as in the Johannine text, would be contextually very appropriate. But there may also be an allusion to the immersion of the body in Christian baptism, in which case the two clauses of this half-verse would be setting forth the inward and outward evidences of the renewing power of Christ.

The second member of the virtuous triad—hope—is introduced in v. 23. The cluster of ideas here recalls 6.18, where *kratēsai* probably refers to the initial act of grasping the proffered hope, whereas in the present context it is holding fast (*katechōmen*) to the hope professed that is enjoined (cf. 3.6, 14 where also *katechein* is used). As in 6.18, the character of the one who made the promise is offered as the ground for maintaining hope. In 4.14, where the addressees are exhorted to hold fast to their Christian profession (*homologia* as here), their having a competent high priest 'who has passed through the heavens' is cited as good reason to remain steadfast. In taking up again the theme of promise (cf. 4.1; 6.13, 15, 17; 7.6; 8.6; 9.15) the writer is acknowledging that he and his friends are not only living in the time of 'the good things that have come' (9.11) but are also waiting for the full disclosure of God's promised salvation. Elsewhere he emphasizes that in this respect they scarce differ from the faithful of Old Testament times who first received the promises (cf. 6.16-20) and who kept believing in God despite living in an era of non-fulfilment (11.13-16). Verse 23 is, in the end, about the *worshipper's* attitude towards God. To abandon the hope proclaimed in the Gospel is, it is implied, to question the trustworthiness of God; if we have a poor view of the God who made us we shall not be much interested in seeking his presence.

Verses 25 and 26 turn to the horizontal relationships within the community of Christian believers. Love, the primary Christian virtue, is not encouraged as some mere abstraction but is associated with good deeds. It is probably the author's intention to suggest that if love is to have meaning it must be incarnated in the 'good deeds' that other New Testament writers also advocate as a necessary concomitant of Christian faith (e.g. Mt. 5.16; Acts 9.36; 1 Tim. 5.10, 25; Titus 2.14; 3.8, 14; 1 Pet. 2.12). With these 'good deeds' we may contrast the 'works that lead to death' in 6.1; 9.14. Already the combination of work (*sic*) and love in the lives of those addressed has been cited as evidence of the genuineness of their faith (6.9-10). Nor is love something that can be practised in isolation from one's fellow-humans, and so the corporate dimension that is explicit in v. 25 appears already in v. 24 in 'let us consider how to provoke one another' (lit. 'let us consider one another with a view to provoking'). Such practical expressions of Christianity cannot thrive in a vacuum (v. 25). For whatever reason, there was a danger of the community members drifting apart and thereby forfeiting the encouragement and mutual support that they were meant to enjoy 'in community'. The word used for 'meeting together' is *episunagōgē,* referring either to the act of meeting or to the company when assembled. The *sunagōgē* element in the word, frequently occurring in the Gospels and Acts to denote Jewish synagogues, might be judged particularly appropriate for a community with a Jewish background, as may have been the case with the 'Hebrews' (the only comparable use of *sunagōgē* is in Jas 2.2, in reference to a Christian assembly of a strongly Jewish complexion), but the cognate verb occurs in 1 Cor. 5.4 in relation to the assembling together of the church in Corinth. It is easy to speculate on the causes of this disinclination on the part of some of the community to attend worship. Disillusionment with a religion so strongly tied to future fulfilment of present expectation could have been a factor (cf. vv. 36-39).

The memory of persecution may also have acted as a deterrent to some members, although a few verses hence the author will suggest that their previous experience had very positive aspects to it (see vv. 32-34). If, on the other hand, they were to meet together they would be able to exhort one another to remain steadfast in the faith. In an earlier admonitory section, the writer prescribed the fairly extreme-sounding remedy for failing hearts of exhorting one another 'every day' (3.13), and later he describes his letter as a 'word of exhortation' (13.22). The reference to 'the Day', by which is meant the day of Christ's return, encourages the addressees to see themselves as an eschatological community (cf. 1.2; 9.26) who, when they meet together, anticipate the very era that appears to be delayed in coming. They do not only stir up one another with what they perceive to be intimations of 'the Day'; they make the future happen. And since the principal occasion and purpose for which the community met will have been the observance of the Lord's Supper, it is legitimate to recall here the eschatological perspective of this institution in both the Gospels and Paul (cf. Mk 14.25, 'I will never again drink of the fruit of the vine until that day when I drink it new in the kingdom of God'; 1 Cor. 11.26, 'you proclaim the Lord's death until he comes'). It is worthy of note that the author can write to people of whose Christian allegiance he cannot be certain in all cases and assume that they, like himself, see signs of the approaching 'Day'. Something quite specific may be suspected as having been in his mind, and there is no likelier candidate than the destruction of Jerusalem and its temple by the Romans in 70 CE. Whether it was the fairly obvious signs of the impending tragedy, in the late 60s, or the tragedy itself, even the more sceptical of the community's members might well have found in these circumstances a harbinger of 'the Day'. For the association of the destruction of the temple with the end of the age they may already have had the Gospel tradition as represented in Mk 13.1-31 and its Synoptic parallels (Mt. 24.1-35; Lk. 21.5-33).

A Severe Warning (10.26-31)

The section recalls the stern tones, if not the actual terms, of 6.4-8. It follows on appropriately enough from the reference to 'the Day', with its implications of judgment, in v. 25, but the development of thought is governed by something more important than the catch-word principle. For the moment the writer sustains the first-person plural reference of the preceding verses, which makes him sound less accusatory as he issues his warning. He feels bound to state as a consequence of the doctrine of the uniqueness of Christ's sacrifice that to reject it is to repudiate the only available means of acceptance with God. Previously we have found the Old Testament's dividing of sins into those committed in ignorance and those carried out 'with a high hand' as central to the writer's theology of forgiveness (see on 5.2; 9.14). This section deals in the second category as it spells out the danger of apostatizing from the faith. 'Willingly' or 'wilfully' (*hekousiōs*) is in emphatic position at the beginning of v. 26; there is an implied contrast with sins committed in ignorance (cf. 9.7). The present participle in *hamartanontōn* suggests a more established pattern of behaviour or attitude of mind (cf. NRSV 'if we wilfully persist in sin')—and in this recalls the Johannine use of the same verb in 1 Jn 3.6. That the sin in question is that of apostasy is indicated by the description of the hypothetical defector as having received 'the knowledge of the truth', by which is meant the content of the Christian message (cf. 1 Tim. 2.4; Titus 1.1). The assertion 'there no longer remains a sacrifice for sins' is a daring inversion of the final sentence of the discourse on the uniqueness of Christ's sacrifice ('Where there is forgiveness of these, there is no longer any offering for sin', 10.18). There the point was that no further sacrifice was needed; here the message is that no alternative is available.

According to v. 27, the consequence of rejecting 'the truth' is the fearful expectation of judgment, which contrasts sharply with the hopeful waiting for the fulfilment of God's promises that is the natural state of the Christian believer as envisaged in *Hebrews*. *ekdochē* ('expectation') is found only here in the New Testament, though the related verb *ekdechesthai* occurs in v. 13 where Christ is said to await the subjugation of his enemies (so giving rise to the fearful prospect referred to here). While God is not mentioned directly at this point, his involvement is implied in 'fearful', as is confirmed by the repetition of the word in v. 31 ('a fearful thing to fall into the hands of the living God'). If we allow that the fear of martyrdom was prominent in the minds of the addressees (see the Introduction), it is ironical that the worse prospect of judgment from God is held out before them (vv. 27, 30-31).

An *a fortiori* argument of a type encountered in 2.2-3, and again invoking the contrast between the Mosaic law and the Gospel, is presented in vv. 28-29. The penalty for breach of certain basic laws was death and it was to be applied 'without mercy', most notably in the case of enticements to idolatry as in Deut. 17.2-7, where the rule about witnesses most nearly parallels the reference here (though for the injunction 'show no pity' see Deut. 13.8[9], also re idolatry; 19.13, 21; 25.12). Three fundamentally grave offences are singled out in v. 29. First, the recipients of the letter are challenged to consider the consequences of rejecting *the Son of God*, from which it may be judged that the writer wants them to be specially clear on the christological question. A similar use of this title, to emphasize the seriousness of rejecting the Christian message, is found in 6.6 ('they are crucifying again *the Son of God*'). This was not an issue unique to Jewish-Christian debate, nevertheless it was a major obstacle to Jewish acceptance of Jesus as messiah, seeing that it was perceived to involve blasphemy (cf. Mk 14.61-64; Jn 19.7). If the recipients of the letter were Jewish converts to Christianity, as seems very probable, this use of the title 'Son of God' will have been intended to focus their attention on one of the most fundamental questions posed by Christianity: who is Jesus of Nazareth?

Secondly, to abandon one's Christian profession is to 'profane the blood of the covenant', which phrasing, while appearing to echo the 'words of institution' at the Lord's Supper (cf. Mt. 26.28; Mk 14.24), refers specifically to the historic sacrifice of Christ as the means by which the unclean are 'made holy' (v. 14). The conclusions regarding Christ's self-offering in 9.1-10.18 depend entirely upon the recognition of Christ as divine and as competent to act in a higher realm than was accessible to any Israelite priest. To turn away from him would be to deny the validity of the new covenant and to treat the blood by which it was established, and by which the believer is sanctified, as 'common' or 'profane' (*koinon*). The addition of the clause 'by which they were sanctified' is striking, but it agrees with the companion section in 6.4-8 in viewing even the apostate as having been a beneficiary of God's goodness. While such a person may have been regarded as 'sanctified' in a limited kind of way (cf. 1 Cor. 7.14), the term may have been chosen partly in the light of the priestly distinction between 'holy' and 'common' (cf. 9.13, 'sanctifies those who have been defiled', *tous kekoinōmenous* and so as to contrast with the preceding reference to treating Christ's blood as 'common'. Notwithstanding that Christ's sacrifice made sanctification possible, the blood of his sacrifice is treated as 'common' when an erstwhile follower reneges on him. Thirdly, it is said of such a person that they have 'outraged the Spirit of grace', which again agrees with 6.4-8, to the extent that there the apostate is described as having 'shared in the Holy Spirit' (6.4). The hopelessness that the writer detects in this situation arises from the fact that the offender is resisting the overtures of a God whose grace inclines him to forgiveness and reconciliation of the offender. The seriousness of resisting the witness of the Spirit in relation to Christ is described in the Synoptic tradition as 'the sin against the Holy Spirit' (Mt. 12.32; Mk 3.29; Lk. 12.10).

The reference in v. 30 to God as 'the one who said' (*ton eiponta*) reminds the addressees of the theme of divine speech in *Hebrews* (see on 1.1); the climax to the main discussion will include the warning not to refuse 'the one who is speaking' (*ton lalounta*, 12.25). Appropriately, in view of the foregoing reference to the violation of the Mosaic law (v. 28), both quotations in v. 30 come from the 'Song of Moses' in Deuteronomy 32 (vv. 35-36). Even the prefatorial 'we know the one who said', which claims knowledge of more than the mere identity of the speaker, may be influenced by the Deuteronomy passage. There the people of Israel are condemned for their lack of discernment, especially as regards the disciplinary ways of God in response to their own disobedience (vv. 28-29). By contrast, our author claims for himself and his addressees a knowledge of God that includes an awareness of his hostility towards those who reject the very basis of their acceptance by him. Again, in the wider context of Deuteronomy 32 the ability of the God of Israel to kill and to bring to life is contrasted with the powerlessness of the nonentities in which others put their trust (vv. 37-39). In a word, the 'Hebrews' are dealing with the 'living' God (v. 31), with all the implications of the term for those who incur his displeasure (cf. 3.12 for the term and the same associations). Nothing about the background of the writer or his friends can be derived from the fact that 'I will repay' in v. 30 corresponds to the Pentateuchal Targum tradition at Deut. 32.35, since the same wording also appears in the Pauline quotation of the verse in Rom. 12.19.

Need for Endurance (10.32-39)

From stern warning the author turns to warm-hearted appeal to his addressees, just as he had tempered some earlier warnings about the danger of apostasy (6.4-8) with commendation of their very considerable virtues and with exhortation to 'show the same diligence' to the end (6.9-12). Something very striking had happened in the recipients' experience when they responded to the preaching about Christ, so much so that the writer could appeal to it, without fear of contradiction, early in his letter. The message first announced by Christ and passed on by those who heard him was attended by 'signs and wonders and various miracles' that helped convince the hearers that this was truly a communication from God (2.3-4). As I have noted in connection with 2.4, a similar appeal, in comparable circumstances and on similar grounds, was made by Paul to the churches in Galatia (Gal. 3.1-5). Those addressed had accepted the new teaching with enthusiasm and had happily put up with the persecutions that befell them on account of their Christian profession. For this decisive experience of conversion the term 'enlightened' (*phōtisthentes*) is used, just as it is in 6.4 where it is the first in a list of features descriptive of the hypothetical apostate envisaged there. The term, which does not occur elsewhere in the New Testament in precisely this way (though see Jn 1.9; Eph. 1.18), is specially appropriate in view of the writer's concern lest any in the community should 'sin against the light', by rejecting the ultimate 'divine speech' (cf. 1.1-2) in Christ. Later they will also be encouraged to recall the example of their leaders from that same earlier period when faith was young and commitment did not count the cost (13.7). They 'endured a hard struggle' (*athlēsin*, for which NIV has 'contest'), and the ideas of endurance (cf. v. 36) and of athletic contest will be developed in 12.1-13 (vv. 1-2, 12-13 for the race, vv. 1, 2, 3, 7 on endurance).

The earlier record of these Christians when faced with persecution had been honourable in the extreme. When publicly exposed (*theatrizomenoi*, v. 33; cf. Paul's reference to himself and his apostolic colleagues as having become a 'spectacle', *theatron*, 1 Cor. 4.9) they had not retired from the scene, and when they themselves were relatively free from trouble they had identified with fellow-Christians in their difficulties. They had been subjected to 'insults' (*oneidismois*), which in the final chapter are identified as sufferings endured for the sake of Christ ('bearing his abuse', *ton oneidismon autou pherontes*, 13.13). More remarkably, the author claims in his review of the Old Testament faithful in ch. 11 that Moses reckoned that 'abuse for Christ' (*ton oneidismon tou Christou*) was preferable to a share in Egypt's riches (11.26). Moses, moreover, is said in the same verse to have been 'looking ahead to the reward', which appears to echo the promise of v. 35 here. This persecution had not as yet seen any of their number suffer martyrdom (cf. 12.4), but other Christians had been called to do so, and we may assume the author's concern that some of the community were wilting at the prospect of being similarly treated. The imprisonment of members of the community obviously created a situation in which the solidarity of the community itself was tested, hence the instruction in 13.3 (cf. 11.36; Col. 4.18). Although it is not spelled out here, their cheerful acceptance of the plundering of their personal possessions, *in expectation of something better*, exhibited just that quality that marked the church's Lord at the point when he embraced suffering and death for their sake—a quality that they will be called upon to replicate (12.2). The reference in v. 35 to throwing away confidence is most nearly paralleled in 3.6 ('if we hold firm the *confidence* and the pride that belong to hope'). To have endured the plundering of their possessions with a sense of joy, because they were focused on the promised eternal inheritance (but see also Acts 5.41), and then to cast their *confidence* to the wind would be a serious come-down for them.

Verse 36 expresses most directly of all the need for endurance (cf. on v. 32): those addressed will 'carry off' (*komisēsthe*) what was promised if they continue to fulfil God's will—which, as has been indicated earlier, was, on Christ's part, the essence of his salvific work on their behalf (vv. 7, 9, 10; cf. 13.21). There follows unannounced, in vv. 37-38, a brace of quotes from Hab. 2.3-4, whence it emerges that faith is the key to the exercise of Christian endurance. These verses, and indeed the whole of Habakkuk 1–2, were also regarded by the Qumran community as speaking to their own situation as an end-time generation. In the Habakkuk *Pesher* the prophetic text is contemporized to the point of making specific references to persons and events contemporary with the Qumran community. The words 'in a very little while' (*mikron hoson hoson*) in v. 37 appear to have been imported from Isa. 26.20 in order to heighten the sense of imminent fulfilment attaching to Habakkuk's prophecy. There are differences between the Septuagint and Hebrew forms of the Habakkuk verses, and the author of *Hebrews* has exploited these as he conveys the two complementary ideas that Christ will come without delay and that the truly righteous will remain steadfast in the meantime through their exercise of faith.

The Septuagint's rendering of 'will surely come' (Hab. 2.3) by the virtual calque *erchomenos hēxei*, that is, with masculine active participle to represent the infinitive absolute of the Hebrew original, may well imply a personal subject. If so, *Hebrews* is simply making the point more explicit by its insertion of the definite article to produce its messianic-sounding reference to 'the coming one' (cf. Mt. 11.3; Lk. 7.19). He for his part, says the writer, will not disappoint. Equally, the righteous in whom God has pleasure will not be found lacking in trust in the promise-giver (though the focus of the trust is not expressly mentioned) (v. 38). The reference to 'living' by faith in verse 38 may, indeed, contribute already to the theme of the overcoming of death as it is developed in ch. 11 (see also the Introduction). The plasticity of the biblical lemma in the author's hands is also seen in the way in which he inverts the two clauses of Hab. 2.4, thus making 'my righteous one' the subject of both. By this means he avoids any suggestion of the 'coming one' shrinking back, as could easily be inferred from the Septuagintal text, and he can summarize the issue in the simple choice between loss (*apōleian*) and the preservation (*peripoiēsin*) of life, as in his nicely balanced sentence in v. 39. Whatever anxieties he may have had about the community, he again ends his admonition with a statement of confidence in the genuineness of their Christian commitment (cf. 6.9). Faith thus comes into focus in vv. 38-39 and prepares us for the grand exposition of the subject in ch. 11.

Hebrews 11: Witnesses to Faith

Introductory Comment

While faith in Christ (cf. Gal. 2.16) was an issue between Christianity and Judaism, faith as a fit human response to God was not (cf. Gen. 15.6; Deut. 9.23; Isa. 43.10). The chapter is a roll-call of characters from biblical and (apparently) postbiblical tradition who are judged to have exercised faith in God at crucial points in their lives. Such faith in God is regarded as having enabled biblical characters from Abel to Rahab, who are mentioned together with their citations (vv. 4-31), to achieve ends otherwise unattainable. Each cameo is introduced by the anaphoric *pistei* ('By faith'). Thereafter comes a list of others, named and unnamed, whose exploits and fortitude in suffering qualify them for similar recognition (vv. 32-38). The chapter is a discrete unit in that it begins with definition of its subject and rounds off its argument, helped by an inclusion (cf. NRSV 'received approval', v. 2; 'commended', v. 39, both translating *marturein* [passive]), with comment on the status vis-à-vis the Christian faithful of those who have just been passed in review. At the same time, the chapter is thoroughly integrated into the argument in this part of the letter. The subject of faith was introduced in 10.38-39, and ch. 12 draws on the 'cloud of (faithful) witnesses' of ch. 11 as it challenges the addressees to keep looking to Jesus 'the pioneer and perfecter of faith' (12.2). There is also development in ch. 12 of an important theme within ch. 11, in that the defiance of death achieved by various of those mentioned here is seen to have been also a feature of the Christ-event (12.1-2).

Fiat to Flood (11.1-7)

First comes a definition of faith—a working definition suited to the form of the argument rather than an attempt at an absolute statement of the essence of faith. The definition is expressed in two parallel clauses: faith gives form and substance (*hupostasis*) to things as yet unrealized in fact; it affords proof (*elenchos*) of things beyond normal human experience. There has been much discussion of *hupostasis*, which also occurs in 1.3 (NRSV 'very being') and 3.14 (NRSV 'confidence'), but close definition in the present setting can be as ill-advised as it is difficult. The psychological interpretation favoured by NIV ('faith is being sure of what we hope for and certain of what we do not see') is probably not far from the essential point that the writer wishes to convey to his readers. The idea of 'seeing' what is normally inaccessible to the natural sight occurs again in the chapter (vv. 7, 13, 27). While the future is certainly included here (vv. 7, 13), the unseen also comprehends those things that are simply beyond the normal bounds of human experience, such as creation (v. 3), or human perception of God himself (v. 27). Nor, according to v. 2, is faith a virtue peculiar to Christian believers. The 'elders', or 'ancients' (*presbuteroi*), whose names and deeds fill the rest of the chapter, won approval because of their faith in God (cf. v. 39).

With a few exceptions, texts that review the history of Israel in terms of its outstanding characters do not usually begin with creation. Hebrews 11 does, and this has the effect of immediately drawing the writer and his readers into the picture: 'By faith *we* understand' (v. 3). On the analogy of the rest of the chapter, we should expect the faith to relate in some way to the act of creation itself, but this is obviously not possible; it is the minds of the writer and his friends that are the locus of faith as they consider a universe whose origins predate anything in their own experience and are beyond their own competence to work out. Two alternative readings of the second half of v. 3 are possible: 'so that what is seen was made from things that are not visible' (NRSV), or 'so that what is seen was not made out of what was visible' (NIV). The point of the NRSV rendering is that, just as in the account of creation in Genesis 1, the worlds were created by the command of God 'from things invisible' (Attridge). The rendering in NIV, however, is couched in the form of a counter-assertion that expressly rejects the idea of pre-existing matter. While it may be possible to translate *eis to mē ek phainomenōn* as if it were *eis to ek mē phainomenōn*, as in NRSV, the point remains that the Old Testament creation narratives do not offer a fresh, scientific cosmology so much as theological statement involving significant elements of counter-statement vis-à-vis alternative, non-Israelite accounts of creation. If Heb. 11.3 is really saying that 'we understand…that what is seen was *not* made out of what was visible', then it is very much in line with this Old Testament approach to the subject.

This heading of the roll-call of the 'faithful' with a reference to creation is sometimes regarded as lacking obvious explanation, although there are partial parallels as in Ben Sira's prefacing of his 'Let us now sing the praises of famous men' in Ecclus 44.1-50.24 with the hymn on

creation in 42.15-43.33. The utterances of the mother of the seven martyred sons in 2 Maccabees 7 may help towards an answer. She is said to
have urged her sons on to faithful martyrdom with reminders of the
creative power by which God had brought them into being:

> It was not I who gave you life and breath, nor I who set in order the
> elements within each of you. Therefore the Creator of the world,
> who shaped the beginning of humankind and devised the origin of
> all things, will in his mercy give life and breath back to you again,
> since you now forget yourselves for the sake of his laws (vv. 22-23).

A little later, in a reference that presents the same translational problem
as is discussed in the preceding paragraph, she says: 'I beg you, my
child, to look at the heaven and the earth and see everything that is in
them, and recognize that *God did not make them out of things that
existed*' (v. 28). So the mother is citing God's creative power as the
means by which he will be able to undo death itself and bring the
martyred youths to life again. Now if one of the purposes of the present
chapter, and indeed of *Hebrews* itself (see the Introduction), is to
highlight the victory of faith over death, then belief in a creator God
who brings visible things into being 'from things that are not visible' is
very much to the point. Saving the benediction in 13.20-21, 12.9 has the
last epistolary echo of this theme of death defeated, or at least frustrated,
in what is also a reference to God as creator: 'Should we not be even
more willing to be subject to the Father of spirits and live?'

The roll-call proper begins with Abel in v. 4. Abel does not feature in
Ben Sira's list of the renowned ancestors, but he is cited in Mt. 23.35 as
the first in the A–Z(!) of the martyrs of Old Testament times: 'so that
upon you may come all the righteous blood shed on earth, from the
blood of righteous Abel to the blood of Zechariah son of Barachiah,
whom you murdered between the sanctuary and the altar'. It is not
explained how his sacrifice was 'greater' than Cain's, nor indeed does
Genesis 4, except insofar as it implies that the attitude of the sacrificer
himself may have helped determine the acceptability or otherwise of the
offering (Gen. 4.4-5, 7; cf. 1 Jn 3.12). In describing Abel as 'righteous'
Hebrews also draws attention to his character, the evidence for which
consists in the fact that God accepted his 'gifts'. His 'still speaking'
almost certainly derives from the reference in Gen. 4.10 to his blood
crying out from the ground for vengeance. This is taken up in 12.24,
where Christ's sacrificial blood 'speaks a better word than the blood of
Abel'. However, the fact that it is 'through it' (feminine)—by which is

meant 'through his faith' (cf. v. 7) or, less probably, 'through his sacrifice'—that Abel still speaks must mean that his speaking is now of a different order. At the least, we may understand the verse to mean that his example can still speak powerfully to later generations of the faithful. However, if one of the main assertions of this chapter is that the way of Christian commitment means not subjugation to death but victory over it, then Abel is the first of those several here mentioned who by one means or another show that death does not have the final say. Philo, commenting on the statement that Abel's blood was still crying out to God after his death (Gen. 4.10), makes a similar-sounding claim, except that it is allegorically motivated: 'He who seems to have died is alive, since he is found acting as a suppliant of God and is using his voice' (*Det. Pot. Ins.* 70). As we shall see, something more of Abel's testimony as developed in postbiblical tradition may be reflected in v. 6.

Enoch (v. 5) is the first biblical character mentioned in Ben Sira's hymn in honour of the ancestors, where he is cited as 'an example of repentance to all generations' (Ecclus 44.16). According to the thumbnail biography of Gen. 5.21-24 he lived for 365 years and then 'was no more, because God took him' (v. 24). The verb in question (*lāqaḥ*, 'take') is occasionally used in connection with the removal of a person's life, but with the word 'life' (*nephesh*) as its object (e.g. 1 Kgs 19.10, 14; Jon. 4.3). However, there is another small group of references where *lāqaḥ* is used to describe God's taking of the specially favoured to the divine presence (2 Kgs 2.3; Pss 49.15[16]; 73.24). This appears to be the significance of the verb in Gen. 5.24. For the most part, Genesis 5 consists of antediluvian epitaphs—we might compare the bald 'born and died' epitaphs noted by Joseph Addison in his essay 'The Tombs in Westminster Abbey'—but v. 24 stands in contrast to the recurrent 'and he died', and the Septuagint had long since interpreted the MT to mean that Enoch 'was not *found*' because God had 'translated' him. The writer of *Hebrews* quotes Gen. 5.24 in more or less its Septuagintal form, which includes the idea of 'pleasing God' where the Hebrew text talks of Enoch's having walked with God. Again, we should note that the theme of the overcoming of death is tied to the exercise of faith.

The idea of *pleasing* God, in the way of Enoch, is developed in v. 6 which acts as a kind of summary comment on what has been said so far and sets out preconditions for the would-be worshipper of God. While the verse follows immediately on from the mention of Enoch and may be implying that Enoch satisfied the 'faith criterion' even though faith is not specifically attributed to him in Genesis, it may as easily have v. 4 and Cain and Abel in mind. For although the verb 'approach' (*proserchesthai*) occurs several times in *Hebrews* in connection with approaching God in worship (see 4.16; 7.25; 10.1, 22; 12.22), and so might be used in a quite general way by our author, it would be particularly appropriate to Abel in the present context, since he is the one who literally makes his approach to God when he brings his sacrifice to the altar. It is also possible that the conditions for successful approach to God may relate to the Cain and Abel story in a special way. In a famous textual crux in Gen. 4.8 the Hebrew says, 'And Cain said to Abel his brother', but fails to report what was said. We might circumvent the problem by translating, 'And Cain spoke to Abel his brother', on the basis of a comparable usage in Exod. 19.25, but this did not occur to the translators of the majority of the ancient versions of Genesis which add something of the order of 'Let us go out to the field.' *Targum Onkelos* remains on all fours with the Hebrew text, but the 'Palestinian' Targums go much further in detailing a discussion that was supposed to have taken place between the two brothers before the killing of Abel. According to the version given in one of the Fragment-Targums, Cain said, 'There is no judgment, nor is there a judge, nor is there another world; there is no giving of good reward to the righteous nor is retribution exacted from the wicked. The world was not created in mercy nor is it governed in mercy.' And Abel replies with affirmations to the contrary, whereupon Cain kills him. Hebrews 11.6 might almost have been written in the knowledge of the Targumic midrash, in view of its insistence upon belief in the existence of the God whom Christians profess (the Targumic 'judge') and in his rewarding of those who seek him (cf. 10.35; 11.26). The Palestinian Targums merely reflect the fact that in rabbinic tradition Cain becomes a topos for Sadducean-type agnosticism as far as afterlife and the idea of an unseen spiritual world are concerned.

The third exemplar of faith in this short section, Noah, is credited with having believed in 'the unseen' in the sense that he acted on information about improbable-sounding events before they took place, and 'to the saving of his house' (AV, v. 7). NIV 'in holy fear' for *eulabētheis* (NRSV 'respected the warning') draws a straighter line to the cognate noun (*eulabeia*) used of Christ's 'reverent submission' during 'the days of his flesh' (5.7). The word neatly balances *chrēmatistheis* in the preceding clause: 'informed...feared'. Noah 'condemned the world', although the

Genesis flood narrative quotes nothing from him until his undistin-
guished utterances after the flood had ended (Gen. 9.24-27); until then
he is presented as a model of unquestioning compliance with the divine
will. The mere fact of his faith-obedience, now exemplified in the con-
structing of the ark, may be sufficient explanation of his 'condemning'
the world, but 2 Pet. 2.5 adds another possibly relevant dimension in
describing him as a 'herald of righteousness'. He thus takes his place in
the line of succession of those who, even in advance of Abraham (see
Gen. 15.6), became heirs to 'the righteousness that is in accordance
with faith'.

The Patriarchs (11.8-22)

The section is mostly about Abraham, though there is a reflective inter-
lude in vv. 13-16, while the last three verses look beyond Abraham to
take note of the other patriarchs, including Joseph. Three facets of Abraham's life of faith are selected for comment, namely his abandoning his
native city for an unknown destination (vv. 8-10), his fathering of an heir
at an advanced age (vv. 11-12) and his willingness to surrender Isaac
when called upon to offer him in sacrifice (vv. 17-19). Between the second and the third of these there is a brief consideration of what motivated Abraham and others like him so that they forsook home ties for a
vision of a heavenly homeland (vv.13-16). In all, the patriarchal period is
represented by seven occurrences of the anaphoric *pistei* ('by faith'; see
vv. 8, 9, 11, 17, 20, 21 and 22).

From One Person (11.8-12)

Formally v. 8 begins in the way of v. 7: 'By faith Abraham, being called...'
(// 'By faith Noah, having been warned...'). Abraham's response to the
call of God parallels that of Noah in that it sprang from a willingness to
obey an inner prompting that ran counter to normal good sense. The
addressees had likewise 'gone out' from familiar things in order to identify with Christ, and later they will indeed be exhorted to maintain their
position of loyalty to him by 'going out' to him 'outside the camp'
(13.13). While the author's intention throughout has been to establish
that Christianity is a religion of substance rather than shadow, that was
precisely because some of his readers perceived it to be otherwise. So
the example of Abraham's abandoning of the assured and the familiar for
the uncertainties of life in Canaan could help to stiffen the resolve of
those who had stepped out in faith without having received any tangible

fulfilment of the promises that had inspired them in the first place.

Arrival in the 'promised land' did not end Abraham's exercise of faith in God, according to v. 9. So long as he remained there without any tangible fulfilment of the promise of inheritance he was 'living by faith'. *parōikēsen*, translated 'he stayed for a time' in NRSV, may be intended to reflect the alien status of Abraham as a *paroikos* ('sojourner') in Canaan for the remainder of his life; on the other hand, the distinction between this verb and *katoikein*, which more usually denotes permanent residence, is often dissolved, as apparently in this verse where the dependent clause uses *katoikein* of the patriarchs' living in tents during the same period of Abraham's sojourning and subsequently. The alien status of Abraham in Canaan is put more starkly in Stephen's speech before the Sanhedrin: '[God] did not give him any of it as a heritage, not even a foot's length' (Acts 7.5). There is obvious contrast between the *tent*-dwelling of Abraham and his successors and the expectation of the well-founded city of v. 10. And while the chronology of Genesis allows us to say that Abraham lived in tents 'with' (lit.) Isaac and Jacob, the mention of these two draws attention to the fact that the pilgrim imperative did not rest solely upon Abraham, but also upon succeeding generations (cf. NRSV, NIV, 'as did Isaac and Jacob'). Abraham's ultimate goal is described in v. 10 as a city of divine origination, identified in 12.22 as 'the heavenly Jerusalem' where the spirits of the righteous, which doubtless includes Abraham, have been made perfect (12.23). The mention of foundations suggests a contrast with the already mentioned tent-dwelling rather than with other cities supposed not to have foundations, though some writers see an allusion to the well-founded (earthly) Zion of Ps. 87.1. The designation of God as 'architect and builder' may be compared with 8.2 ('the sanctuary and the true tent that the Lord, and not any mortal, has set up'). There is nothing in the Genesis narratives to indicate patriarchal preoccupation with a heavenly city, and indeed even the earthly Jerusalem features only once (if Salem in Gen. 14.18 refers to Jerusalem). Later speculation about the extent of the insights granted Abraham is, however, represented in a passage like *2 Bar*. 4.2-7, in which Abraham, like Adam before him and Moses subsequently, is given a vision of the heavenly sanctuary, on the occasion described in Gen. 15.7-21.

Both NIV and NRSV construe v. 11 with Abraham as subject, even though the syntax favours Sarah. The reasons for agreeing with these versions are strong: the expression *eis katabolēn spermatos* more naturally refers to the male part in procreation, and the subject/referent in the adjoining sentences is unquestionably Abraham. Moreover, the requirements of grammar can be satisfied if by the smallest of changes the words *autē Sarra steira* are converted into a dative of accompaniment ('[and] Sarah herself was barren'). Otherwise the translation has to be as in REB ('By faith even Sarah herself was enabled to conceive...'). While it is not at all a crucial point, 6.13-14 speaks of God having made the promise about descendants *to Abraham* (cf. 'considered him faithful who had promised' here). The mention of both Abraham and Sarah is at any rate appropriate in view of the echoing in v. 12 of Isa. 51.2 and the circumstance that Abraham was 'but one' when God called him (cf. *kaloumenos*, v. 8): 'Look to Abraham your father and to Sarah who bore you; for he was but one when I called him, but I blessed him and made him many'. This Abrahamic solitariness is also remarked upon in Ezek. 33.24, in speech attributed to the Judaeans who remained in the land at the time of the Babylonian exile: 'Abraham was only one man, yet he got possession of the land.' We might also compare the Targumic version of Mal. 2.15, which seeks to relieve the obscurities of the Hebrew text by introducing the figure of Abraham: 'Was not Abraham one alone from whom the world was made?' Abraham's physical 'deadness' (NRSV 'even though he was too old') is also a matter for comment in Rom. 4.19 where his body is likewise described as 'dead' (NRSV 'as good as dead'). In both instances Abraham is dead in the sense of being impotent. Here the description contributes to the theme of the overcoming of death in whatever form the faithful may encounter it.

Strangers and Foreigners (11.13-16)

Significantly, the author has followed unfulfilled promise (vv. 8-10) with a clear instance of fulfilled promise (vv. 11-12) before pausing here in vv. 13-16 to reflect on the 'not yet' of patriarchal expectations. The parenthetical character of the section is indicated by the temporary suspension of the anaphoric 'by faith' and the substitution of the synonymous *kata pistin*, an expression that may in any case have been regarded as more appropriate in a straightforward reference to dying (v. 13), since *en pistei* otherwise is used of more positive action, granted that death and dying may be part of the attendant circumstances of the action (e.g. vv. 21, 22). The referents of 'these' in v. 13 are most naturally the patriarchal and matriarchal figures mentioned in vv. 8-12, since it was they who had in a literal sense left their native land (cf. v. 15). In 6.15 Abraham is said to have 'obtained the promise', but there is no tension with the present passage since it is the promise of multitudinous descendants that is in question there, whereas here it is the possession of the land. Verses 11-12 have already expressed agreement with 6.15 as regards descendants. These faithful both 'saw' and 'greeted' the things promised, which must include in particular the well-founded city of v. 10; 'greeted' more or less implies the arrival of those who never actually did 'arrive' while on this earth. They had the assurance that what was promised was truly before them, and they lived in the light of this conviction. Time as much as distance is thus implied in the use of *porrōthen* (NRSV 'from a distance'). The dominical saying about Abraham rejoicing to see the time of the messiah (Jn 8.56) attributes the same kind of long-sightedness to the patriarch, with the implication that fulfilment lay in the historical 'Christ-event'. The writer of *Hebrews* may have had in mind the sort of vision of the end-time that is sometimes granted biblical worthies, in biblical and postbiblical literature, but more likely is showing how faith produced in them 'the conviction of things not seen' (v. 1).

The confession of Christ as Lord was obviously as important to the author as to the early Christian communities generally, but there are other aspects of Christian 'confessing' and in this respect the patriarchs proved helpful allies (NIV 'admitted' is surely too weak for *homologēsantes* [NRSV 'confessed'] in v. 13). 'I am a stranger and an alien residing among you', says Abraham to his Hittite neighbours (Gen. 23.4), and the extent of his alien status is seen in his having to negotiate over a plot of ground where he could bury his wife Sarah. Our author has already written of Christians' confession of Jesus as their apostle and high priest (3.1; cf. 4.14) and of the hope that Christians confess (10.23). In Pauline parlance, this confession is made 'with the mouth' (cf. Rom. 10.10): it involves public affirmation of allegiance to Christ, and so 'those who say such things' (v. 14) resonates as much in a Christian as in an ancient patriarchal context. This broadening out of the issue is already evident in the addition of the phrase 'on the earth' at the end of v. 13, since the patriarchal rootlessness even in Canaan is interpreted to mean that Canaan was not the goal of their travels. It is implied that no territorial possession would have answered to their aspirations, so that even in Canaan they were in search of a 'homeland' (*patrida*, v. 14). Their situation is therefore directly comparable with that of the addressees who had not even the promise of eventual territorial possession to spur them on.

As v. 15 observes, it was open to the earlier generations of the faithful, if they had been seeking a haven on earth, to return to the land whence they had come. And so also could those of the 'Hebrews' who, having stepped out from their ancestral religion, longed for the certainties and security that it had once afforded them. However, in 13.13-14 the author will remind them that they do well to 'go out' precisely because the present order of things can provide no enduring city. Verse 15 is, thus, a challenge to the 'Hebrews' to be single-minded in their living out of their Christian profession. By speaking as he has in this section the author may also have wished to convey to them that true faith in God never should be tied to residence in, or possession of, a stretch of real estate on this earth. He is not at all explicit about this, but not for the only time in the letter it is possible to interpret what he says as being intended to discourage the 'Hebrews' from complicating their Christian faith with the addition of a this-worldly land perspective (cf. 13.14, 'here we have no lasting city').

There is in this section a tendency towards the use of the vivid present tense (vv. 14, 16), which also suggests a merging of the horizons of the Hebrew patriarchs and the 'Hebrews', for it may be predicated as much of the latter as of the former that they 'desire a better (country)' (v. 16). The description of the celestial land as 'better' puts it in the company of those other elements of Christian experience favoured with the use of the same term in this letter (e.g. 7.19, 22). As well as being the god of the ancient Hebrews in a general sense, the God of the Old Testament is occasionally described as 'the God of Abraham, the God of Isaac, and the God of Jacob' (cf. Exod. 3.6; 4.5). And in view of the heavenly character of their aspirations, says our author (v. 16), God may be said to wear his title (in whichever of these two senses) with pride (cf. NRSV 'indeed, he has prepared a city for them'). Already, the writer has informed his readers that Christ is not ashamed to call them his 'brothers' (2.11), at which point we noted the possible implication that it would be unworthy of them to be ashamed of him who had so honoured them. There is, however, the further possibility here in 11.16 that God is said to be unashamed because, in having prepared a city for the patriarchs and their ilk, he has fully met their expectations of him (cf. NIV 'for he has prepared a city for them'; cf. v. 10).

Faith and the Future (11.17-22)

The writer is not finished with Abraham, whose faith is further illustrated in the unique episode of the 'binding of Isaac' (vv. 17-19; cf. Gen. 22.1-19). There is even a suggestion of alacrity on Abraham's part, in response to the divine command to offer up Isaac, in that the circumstantial participle *peirazomenos* ('being tested') is delayed in favour of the clause 'By faith Abraham offered up Isaac' (contrast the position of the participles *chrēmatistheis*, 'warned', and *kaloumenos*, 'called', in vv. 7, 8). In contrast with its occurrence in the perfect tense in the opening clause, the verb *prospherein* ('offer up') is used in the imperfect, probably with an ingressive or conative sense (cf. NIV 'was about to sacrifice'), later in the verse. What excites our author's interest, as it must that of any reader of the Abraham story, is the apparent irreconcilability of the divine promises centred on Isaac and the command to offer up this embodiment of the patriarch's hopes, and thus apparently terminate all hope of fulfilment of those same promises: 'He who had received the promises was ready to offer up his only son' (v. 17). The dilemma is underlined in v. 18 by the quotation of a sentence from Gen. 21.12, a quotation that is important also in that it comes from the section dealing with Abraham's dismissal of Hagar and Ishmael—for, of course, Isaac was not Abraham's *only* biological son. The use of *monogenēs* (NIV 'one and only') to describe Isaac in v. 17 no doubt reflects the Hebrew *yeḥîdekā* ('your only [son]') of Gen. 22.2 where Isaac, following Ishmael's departure, now appears as the focus of Abraham's hopes.

Abraham is not commended for an irrational, ill-considered response to a situation in which he found himself overwhelmed by a divine imperative. He is credited with having already reconciled the irreconcilable in his own mind before he laid Isaac on the altar, reckoning that God could restore the boy to life (v. 19). On the one hand, belief in the resurrection of the body is not expressed anywhere in the Pentateuch, as may also be judged from the way in which Exod. 3.6 is cited as a Pentateuchal prooftext (for the benefit of Sadducees) in relation to resurrection in Mt. 22.31-32. At the same time, our author may have based his remarkable statement about Abraham's resurrection faith on the patriarch's own words to the young men who accompanied him to Moriah: 'we will worship, and then we will come back to you' (Gen. 22.5). In one sense, the text goes on to claim, Abraham did receive Isaac back from the dead, possibly because, for the author, Isaac was 'as good as dead' (cf. v. 12!) when he lay on the altar. Such a 'resurrection' could be described as 'figurative' (cf. NIV, NRSV), but the expression *en parabolēi* may perhaps be better rendered 'as a symbol'—a symbol, that is, of something greater than what happened at Moriah (cf. *parabolē*, translated 'symbol' in NRSV, at 9.9). Whether the reference is then to the resurrection of humans in general or specifically to the resurrection of Christ is not easily decided. In *Hebrews* there is no certain reference to Christ's resurrection as such until the benediction in 13.20. When Isaac appears in his own right in v. 20 his contribution is brief, rather as it is in Genesis itself. On the occasion referred to, his blessing of Jacob and Esau looked beyond their immediate circumstances to include their future prospects (Gen. 27.27-40), and since the blessing pronounced over Jacob partly echoes the original promise to Abraham (compare Gen. 27.29 with Gen. 12.3) it can the more readily be seen as belonging to the continuum of patriarchal faith. NIV 'blessed Jacob and Esau *in regard to their future*' is therefore more specific-sounding than 'concerning things to come' (*peri mellontōn*) implies.

Two death-bed scenes in vv. 21-22 round off the section on the faith of the patriarchs, both therefore contributing to the theme of faith's triumph over death. Jacob's story in Genesis is of sufficient length and detail to have provided the author with opportunities to highlight some act or aspect of faith in the patriarch's life, but his blessing of Ephraim and Manasseh so near the end of his life clearly illustrated best the idea of the life of pilgrim faith and transmitted hope that is central to the encomium of the present chapter. Verse 21 contains a hysteron proteron in that Jacob's blessing of Joseph's sons (Gen. 48.9-20) is followed by the mention of his worshipping upon his staff (Gen. 47.31). In this respect the text is ill-served by the NRSV circumstantial participle, 'bowing in worship', which telescopes the two episodes in a way that the Greek does not. As is well-known, v. 21 follows the Septuagint in having 'staff' (Heb. *maṭṭeh*) where the Hebrew text has 'bed' (Heb. *miṭṭâ*), but it is unwise to attribute an authorial motive on this account in view of the writer's regular citing of the Septuagint in *Hebrews*. The point of the quotation from Gen. 47.21 apparently is to recall the circumstances in which Jacob engaged in worship, namely his securing from Joseph a promise that he would not be buried in Egypt, but back in Canaan. This is but one of a variety of ways in which the patriarchal attachment to Canaan is expressed in Genesis, and all based on the conviction that the future of the Abrahamic family lay there rather than in Egypt or Mesopotamia. If Jacob's worship in Gen. 47.21 was thought to include some insight into the long-term prospects of his descendants, then our author may have regarded this as an instance of a patriarch's 'greeting' of divine promises from a distance (cf. v. 13). This patriarchal attachment to Canaan is even more explicit with Joseph who, close to death, gave orders about the transference of his bones to the promised land (v. 22; cf. Gen. 50.24-25; see also Exod. 13.19; Josh. 24.32). Joseph makes direct mention of the exodus, and in that hopeful context requires his fellow-Israelites to swear that they would take his remains with them when they left Egypt. No hint of a resurrection hope is discovered by the author of *Hebrews* in the mention of Joseph's bones, nor, indeed, is there any suggestion in these verses that Canaan (> Israel) was 'the land of the living (= resurrected)' in the sense in which it was commonly so regarded in postbiblical Jewish writings, where one may find the view expressed that only those buried in 'the land' could hope to participate in the resurrection.

From Moses to Maccabees (11.23-40)

In the second half of the chapter the author moves on from the patriarchs to the time of the Israelite exodus from Egypt and the conquest of Canaan (as it certainly is from the perspective of vv. 30-31). Here Moses is the major figure (vv. 23-28), standing in relation to the rest of the text much as Abraham does in the first part of the chapter. Again there is a heptad to be reported: the anaphoric *pistei* ('by faith') occurs in vv. 23, 24, 27, 28, 29, 30 and 31 (cf. above on vv. 8-22). Then in vv. 32-38, following the sample citing of a few worthy names, the sufferings and the triumphs of the faithful down through the biblical centuries are passed in rapid review.

By Faith Moses... (11.23-28)

In the first instance it is the faith exercised by Moses' parents (*Hebrews* follows LXX in attributing the action to both, *pace* the focus on the mother in the standard Hebrew version) that is decisive in the history of faith. As in vv. 7, 8, 17, 21 and 22 the background is summarized with the use of a participle, in this case *gennētheis* (lit. 'having been born'). Formally, then, it looks as if an aspect of Moses' own faith is being commended, whereas he was totally passive—and as a child could do naught else—in the situation. No explicit mention is made of the threat of death that hung over the child's birth or of the parents' thwarting of the threat, but the pharaonic edict required the killing of all Israelite boys and so the reference implicitly relates to faith's vindication over against death and the fear of it. The reason given for the parents' action is that they recognized that the child was 'good' (*asteion*; NRSV 'beautiful'), which leaves unsaid what it was or how they recognized the special characteristic that merited the risk they took. A fuller expression, *asteios tōi theōi* (NRSV 'beautiful before God'), is used in Stephen's speech in Acts 7.20 and, though the use of 'God' may be explained as an elative, in a manner more characteristic of Semitic idiom, it is tempting to retain the reference to the divine and to treat the *Hebrews* occurrence in the light of the fuller form. NIV has 'no ordinary child' in both places. That Moses' parents did not fear the king's edict is mentioned as significant, just as Moses himself will be commended in v. 27 for a similar disregard of the royal wrath.

Prior to that, however, he made his own declaration of faith when he refused to be known as the son of the Pharaoh's daughter (v. 24). The biblical storyline is sparse on this matter, recounting only how the adult Moses was witness to the privations of his fellow-Hebrews and intervened to save one of them from ill-treatment (Exod. 2.11-12). For the author of *Hebrews*, however, it was important to present Moses' identification with his people as the conscious act of renunciation that it was. And as v. 25 indicates, this renunciation involved actively embracing the afflictions of 'the people of God', which term seems to reach beyond the Hebrews of the exodus narratives to the Christian community of the writer's own time (cf. 4.9; 8.10; 1 Pet. 2.10). This, as we shall see, is not the only way in which the summary of Moses' life of faith seems to be brought to a point of near convergence with the circumstances of those addressed (see on vv. 26, 27). Need we, on the other hand, assume that 'the fleeting pleasures of sin' held a particular attraction for the recipients of the letter? It is certainly not difficult to see how the expression might apply to an aspiring Egyptian prince such as Moses chose not to be, though the 'pleasure(s)' (*apolausis*) may have been not so much in the area of sensual self-indulgence as in the gratification of ambition and the power-lust. At the same time, the author of *Hebrews* does not limit his discussion of sin to the theological issue of how it was expiated by Christ. Elsewhere he expresses concern lest his readers be 'hardened by the deceitfulness of sin' (3.13) or, by continuing to sin wilfully, put themselves beyond the efficacy of Christ's sacrifice for sins (10.26), while in 12.1 he encourages them to lay aside the sin that besets them, following this up with the chastening observation that in their struggle against sin they had 'not yet resisted to the point of shedding [their] blood' (12.4). In 13.4 he issues a strong warning against sexual misbehaviour. It is clear that one particular sin against which our author wished to warn his addressees consisted in choosing the easy option and 'turning away from the living God' (3.12), in which case there was much that Moses could teach these latter-day 'people of God'.

In v. 26 the ill-treatment that Moses embraced is described rather strikingly as 'abuse suffered for Christ' (*ton oneidismon tou christou*). Even if we opt for 'the Christ' (NRSV) or 'the Messiah' (NRSVn) the anachronism remains, if less starkly. Presumably it is the writer's intention, in this the only specific reference to Christ in the chapter, to demonstrate the complete subordination of Moses to Christ by portraying the great law-giver as one who in his own experience anticipated the sufferings of Christ's followers. Already in 3.5 Moses is seen as 'testifying to what would be said in the future' (so NIV), which partly prepares us for the claim made in the present verse. As previously in the chapter, the author focuses on the prospect of reward for the faithful (v. 6; cf. 10.35), summarizing Moses' choice in appropriate terms: abuse suffered for Christ is 'greater wealth' than Egypt's 'treasures'. But, as the concluding clause in v. 26 points out, without faith's vision the choice would have been more difficult to make—which was also a fair reflection of the circumstances of the recipients of *Hebrews*. Soon they will be exhorted to dissociate themselves from previous ties and take their share of the reproach attaching to the name of Christ (13.13). With 'considered' (NRSV for *hēgēsamenos*) in v. 26 we may compare 'considered' (NRSV for *logisamenos*; 'reasoned', NIV) in v. 19: Abraham and Moses are alike regarded as exemplary in that theirs was not an unreasoning faith in God.

Moses, for his part, left Egypt behind (v. 27), on a couple of occasions at least. Whether v. 27 refers to his hurried departure after his murder of the Egyptian (Exod. 2.11-15) or to the exodus itself is disputed. On the occasion described in Exodus 2 Moses is said to have been fearful of the Pharaoh's reaction to news of the murder, and so he fled to Midian. NEB, in apparently opting for this first 'exodus', makes a virtue of the tension between Exodus and *Hebrews* by making the latter imply that the real motivation was something other than fear: 'By faith he left Egypt, and not because he feared the king's anger'. (REB is regressive by comparison: 'By faith he left Egypt, with no fear of the king's anger.') We might in that case read the next clause, which says that Moses 'saw him who is invisible' (NIV, which has as much to be said for it as NRSV 'as though he saw him who is invisible'), in the light of his encounter with God at the burning bush (Exod. 3.1-22), even though *Hebrews* does not refer directly to this episode. The case against identifying Moses' departure with the 'national exodus' of Exodus 12 consists partly in the fact that pharaonic wrath was not then so much of a consideration, though Exod. 10.28-29 has the Pharaoh issue a threat that Moses appears to take seriously. It is also noted that v. 28 mentions the observance of Passover, which, of course, precedes the exodus itself in the book of Exodus. Again the objection is not fatal, since we have already found an instance of obvious dischronologizing of biblical events in v. 21. Moses' intrepid forsaking of Egypt, whenever it happened, matches the bold action of his parents commended in v. 23, where it is through disregard of the Pharaoh's edict that the infant Moses is saved. These two examples of fearlessness in the face of royal edict and anger are probably meant to speak quite specifically to the recipients' situation, and the deliberate and contrived manner in which the idea is resuscitated in v. 27 makes the suggestion all the more appealing. The 'Hebrews' are not to fear the Pharaohs of their own day, whether in the form of the Roman emperor or of some more local despot. So much is implied in 1 Pet. 2.17, which seeks to direct 'fear' where it properly belongs, even while advocating good Christian citizenship: 'Fear God. Honour the emperor' (cf. Acts 5.29). Whether or not Moses' seeing 'him who is invisible' contains an allusion to the burning bush, he evidently satisfies another of the criteria set out in v. 6, namely belief in the existence of the unseen One who rewards those who seek him. The final acts associated with Moses are the keeping of Passover and the apotropaic sprinkling of blood that kept the destroying angel away from Israelite homes on the night of the first Passover. Once more, then, it is a question of death and its thwarting through faith.

Exodus and Conquest (11.29-31)

No further actions of Moses personally are cited, but the Israelites' crossing of the Red Sea (under his leadership) provides another instance of faith, now on the part of the people generally, preserving the faithful from death. It is almost as if, in the author's estimation, the absence of faith on the part of the pursuing Egyptians was what accounted for their destruction (cf. on v. 31), though the biblical narrative naturally thinks of the disaster in other terms (e.g. Exod. 14.15-18). From the Red Sea the author proceeds straight to Jericho, and so a letter that elsewhere makes so much of the wilderness phase of Israelite history, and of the cultus associated with that period, passes over it in this chapter. One possible explanation is that the writer regarded the period as one of 'disobedient history' and therefore unworthy of a place in his review. On the other hand, his telescoped account may be intended to make the point that, wanderings notwithstanding, the goal of Canaan was achieved. Two features of the conquest account in Joshua complete the roll-call in this section. The claim that it was faith that undermined the walls of Jericho may sound simplistic even from the perspective of the biblical narrative, but not for the author who doubtless draws his inference from the Israelites' eschewal of military action at Jericho. By mentioning the seven-day circumambulation of the city walls he does enough to draw attention to the remarkable outcome of the venture.

The common factor at the Red Sea and at Jericho consisted in the Israelites' disregarding—perforce in the first instance—what good sense and ordinary experience dictated as possible. Finally, to even the prostitute Rahab is attributed the faith that saves from death, and the all-pervasiveness of the theme of faith in the chapter leads to the characterization of the citizens of Jericho as 'those who disobeyed' (v. 31). It was a bold move to round off the main list of faith's notables with a Gentile prostitute—Jewish tradition sought to make an innkeeper of her (so *Targ. Josh.* 2.1 and Josephus, *Ant.* 5.7-8 [and cf. Whiston's footnote in his edition!])—but Rahab appears in distinguished company elsewhere in the New Testament, in the genealogy of Christ in Mt. 1.5 and as an exemplar, with Abraham, of practical faith in Jas 2.25 (cf. vv. 21-23). Her inclusion, then, defies any restriction of faith's prerogatives to the people of the old covenant. Her faith is seen in her hiding of the Israelite spies, though the writer could have found supporting material in her confession of the God of Israel as made in Josh. 2.9-13.

Here the main review of the history of the faithful breaks off (cf. v. 32), with Israel having crossed the Jordan and campaigning in Canaan. It was not the writer's intention to go endlessly on with his review, yet his semi-colon after Jericho and Rahab may have more than convenience to account for it. The next section is indeed poorly supplied with references to achievements in the monarchical period when, after a manner of speaking, Israel *had* a 'continuing city' (cf. 13.14). Again this may reflect the author's assessment of the religious condition of Israel during the monarchical period (cf. on vv. 29-31, in relation to the wilderness phase), or it may be that the mere fact of Israel's nation status was less congenial for a portrayal of the 'life of faith' in terms of pilgrimage and patient hope.

Of Whom the World was not Worthy (11.32-40)

Verse 32 seems to indicate in its use of a participle with a masculine ending ('time would fail me telling [*diēgoumenon*]') that, like so many other biblical writers, this one was male. It is a small contribution to a centuries-old debate. Any likelihood of a Priscilla having authored *Hebrews* is almost automatically ruled out by this verse. For the writer, biblical history is full of illustrations of the faith that overcomes, but it would have taken a much longer letter than it was his intention to write (cf. 13.22) if he had tried to do justice to the fuller story. His review of biblical characters who exemplified faith in one way or another breaks down in this section first into a list of names and then into a recitation of the kinds of daunting circumstances in which these and others like them 'conquered through faith' (v. 33). The name-list carries the review forward from the conquest into the periods of the judges (Gideon, Barak, Samson, Jephthah) and the monarchy (David, Samuel and the prophets). David is the only representative of the monarchy to be mentioned, possibly for the kind of reason suggested in the previous paragraph.

In the expression 'Samuel and the prophets' Samuel is not so much distinguished from the prophets as regarded as the first in the prophetic succession that lasted throughout the monarchical period. (Moses is less prophet and more law-giver and 'head of house' in *Hebrews* [cf. 3.3-5; 7.14; 8.5; 9.19; 10.28].) Chronologically Barak precedes Gideon in the book of Judges, but the latter doubtless came to mind first as the better known of the two. They are cited in the same order in 1 Sam. 12.11, if the otherwise unknown Bedan of the Masoretic tradition is a mistake for Barak. (Gideon is mentioned by his other name of Jerubbaal in the Samuel reference.) Fame, or notoriety, probably also accounts for the inversion of the names of Samson and Jephthah. Some of what is said about these characters in Judges is anything but heroic, and Barak is even condemned for his lack of courage by the woman who might have occupied his place in this list (cf. Jdgs 4.9). At this point victory against foreign enemies seems almost to be taken as a sign of faith on the part of the victor (cf. v. 34). Again, David is mentioned ahead of Samuel who, in the Old Testament account, is in his declining years by the time David comes to prominence.

The actions described in vv. 33-38 are said to have been achieved 'through faith' (*dia pistēs*), which marks a departure from the anaphoric 'by faith' (*pistei*) of the chapter so far (cf. also *kata pistin* in v. 13), but without any special significance attaching to the change. The actions associated with faith in the chapter are sufficiently diverse to make pointless any attempt at distinctions between one set and the other. The sentence begun in v. 32 runs to the end of v. 34, concluding in nine short asyndetic clauses that describe the transforming effect of faith in adverse circumstances. The first and last in the series highlight military feats in a way that may be intended to suggest that these were a feature of the entire history of the people of God, right down to the Maccabaean times that seem to be in view in v. 35. But it is not just military conquest for its own sake that the writer lauds, for the overthrow of kingdoms in v. 33 is followed by the establishing of justice, and the two ideas may have been closely linked in his mind (cf. Ps. 45.4-7). In being victorious, moreover, the heroes of v. 32 could be said to have 'obtained promises', which means the realizing of expectations built on traditions of divine undertakings recorded in Scripture (e.g. Gen. 15.18-21), without at all suggesting the attainment of *the* promises that the writer has expressly said were beyond the grasp of still earlier generations (v. 13; cf. v. 39).

REB imposes its own stylistics on the text by dividing the nine clauses of vv. 33-34 into three triads, so bringing the obtaining of promises into close association with the conquest of kingdoms and with the establishing of justice in the way that we have suggested. Such a connection is justified to the extent that linking these three clauses with the one following ('shut the mouths of lions') is exegetically not very productive. Apart from the highlighting of military success in this section, there is renewed emphasis on the circumventing or overcoming of death, in keeping with the tendency already noted for *Hebrews*, and especially for this chapter. The shutting of lions' mouths (v. 33) and the quenching of flames (v. 34) are both in obvious debt to the book of Daniel (chs. 3; 6). Escape from the edge of the sword on the part of the faithful could have been exemplified from a number of Old Testament references (e.g. 1 Kgs 19.1-3). Instances of actual resurrection are claimed in v. 35, whereas up until now the writer has talked only of figurative or symbolic resurrection (v. 19).

Verses 35-36 break with the short clauses of the preceding two verses and, in the mention of women receiving back their dead (v. 35), break also, if but briefly, from the list of masculine heroes who are named in v. 32 and implied in vv. 33-34. The fact that the Old Testament stories of resurrection-resuscitation in 1 Kgs 17.17-24 and 2 Kgs 4.18-37 involve mothers and their sons (cf. 'their dead', v. 35) makes this change of perspective specially appropriate. Equally, the history of Maccabaean times, especially, provided examples of resolute Jews who submitted to torture and death 'in order to obtain a better resurrection' (cf. 2 Macc. 6.1-31; 7.1-42). The probable allusion in *etumpanisthēsan* (NRSV, NIV 'tortured') to the fate of the aged Eleazar who was killed on the rack (*tumpanon*; cf. 2 Macc. 6.19, 28) is not to be missed here. For those who renounced their hold on life rather than compromise their faith the expectation was of a resurrection attended by greater glory than would otherwise have been achieved. Whether the writer was thinking in the specific terms of Dan. 12.2—resurrection 'to everlasting life' or 'to shame and everlasting contempt'—is not so clear. The contrast, if any, implied in 'better resurrection' may simply be with the resurrections already mentioned in v. 35, for those so raised would have to face death again. Mocking and flogging (v. 36) may bring us back to the Maccabaean martyrs (cf. 2 Macc. 7.1, 10), though such abuse had been experienced by a long line of the Jewish and Christian faithful, including the addressees themselves at an earlier stage (see 10.32-34). The earlier phase of persecution had also meant imprisonment for some of the community (10.34), and that kind of deprivation was not yet at an end, to judge from the injunction in 13.3. Verses 37-38 start with simple verbal clauses ('they were stoned', 'they were sawn in two', 'they were killed by the sword') but then develop a series of participles describing the wretched lot of those who, while escaping death in the meantime, lived as persecuted outcasts 'of whom the world was not worthy' (AV, v. 38). 'They were outlawed as people who were unfit for civilized society; the truth was that civilized society was unfit for them' (F.F. Bruce, *The Epistle to the Hebrews*, p. 342).

The chapter ends in resumptive manner, noting how the ancients were commended for their faith (vv. 39-40; cf. vv. 1-2). They were exercising their faith in a 'not yet' situation, and the author is sufficiently bold to imply that, if the realization of what was promised had been achieved in advance of Christ and the church, it would of necessity have been a poorer promise in the first place. He is saying, in effect, that the perfecting of these pre-Christian faithful (v. 40) could not be achieved 'apart from us' because it could not be achieved apart from Christ. The chapter therefore ends as it had begun, with a first person plural reference embracing the writer and his friends (cf. 'By faith *we* understand', v. 3). This summing up after the roll-call of the faithful noticeably conflicts with the more developed forms of 'dispensationalism' that make sharp distinctions between Israel and the church and their respective destinies—just as the chapter consistently affirms that the basis of faith upon which the individual finds acceptance with God remains unchanged through the generations.

Hebrews 12: Journey's End

Introductory Comment

From the celebration of Israel's faithful the writer moves on to Christ himself, not simply as an exemplar of faith but as the 'pioneer and perfecter' of faith (v. 2). In vv. 1-17 he commends discipline and endurance to his addressees as he encourages them to regard these as corollaries of their acceptance into God's family rather than as reasons for abandoning the faith. The remainder of the chapter adopts a journey's-end approach to the situation of the 'Hebrews': although as Christians they have not encountered a physical equivalent of Mt Sinai they have already reached Mt Zion and 'the heavenly Jerusalem' (v. 22), though this, as he points out, gives no occasion for careless hearing (vv. 25-29).

Looking to Jesus (12.1-3)

The concluding verses of ch. 11 had brought the review and the argument back to the recipients of the letter, which from now on consists largely of exhortation of the sort that has punctuated earlier chapters. The Christian life is pictured as a race in vv. 1-2, and the idea of the race is revisited in vv. 11-13, and perhaps also in the injunction to 'pursue peace' in v. 14. Much of the imagery is paralleled in *4 Maccabees*, in its eulogizing of the Maccabaean martyrs who engaged in a 'divine' contest, with the world and the human race spectating, endured torture 'even to death' and received the prize of 'immortality in endless life' (17.9-14). It is tempting to conclude that the 'cloud of witnesses' in v. 1 are spectators of the race in progress. They as the 'cloud' 'surrounding' (*perikeimenon*) urge on the 'Hebrews' to run the race 'set before' (*prokeimenon*) them. However, their chief function is to testify, for the benefit of these later competitors, to the invincibility of faith. Yet if the 'Hebrews' are to run their race mindful of the example of these 'witnesses' to faith, they must nevertheless focus on Jesus who, having himself triumphed, was exalted to the heavenly throne.

As previously (see on 2.9), it is Christ who by his incarnation identified with humanity and who bore the earthly name Jesus, who is held up as the inspirer and sustainer of his people's faith. 'Looking to

God' says 4 Macc. 17.10 of the Maccabaean martyrs, and similar senti-
ments are found in other Jewish and non-Jewish writings. There may
therefore be a christological implication in 'looking to Jesus' that the
author would have been happy for his readers to recognize. He does not
put Christ on the same level as those whose faith has been celebrated in
ch.11; instead, he describes him as 'the pioneer and perfecter of faith',
by which he probably means something like 'the one with whom faith
begins and ends'—itself a paraphrase that is not completely transparent.
Already the words of Isa. 8.17, 'I will put my trust in him', have been
reinterpreted as an utterance of Christ in 2.13, so that faith has been seen
as an aspect of the life of Christ. But what is specifically highlighted in
v. 2 is his endurance (*hupemeinen*, 'endured', picking up *di' hupo-
monēs*, 'with endurance' [NRSV 'with perseverance'], in v. 1) of even a
cross, in expectation of (*anti*) 'the joy that was set before him'. There is
ironic reversal in 'scorning its shame' (NIV); the idea is as in Col. 2.15
where the Crucified makes 'a public example' of principalities and
powers while on the cross. The conclusion to all this—glory for shame
—is expressed in terms of the author's favourite psalm: Christ sat down
'at the right hand of the throne of God' (v. 2; cf. 1.3; Ps. 110.1).

The addressees are bidden in v. 3 to 'consider' Christ and his response
to suffering in order to gain strength for their own trials. Since their
problem consists in a flagging of spirit the contemplation of the great
exponent of faithful endurance will itself be beneficial. There is, moreover, a special benefit in focusing on the 'case-history' of Christ for,
whereas the faithful of ch. 11 did not receive what had been promised
them (11.39), Christian faith embraced the victorious session of Christ
on the heavenly throne. In 'consider' (*analogisasthe*) there is perhaps
the suggestion that the 'Hebrews' should make a comparison between
their circumstances and his. Comparison of the sort has certainly affected
the author's way of referring to the sufferings of Christ in this verse, for
there is nothing here of a theology of the cross (*pace* v. 2), whether in
sacerdotal or transactional or other theologically relevant terms. Those
sufferings are seen as consisting, rather, in the hostility of 'sinners'
against Christ's person, for the writer wishes to show how Christ's experience most nearly parallels that of the addressees. However, if we
consider the references to 'sin' and 'sinners' in vv. 1-4 we may also
discover a contrast between Christ and his suffering people that is
almost certainly intentional on the part of the author. *They* have been

bidden to divest themselves of 'the sin that clings so closely' (v. 1) and they are about to be reminded that in their struggle against sin they have not had to make the ultimate sacrifice (v. 4). Christ's 'struggle', on the other hand, is not with sin as such but with gainsaying sinners. The author eschews the thought that in respect of sin and sinfulness there is any comparison between the author of faith and those following in faith (cf. 4.15). The strongly supported alternative reading in v. 3, 'such hostility from sinners against themselves' (NRSVn), has generally been considered as difficult and secondary, even when cross-referred to a similar-sounding phrase in LXX Num 17.3 (MT 16.38). If the reading is accepted, the point is then that those who opposed Christ harmed themselves more than they harmed him.

Family Discipline (12.4-13)

In these verses the figure of the race is temporarily lost to view, though it emerges again in vv. 11-13. Meanwhile the more generalized idea of struggle—an idea not incompatible with the metaphor of race—informs the writer's appeal. He notes that, whereas the opposition that Christ encountered in his public ministry culminated in his rejection and crucifixion, those addressed had not yet suffered in such an extreme way (v. 4). Even the privations recalled in 10.32-34 fell short of martyrdom. 'Not yet', of course, not only states a fact but also warns of a possibility, and the writer's concern is intensified by the thought that wilting at this stage augured poorly for the time when to be a Christian would prove still more costly. He senses, too, a tendency to infer from the experience of persecution that the whole Christian enterprise was questionable, since the community's experience of suffering could well be an indication that God was not with them. On the other hand, there is good evidence that the earliest Christian preaching, if only because of the circumstances in which it was often conducted, included realistic advice about the likely consequences of conversion (cf. Acts 14.22; 1 Thess. 3.4).

In vv. 5-11 it is indeed asserted that God is involved in what has overtaken the 'Hebrews'. For the writer to say that their suffering in any way derived from God is daring, and especially in this context. Nor does he take refuge in the suggestion that the suffering relates to God only indirectly, or comes only by his permission. But by quoting from Prov. 3.11-12 in its Septuagintal form and bringing their suffering within a family context—here the 'father–son' relationship—he makes a statement

about the legitimacy of their Christian faith at the same time as he subjects them to the paternal discipline of the God who has accepted them.
The Proverbs quotation addresses *them,* and because the function of the
Hebrew scriptures is conceived in this way he is the more able to apply
directly to them the word of encouragement that they have overlooked.
Previously he has advised them to 'encourage one another daily' (3.13)
and he has counselled them to continue to meet together for their
mutual encouragement (10.25). Given that ordinary Christians were
dependent upon church meetings for the hearing as much as for the
exposition of Scripture, it is reasonable enough to trace a connection
between the forsaking of church meetings and the forgetting (in whatever precise sense) of Scripture.

On the basis of the quotation from Proverbs the writer makes the
point that discipline is a condition of being a member of God's family.
(We have already noted that the assumption in 5.8 about the nature of
Christ's sonship makes suffering obedience a concession rather than the
consequence of that unique status of sonship.) The occurrence of 'lose
heart' (*ekluou*) in the quotation in v. 5 uses the same verb as in v. 3
(*ekluomenoi*). Possibly the writer was already thinking in terms of LXX
Prov. 3.12 when he wrote v. 3. In the last line of the quotation the
Septuagint differs substantially from the standard Hebrew text, which
runs: 'as a father the son in whom he delights'. The removal of the simile
and its replacement by a direct statement about God's chastising of
'everyone he accepts as a son' (NIV) enables the writer of *Hebrews* to
develop the idea of Christians being children of God in a way that is
characteristic of the New Testament while standing at a considerable
distance from the meaning of the Old Testament text quoted. It is one
among a good number of creative reworkings in the New Testament of
Septuagintal misrenderings of Old Testament passages.

The word 'discipline' in its noun and verb forms (*paideia/paideuein*)
occurs twice in the Proverbs quotation in vv. 5-6 and no fewer than six
times in the succeeding argument in vv. 7-11. Whatever the external
circumstances and the addressees' own interpretation of them to this
point, the writer clearly wishes to convince them that God is subjecting
them to family discipline and has definite goals in mind (vv. 10, 11).
There is no talk of advancing the kingdom through suffering, or of
bringing glory to God in the face of a hostile world, or of their suffering
being a necessary element in the messianic woes in which the church
must have a part. The concern is with their character development and

it becomes unapologetically individualistic (vv. 15-16), just as any serious expression of Christianity must be before ever it can look to the corporate dimensions of the faith.

On the premise that paternal duty includes the disciplining of one's offspring, vv. 7-11 explore the idea in relation to God as 'the Father of spirits' (v. 9). At first blush this expression might suggest that the writer is thinking simply of God as the creator of all human life, nevertheless his considering the possibility of the 'Hebrews' being shown to be illegitimate and not true children of God shows that he has a more particular kind of family in mind (see also below). So v. 8 states an absolute: that to be a Christian is in some way to experience God as a father who deals out discipline as a necessary element in the parent-child relationship into which he has entered. It is a reflection on the relationship between God and the Christian believer that can usefully be inserted into discussions of the supposedly antinomian character of, in particular, the Pauline preaching of salvation by the grace of God (cf. Rom. 3.5-8; 6.1). Since 'everyone' experiences fatherly discipline the writer can slip naturally into the first person plural in v. 9, and it is as if his addressees and he join up again after the disconcerting possibility entertained at the end of the previous verse. I have already noted the expression 'Father of spirits' as possibly hinting at more than the general idea of God as 'father', in the sense of creator, of all (cf. '[son] of Adam, [son] of God', Lk. 3.38). There are near-parallels to the expression in the Old Testament (notably Num. 16.22; 27.16) and elsewhere (e.g. 'Lord of spirits' in *1 En.* 37.2-4; 38.4). Here there is obvious contrast—in a basically chiastic arrangement—between 'fathers of our flesh' (NRSV 'human parents') and 'the Father of spirits'.

Finally, in v. 9, the outcome of submission to the divine Father is that his children 'live'. This is very much the goal of the wisdom teaching of the book of Proverbs, from the third chapter of which the author has already quoted (see on vv. 5-6 above). Proverbs 3 itself advertises prominently this aspect of wisdom: observing parental instruction will give 'length of days and years of life' (v. 2); wisdom holds long life in her right hand (v. 16); wisdom is 'a tree of life to those who lay hold of her' (v. 18); sound wisdom and prudence 'will be life for your soul' (vv. 21-22), and in the next chapter a father's advice received in childhood is passed on to the next generation: 'keep my commandments, and live' (Prov. 4.4). This is all, indeed, of a piece with the decalogal command to honour one's parents so that long life in the promised land may be granted (Exod. 20.12). However, against the background of 'the fear of death' within this letter the verse gives the assurance that God's disciplinary actions are not intended to bring death but will, rather, in the spirit of ch. 11 and its theme of the defeat of death, issue in true life now and hereafter. In two balancing clauses in v. 10 the contrasting motivations behind human and divine disciplining are set out. Human fathers are said to do what seems right in the circumstances, but the implication is that God acts unerringly for the benefit of those whom he disciplines, by promoting their holiness. When the writer refers to ordinary parental discipline as lasting 'for a short time' he may be implying that God's chastening takes longer. There is a 'being made holy' that is a once-for-all reality by virtue of Christ's sacrificial death, according to 10.10, but that has its counterpart in the realm of moral endeavour, as soon enough becomes apparent: 'Pursue peace with everyone, and the holiness without which no one will see the Lord' (v. 14; cf. 2 Cor. 7.1).

Verse 11 presents another contrast, this time of a 'before' and 'after' sort. Now the previous reference to holiness is complemented by the mention of righteousness, and the two are probably meant to function as synonyms. This is also suggested by the degree of correspondence between vv. 11 ('the peaceful fruit of righteousness') and 14 ('Pursue peace with everyone, and the holiness...'). The comparison may also shed light on the significance of 'peaceful' in v. 11. It is possible that the writer is thinking of a mind at peace because it is resigned to the acceptance of God's will, but he may also be referring to the social benefits, even within the Christian community, produced by peacemakers—those deserving of being called 'sons of God', according to the Beatitudes (Mt. 5.9). Discipline is now seen as training (v. 11), which brings back to the surface the athletic imagery with which the chapter began. Verses 12-13 continue in this vein with encouragement not only to attend to one's personal fitness but also to ensure that the running track is fit to run on, in view of the aggravation of injury that can be inflicted by an uneven surface. Verse 12 probably qualifies as a paraphrase of Isa. 35.3, which comes in a section announcing the advent of God and the return of his delivered people to Zion. In the injunction to 'make straight paths' the writer has returned to the book of Proverbs for further counsel from father to son (Prov. 4.26), so reinforcing his point that the tribulations through which his addressees are passing are to be viewed in the light of their relationship to God as Father.

A Bad Example (12.14-17)

This section is in the nature of an 'awful warning' about the danger of failure to 'obtain the grace of God' (v. 15). Initially the advice is couched in the form of basic Christian instruction: to be at peace with one's fellow-humans and to replicate the divine holiness (cf. on v. 10). It is not just a peaceable attitude within the Christian community that is enjoined, but one that embraces all, and perhaps specially those responsible for the persecution that has been dignified as 'discipline' in the earlier verses. The mention of holiness, however, marks a change of mood as compared with even the parenesis of the preceding section. Holiness is the stated *sine qua non* for seeing the Lord, by which is meant the personal realization of the Christian hope preached in the Gospel. In the Old Testament the so-called 'entrance liturgy', as in Psalm 15, stresses the moral and ethical requirements laid upon those who would approach the worship of God in his sanctuary. Now the cultic apparatus has gone, as far as the 'Hebrews' are concerned, but the moral and ethical conditions must still apply. Three possible categories of failure are noted in three parallel clauses beginning 'lest anyone' (*mē tis*; 'See to it that', NRSV) in vv. 15-16. The first possibility, that anyone should 'fail to obtain the grace of God', recognizes the possibility of denying the basis of, and so rendering inoperative, the very gift that lifts the individual to God (cf. 2 Cor. 6.1; Gal. 5.4). In its original setting the 'root of bitterness', which is the second danger to be avoided, is the inclination towards idolatry on the part of Israelites poised to enter the promised land (Deut. 29.18). Here the nature of the bitterness is not indicated, though we may suspect that it is the bitterness of disillusionment with the Christian life. As in the Deuteronomy passage, the concern is lest the disaffection should spread, so that even here the individualistic emphasis already noted (see on vv. 7-11) has a community dimension. Far from the desired end of holiness, the result will be the defilement (cf. *mianthōsin*) of 'many'. (The alternative reading 'the many' could refer to the community as a whole [cf. 2 Cor. 2.6].)

In v. 16 Esau provides the third example of an aberration to be avoided, probably because the writer detected in his addressees a comparable danger of selling their spiritual birthright for short-term benefit. Again the choice of 'profane' (*bebēlos*) contrasts with the holiness that is the goal of Christian living (v. 14); the corresponding verb is used in Mt. 12.5 of priests 'profaning' the sabbath. The first of the two categories in v. 16 (*pornos*, 'sexually immoral', NIV) offends no less

against the holiness inculcated in both Testaments (cf. 13.4; 1 Thess. 4.3-
8). Although there is nothing in biblical tradition that would specially
associate Esau with sexual immorality, later Jewish tradition did not
spare him in this or in other respects, so that it is possible that 'sexually
immoral' is meant to refer to Esau in the same way as 'profane'. That
Esau is said to have surrendered his birthright 'for a single meal' could
be significant in the setting of *Hebrews* if we but knew more about the
author's concerns in relation to the addressees. In 13.9 he will stress that
Christian faith is not strengthened by 'foods' (NRSV 'regulations about
food', NIV 'ceremonial foods'). From further consideration of Esau's
plight (v. 17) the writer issues an implicit warning that recalls the
explicit terms of 6.4-8. The point is that, just as to sell one's birthright is
to disinherit oneself once and for all, so the 'Hebrews' should take care
lest they pass a point of no return by repudiating their original profession of Christian faith. On the contrary, their calling is to participation
in the church of the firstborn whose names are ineradicably written in
heaven (v. 23). The warning against apostasy issued in 6.4-8 is echoed
most clearly in the reference to the impossibility of repentance in such a
situation (cf. 6.4). This warning from the story of Esau is the more
interesting in that it may suggest that, if any of the addressees were
converts fom Judaism, to go back to their ancestral faith would not mean
a return to 'Jacob-Israel' but an identifying with Esau, who was the
bearer of no special hopes or promises for the descendants of Abraham.
It may, then, imply an appropriation of the term 'Israel' by the church,
as arguably is made in Gal. 6.16.

Not Sinai, but Zion (12.18-24)

'Seeing the Lord' (cf. v. 14), and under what conditions, is still the issue
in this section. The essential point of the argument comes in v. 25 when
the writer capitalizes on the contrast that he has drawn in the preceding
verses in order to warn his addressees against rejecting a divine
communication more awesome even than that delivered at Mt Sinai. In
vv. 18-21 they are reminded first of what had not characterized their
experience of Christian faith ('You have not come', v. 18), and seven
aspects of Sinai are listed (palpability-fire-darkness-gloom-tempest-
trumpet-voice). This is offset in vv. 22-24 ('But you have come', v. 22)
with a rehearsal of some of the 'impalpable realities' to which, as
Christians, they have been introduced. Sinai is not mentioned by name
in v. 18, nor indeed does the word 'mountain' occur in a significant part

of the manuscript tradition. The emphasis is on Sinai as representing what was tangible, visual and aural in the tradition of the giving of the law to Moses, and, by extension, in the Jewish religion in general. If originally Jewish, the 'Hebrews' would have been encouraged by such texts as Deut. 4.9-14; 5.3-4 to consider themselves as part of the original Sinai congregation, in solidarity with that generation that had received the revelation of the law. As Christians, however, they have not come to 'something that can be touched' (NRSV).

The epiphenomena of Sinai—the fire, darkness, gloom, tempest—themselves convey the overwhelming nature of the Israelites' experience at the mountain, but the writer goes on to describe the effect on both the people and Moses their leader. The people's dread is expressed in *a fortiori* fashion, focusing on the interdiction concerning any animals that might come in contact with the holy mountain. In the Old Testament narrative itself the ruling applied in the first instance to humans (Exod. 19.12-13). Moses' own reaction is summed up in an utterance that finds its nearest parallel in Deut. 9.19, which in its Septuagintal form also uses the adjective *ekphobos* in first person speech by Moses. There he is referring to his fear of divine reprisals for the making of the golden calf rather than to his response to the theophany *per se*. This attribution of extreme dread to Moses contrasts with the absence of fear, as noted by the author, that enabled his parents to disregard the pharaonic edict at the time of his birth (11.23), and also contrasts with the author's own claim that it was not fear of the royal wrath that drove Moses out of Egypt (11.27).

Verses 22-24 describe the unseen realities that had become accessible to the 'Hebrews' since their conversion to Christ. '[But] you have come' (*proseléluthate*) is a verb used by Philo to represent proselyte conversion (*Spec. Leg.* 1.51), but, although it is the effects of Christian conversion that are being described in the present passage, the word may simply denote cultic approach such as would be appropriate to both Mt Sinai and the heavenly Zion. Even so, participation as much as mere approach is suggested by the language of these verses. The addressees themselves, inasmuch as they could be said to belong to the 'church of the firstborn' and to have become beneficiaries of the new covenant, had begun to experience the life that is characteristic of the heavenly city. In this respect they had transcended the experience of Abraham who 'looked for the city with foundations' (11.10 [cf. 14]; 13.14). The familiar contrast between Sinai and Zion served well the author's purpose of contrasting Judaism and Christianity. Sinai, as much as being a locale associated with law-giving, was a staging-post on the way to a destination, namely Canaan, and ultimately the holy city of Jerusalem. The language here is again suggestive of heavenly prototype and earthly counterpart in a Platonic sort of way, but there is a more immediate Jewish parallel for it in *2 Bar.* 4.2-7, as also in the Pauline writings (see Gal. 4.26).

The idea of a heavenly city to which the faithful aspired is also implicit in some of the Old Testament texts in which the concept of 'life with God' is developed, as in Psalm 16 ('You show me the path of life/In your presence there is fullness of joy/in your right hand are pleasures for evermore', v. 11) or Psalm 23 where the psalmist's expectation that he would 'dwell in the house of the Lord for ever' (v. 6, NIV) surely means more than a permanent domicile in the Jerusalem temple (NRSV 'my whole life long' is unnecessarily restrictive). If, at the time *Hebrews* was written, the earthly Jerusalem had not yet been destroyed by the Romans, it would soon happen; in which case the spiritual, immaterial comforts of a 'heavenly Jerusalem' could be expected to appeal the more strongly to the addressees. 'Living God' is a term favoured by our author (see also 3.12; 9.14; 10.31), and its use tends to underline the awesomeness of the God before whom his creatures live. It is used also in connection with the theophany at Sinai ('For who is there of all flesh that has heard the voice of the living God speaking out of fire, as we have, and remained alive?', Deut. 5.26). Here the association with Zion might suggest a less forbidding connotation, in which case there is obvious contrast with the death and dread of the verses immediately preceding. At the same time, it is a feature of vv. 22-24 that, in an almost disconcerting fashion, elements of awe and dread mingle with others of celebration and joy in the description of the features of the heavenly Jerusalem.

The mention of the angelic assembly both recalls the Sinai narrative and reminds the 'Hebrews' of the company that they now keep. At Sinai the giving of the law was attended by myriads of angels, according to Deut. 33.2 (cf. on 2.2 above). Those who people the heavenly Zion are said to be 'in festal gathering' (*panegurei*), which term is occasionally used of the Israelite festivals (cf. LXX Hos. 9.5; Amos 5.21; Ezek. 46.11) and may or may not be appropriate for the solemn proceedings of Sinai. Since the writer has already plotted the relative positions of angels and redeemed humanity in the hierarchy created by God, this reference to the angelic companies doubtless has to be read in the light of such earlier texts as 1.14 and 2.16. (It is possible, on the other hand, to take *panēgurei* with what follows, as in AV 'the general assembly and church of the firstborn', though the structuring of the clauses in vv. 22-23 seems marginally against this.) The 'assembly of the firstborn' (v. 23), on the other hand, reads more naturally like a reference to the church as being composed of human beings elevated to firstborn status by their association with Christ, and this is confirmed by the statement that these firstborn are 'enrolled in heaven', in view of the biblical parallels for this figure (cf. Exod. 32.32; Lk. 10.20). Remarkably, this mention of the 'assembly of the firstborn' is followed by a reference to God himself, introduced as 'a judge [who is] God of all' (lit.). There follows a reference to those who have passed from this life to the world beyond ('the spirits of the righteous made perfect'), perhaps with the suggestion that they have passed the scrutiny of the divine judge as they have proceeded to the realm of the blessed dead. These righteous no doubt include the Israelite faithful as represented in ch. 11 (see on v. 40), as well as those Christians who had already died. Both, in the parlance of *Hebrews*, had been 'made perfect' by Christ's sacrifice on their behalf (10.14).

The means by which such perfecting came about is addressed in v. 24. Here again, and somewhat in contrast with the august setting, the author refers to Christ by his ordinary name Jesus, as on various other occasions in his letter. In the exposition of the 'new covenant' in ch. 8 Christ is described as 'the mediator of a better covenant' on the ground that the new version was founded on better promises (v. 6). Here the contrast is between the sprinkled blood associated with the making of the new covenant and the blood of Abel. Since 9.14 links the purification of the conscience with the sacrificial death of Christ, an easy contrast suggests itself in the present text: whereas Abel's blood cried out from the ground for vengeance, Christ's sacrificial blood speaks the 'better word' (Gk simply *kreitton*) of forgiveness for those who seek it. Moreover, 9.15 links this purification of the conscience through Christ's blood with his role as the mediator of the new covenant. The likelihood of a contrast of this type would be strengthened if it were clear beyond doubt that a blood ritual was in the author's mind at 10.22 when he spoke of 'hearts sprinkled clean from an evil conscience' (see on 10.22, however). It is no problem that in 11.4 Abel's 'speech' is commended— and hardly as a cry for vengeance—since there it is through his *faith* that he is said to be speaking still. Although the Greek in v. 24 reads literally 'than Abel', this may be elliptical for 'than the blood of Abel'. To that extent a contrast can be made between the 'speakers' in vv. 4 and 24.

If not an actual aim of the author, one possible effect of his argument in these verses was to minimize in the estimation of his readers the importance of the earthly Jerusalem as a place of pilgrimage. Even diaspora Jews commonly made pilgrimage to Jerusalem on the great festival occasions, but Jewish converts to Christianity, on hearing that they had come 'to Mount Zion and to the city of the living God, the heavenly Jerusalem', might well draw conclusions about the earthly city that they had long venerated. The implications of 13.12-14 are arguably even stronger in this regard. At the same time, the main point in the present section is the contrast between Sinai and the heavenly Zion, as the following verses also indicate.

Speaking and Shaking (12.25-29)

Now that the main body of the letter is reaching its conclusion—ch. 13 deals with more personal and practical matters in the way of some other New Testament letters that are similarly divided between the theological and the applied—it is appropriate that the theme of divine speech is developed in these verses. In a way, the emphasis follows naturally from the preceding paragraph (see especially vv. 19-20), but the perspective is the grander one with which the letter began ('Long ago God spoke', 'in these last days he has spoken', 1.1-2). God is 'the one who is speaking' in v. 25, and in the remainder of the verse a contrast is made between Mt Sinai and God's current speaking, in respect of the locale of the speaking. Sinai is characterized as a divine speaking 'on earth', whereas the message with which the author is mainly concerned is dignified as speech from heaven. To heighten the contrast the writer indulges in hyperbaton, the effect of which is to bring the words 'on earth' up front. He will have been aware of such texts as Exod. 20.22 and Deut. 4.36, according to which the divine voice at Sinai issued from heaven (cf. Neh. 9.13); it is just that he regards the one kind of speaking as so much more final than the other as to belong in a different category. Some drawing upon the palpable Sinai/heavenly Jerusalem contrast of the preceding verses is also doubtless involved in the distinction made here in v. 25. Although the verb translated 'refuse' has already been used to describe the Israelites' request in v. 19 (NRSV 'beg'), the warning has much more in common with 2.2-3 where the 'Hebrews' are reminded that the laws of Sinai were hedged about with sanctions. (There is a sense in which the whole Pentateuchal wilderness tradition, indeed, provides a commentary on the effects of 'refusing' the divine speaker who communicated with Israel at Sinai.) These sanctions, rather than the very specific prohibition mentioned in v. 20, are probably recalled here. At this point in the letter, however, it is not 'neglect' (cf. 2.3) but straightforward refusal to listen that concerns the writer. And it is a refusal to listen, not so much to the message, as to the speaker himself, namely God. For the present purpose, even the Sinai experience is seen as direct communication from God, without reference to the mediation of angels (contrast 2.2) or the role of Moses.

The writer proceeds in v. 26 to claim that he whose voice 'shook the earth'—the Old Testament traditions about Sinai speak of earthquake as a concomitant of the divine presence (Exod. 19.18 [MT; LXX otherwise]; Jdgs 5.4-5; Ps. 68.8)—has promised a further intervention in the created order that will affect 'not only the earth but also the heaven'. The earth-heaven contrast is sharpened by the insertion of 'not only' and 'but also' in this quotation from Hag. 2.6, as also by the inversion of the terms 'heaven' and 'earth' and the omission of the reference to the sea and the dry land. Moreover, the words 'yet once more' (*eti hapax*) are taken to imply that no such upheaval will ever take place subsequently: it is a case of 'one more time' (v. 27). In fact, the author explains, the final 'shaking' of the earth and the heavens will remove the temporal, visible order of things, leaving only that unseen world that alone is true and real. This transience of the created world is acknowledged already in the penultimate Old Testament quotation in ch. 1, where the impermanence of creation is seen in contrast with the eternal character of deity (1.10-12). *Hebrews*, then, does not portray the renovation of the heavens and the earth in the way of Isa. 65.17; 66.22, or even of 2 Pet. 3.13 ('we wait for new heavens and a new earth, where righteousness is at home'; cf. Rev. 21.1), though the permanence of what emerges in the new order is similarly stressed in Isa. 66.22 ('For as the heavens and the new earth, which I will make, shall remain [LXX *menei*; cf. *meinēi* here in v. 27] before me...'). At this point the author comes especially close to an expression of Platonic dualism, since Old Testament precedent is not forthcoming in the way that it is with, for example, the heavenly prototype/earthly form duality represented earlier in the letter (cf. 8.5). If the addressees were meant to draw the inference that a simple cultus that concentrated on spiritual dimensions of worship best fitted in with such eschatological expectation, this would agree well with the writer's purpose as reflected in other parts of his letter.

In Hag. 2.20-23, which partly repeats and expands Hag. 2.6-7, the predicted convulsions in the natural order have as their particular focus the overthrow of the 'kingdoms of the nations' (v. 22). The linking of these related passages in Haggai 2 may possibly account for our author's reference in v. 28 to the 'kingdom that cannot be shaken'. For the specific idea of *receiving* a kingdom he may, on the other hand, have been indebted to Dan. 7.18 where the 'holy ones of the Most High' 'receive the kingdom' when the Danielic quartet of world empires has been overthrown. The receiving of this kingdom, he suggests, is grounds for thanksgiving on the part of himself and the 'Hebrews' (v. 28). To have said that they had already received the kingdom would have fitted ill with the eschatological emphasis of v. 27, nevertheless he may have wished his addressees to consider the kingdom as being in some sense their present possession, just as he has been able to speak of their having come already to Mt Zion and the heavenly Jerusalem (v. 22). Their thanksgiving would then be based not merely on future expectation but on present reality. Thanksgiving, as he observes in a statement that anticipates a point developed in 13.9-16 (see especially v. 15), is that in which the truly acceptable worship of God consists. For 'offer...worship' (so NRSV) he has used the verb *latreuein*, the term by which he indicates the cultic service of the Israelite priesthood (8.5; 13.10) and of the worshippers who approached God within the context of that cultus (9.9; cf. 10.2). Finally, he notes that Christian worship, no less than the worship of the Israelite cultus, must be offered 'with reverence and awe' (v. 28). This is supported by a quotation from Moses' words to the Israelites in Deut. 4.24: 'For the Lord your God is a devouring fire, a jealous God'—except that the use of the possessive pronoun 'our' acknowledges this description of God as intrinsically Christian as well. For just as the God of the Old Testament is a God of compassion and mercy, as well as of severity and judgment, so the God of the New Testament is depicted as both dread and awesome and also loving and forgiving.

Hebrews 13: Continuity midst Change

Introductory Comment

The final chapter of *Hebrews* is different from the rest of the letter, and yet not so comprehensively as to justify the various attempts that have been made to reduce it to secondary status. The continuity between the central section, on the subject of the legitimacy and proper expression of Christian worship (vv. 9-16), and earlier chapters is itself a strong argument for integrality. Continuity is also important in another respect, in that the previous emphasis on *dis*continuity as between the Hebrew and Christian systems of worship is balanced here by reminders of things that make for endurance and stability in Christian experience. This is not to say that 'continuity' is an absentee theme in earlier chapters, for example in the discussion of Christ as a 'priest according to the order of Melchizedek' (chs. 5–7); nevertheless, there is a practical, pastoral deliberateness about its treatment in the early verses of ch. 13. Love, purified of its perversions, is mentioned first (vv. 1-6), and then Christian leadership (v. 7), and especially as represented by the Lord of the church (v. 8). Conversely, the warning against 'being carried away' by 'strange teachings' introduces a section on the validity of Christian life and worship in spite of their lowly associations (vv. 9-16). After a further reference to leadership in v. 17, which acts with vv. 7-8 as a frame to the section on worship (vv. 9-16), the chapter concludes with more personal observations (vv. 18-19, 22-25) and a benediction (vv. 20-21).

Let Love Continue (13.1-6)

The section, which forms a fairly discrete, yet not wholly self-contained, unit within the chapter, consists of several loosely structured exhortations that culminate in two quotations from the Old Testament (vv. 5, 6). Love and two of the commonest perversions of it combine to form a plausible connecting theme, as is also suggested by the presence of the *phil-* elements in *philadelphia* (NRSV 'mutual love', v. 1), *philoxenias* (NRSV 'hospitality to strangers', v. 2) and *aphilarguros* (NRSV 'free from the love of money', v. 5). First and foremost, 'mutual love' is to *remain* (*menetō* , v. 1; NRSV 'continue'). The use of this verb unites the section with what immediately precedes, since the 'shaking' of the world order is there said to take place so that 'what cannot be shaken' may *remain* (12.27). While the earlier reference gives no indication of what these imperishable things might be, the writer now nominates love as having this enduring quality—much as does the great Pauline encomium on love in 1 Cor. 13 (see vv. 8-13). The exhortation is hardly otiose; the need for mutual love has already been mentioned in the context of the neglecting of opportunities for fellowship and, consequently, for demonstrating concern for fellow-members in the church (10.24-25). This mutual love, according to vv. 2-3, is to be translated into acts of practical kindness. In the context, the strangers are Christian travellers, of whom there may have been a good number in some parts of the empire. In addition to normal business travellers there will have been others engaged in itinerant missioning, and at times yet others suffering displacement because of persecution. The writer offers an incentive to hospitality, perhaps because he thought that one was needed: in the course of welcoming strangers one might possibly entertain angels. In this respect the mutual love that must 'remain' is shown to have an ancient pedigree, for the reference to those who unsuspectingly entertained angels must have Abraham and Sarah principally in mind (cf. Gen. 18). If so, there may also be the unspoken suggestion that those celebrated for their faith in the honours list in ch. 11 (cf. vv. 8-19) were possessed of a truly practical form of charity. The present reference to angels is proof, if such were needed, that the attention given to angels in chs. 1-2 should not be interpreted to mean that the 'Hebrews' were given to angel worship. For it would be singularly inappropriate to incite people to hospitality in the hope of entertaining extra-terrestrial visitors if part of the larger agenda was to deter the same people from the worship of angels.

Because the mutual love advocated is in the first instance in relation to fellow-Christians, the imprisoned and afflicted (NRSV 'tortured') who are the writer's concern will have included those who owed their misfortune to their fidelity to Christ. The 'Hebrews' had already proved themselves in this matter of caring for prisoners (10.34). For the present they themselves might not be in prison, but they were 'in the body' (lit. 'as also [your]selves being in [the] body'), and to that extent capable of empathizing with their fellow-Christians in trouble. Attridge expresses a stronger idea in his translation, 'as if you yourselves were in (their) body', since he holds that *hōs* ('as if') should function as in the preceding clause, 'as if bound with them'. He quotes a helpful parallel from Philo: 'feeling themselves maltreated in the bodies of others' (*Spec. Leg.* 3.161). Both NRSV and NIV seem to concede the grammatical point with, respectively, 'as though you yourselves were being tortured' and 'as if you yourselves were suffering'.

Verse 4 is about *marital* love and warns against the forming of sexual liaisons outside the institution of marriage. The first two clauses are verbless in the Greek but are properly taken as commands, as in NRSV (*pace* AV 'Marriage is honourable in all') and as the analogy of the opening, and formally parallel, clause in v. 5 would suggest. There is a similar construction, involving the noun-predicate order, at Rom. 12.9, which begins a similarly parenetic section. The exact sense of *en pasin* ('by all' [NRSV] or 'in all respects'?) is not certain, but it is clear that a sweeping claim is being made on behalf of the institution of marriage. Unchastity is viewed as a defilement (*amiantos*, 'undefiled') which is not merely ceremonial but moral, and so depriving the individual of that holiness 'without which no one will see the Lord' (12.14). Disregard of marriage may take more than one form, including that of the exaltation of celibacy above the married state. There is no attempt here to carve out a place for celibacy, even if it is exercised as part of a Christian commitment. Implicit in the warning of judgment at the end of v. 4 is the idea that, even if prevailing sexual mores or individual behaviour may repudiate the idea of a calling to account, God is the monitor and the judge in the area of sexual morality.

Another form of avarice is addressed in v. 5. (Such is the closeness between sexual lust and avarice in some New Testament thinking that the language of the two is combined in 1 Thess. 4.3-8 in Paul's warning against sexual exploitation of one's fellow-Christian [cf. v. 6].) Structurally the verse begins as does v. 4. There follows in the second clause an unattached participle (*arkoumenoi*, lit. 'being content') with imperatival force, for which Rom. 12.9 again supplies a close parallel (cf. also Col. 3.13). *aphilarguros* (contrast Luke's description of the Pharisees [Lk. 16.14]) represents a state of mind commonly recommended in the New Testament and further described in the next clause (cf. Phil. 4.11-12). The basis for such insouciance is said to reside in what 'he'—probably God, the referent at the end of the previous verse—'has said'. (The perfect tense of this verb occurs elsewhere in *Hebrews* [e.g. 1.13; 4.3] and does not necessarily emphasize the continuing effect of what has been 'said'.) What he is represented as saying here is most nearly paralleled in Deut. 31.6, 8, with the difference that the third person utterance there is converted into the first person here. Interestingly, the warning against covetousness suggests an improvement in circumstances as compared with the situation recalled in 10.32-34. Verse 6, with its quotation of Ps. 118.6, both acknowledges a surer source of confidence than that of accumulated wealth and also takes account of the possibility of further persecution: 'What can anyone do to me?' 'We say with confidence' is a more literal rendering than 'we *can* say with confidence' and is preferable because it may properly be taken to imply the use of the Old Testament psalms by early Christians, whether congregationally or in personal devotions. The other rendering does not, of course, rule out that possibility.

We Have an Altar (13.7-17)

Church leadership is introduced in v. 7 as another agent making for stability in the community or communities being addressed. The leaders in question are evidently now dead, which circumstance agrees with previous hints about the addressees living in the second or third generation after Christ and the apostles (see on 2.3). 'Leader' (*hēgoumenos*), which term occurs also in vv. 17 and 24, is the author's preferred designation for the church eldership among the 'Hebrews'. Nomenclature in respect of leadership was a matter of some indifference among the first-century churches, to judge from the New Testament evidence. The role of leader consists here principally in the committal to the flock of the 'word of God', which might suggest a ministry of teaching and exposition based on the Hebrew scriptures—which in their Septuagintal form constituted the Bible of many of the earliest Christian communities—and such records and traditions of a Christian nature as were available. However, 2.3 speaks of the message of salvation, which had first been announced by Christ himself, as having been passed on to the addressees by those who had heard him. In Acts 'the word of the Lord' (or 'the word of God') is an expression used specially of the preaching and confirmation of the Christian message among its first hearers (8.25; 13.46; 16.32; cf. 14.25; 16.6). If these leaders represented a link with the first generation and had introduced the Hebrews' to the Gospel then the call to remember is all the more poignant.

Two things are required of those remaining: to consider the outcome of the lives of these leaders and then to imitate their faith. What exactly is intended by 'outcome' (*ekbasin*) is unclear, though something that differentiated the 'outcome' of these leaders from that of others obviously is indicated. Martyrdom seems unlikely, even though the reference has sometimes been interpreted in this way. If the writer has indeed been trying to wean the 'Hebrews' from the fear of death (cf. on 2.15, etc.), the effect of contemplating any martyr 'outcome' experienced by these leaders could well have been the opposite of that intended. Clearly, and whatever the external circumstances, the departed leadership had been exemplary in maintaining their Christian profession, which included 'the hope of glory'. They had 'died in faith' like those mentioned in ch. 11, and so the present generation are enjoined to 'imitate their faith', just as in 6.12 they were encouraged to become 'imitators of those who through faith and patience inherit the promises'. This call to imitate echoes a common theme in the New Testament epistles, and especially in Paul's writings. In 1 Cor. 11.1 Paul challenges the Corinthian church to become 'imitators of me, as I am of Christ', by which he suggests that Christian imitation is ultimately the imitation of Christ, which was possible only indirectly for most of Paul's own converts since they had never encountered Christ in person (cf. also 1 Thess. 1.6). This is suggestive in the present context, in view of the statement about Christ in v. 8.

This verse is best seen as transitional: it fills out v. 7 inasmuch as Christ was the focus of the faith of the departed leaders, and it anticipates the argument beginning with v. 9, by asserting that Christ is the unchanging one—who, as always present to the addressees, can enable them to resist 'strange teachings'. The sentence is constructed so as to emphasize that their perception of Christ as unchanging can be maintained indefinitely: 'yesterday and today the same—and forever'. In a letter that sometimes prefers to refer simply to 'Jesus' the fuller reference to 'Jesus Christ' is more formal-sounding, as in v. 21 (cf. 10.10). The three phases or aspects in relation to which Christ is 'the same' correspond loosely to the Jewish exposition of the Hebrew tetragrammaton—the divine name—as reflected in Rev. 1.8 ('who is and who was and who is to come'), but the writer has more than mere ontology on his mind at this point. Rather, his concern is to convince the 'Hebrews' that the earthly Jesus about whom they had been taught remained unchanged and worthy of their commitment in the present and ever thereafter. In this respect Christ stands in contrast with the generation of leaders already gone (v. 7); they were no different from the generations of Jewish priests who 'were prevented by death from continuing in office' (7.23). In 1.12 the words 'you are the same', which refer to God in their original setting in Ps. 102.27, are addressed to Christ and have more specific ontological intent.

The deposit of Christian teaching that the author commends to his addressees was supposed to provide anchorage for their faith. In v. 9 he warns them against the danger of being swept away by any of a variety of 'strange teachings' that could unsettle them. The use of the plural attests to the heterogeneity of what is being opposed, elsewhere in the New Testament 'teaching' being used only in the singular (e.g. 'the apostles' *didachē'*, Acts 2.42). The teaching particularly deprecated had to do with 'foods', but in what precise respect is not indicated. 'Grace' is given an emphatic position in the second sentence. This, rather than reliance upon such 'foods', is commended as the means by which a person's spiritual life ('heart') may be strengthened. That the foods in question are connected with Jewish religious observance is suggested by the argument of the following verses. The author has already declared himself on the limited usefulness of 'food and drink and various baptisms' (9.10). Residual attachment to dietary regulations is also addressed in the letter to the Colossians, where the addressees are told not to countenance anyone judging them in such matters (Col. 2.16, 20-21). Such observances are also pronounced ineffective there (vv. 22-23; cf. Jn 6.63). While it is unlikely that the author is concerned here with a misplaced emphasis on the eucharist, what he writes is hardly compatible with an over-developed eucharistic theology. A similar sentiment is expressed in 1 Cor. 8.8 ('Food will not bring us close to God'), though the force of this passage depends on whether the statement is Paul's own or his quotation of a slogan current among some in the Corinthian church. (Even so, he noticeably does not reject the basic premise.)

This rejection of 'foods' is followed in v. 10 by another of the writer's assertions about what Christians 'have' (6.19; 8.1; 10.19; cf. 4.14)—in this case an altar, and, moreover, an altar not accessible to the officiants at the Israelite tabernacle. It is a bold reversal of positions to suggest that it is the adherents of temple and sacrifice who are now cultically debarred. Verse 11 then states a general principle about the treatment of the carcasses of animals killed as sin offerings at the Old Testament tabernacle: the carcasses of animals whose blood was taken into the 'holy place' were burned outside the Israelite camp. This is the general rule according to Lev. 6.30(23): 'But no sin offering shall be eaten from which any blood is brought into the tent of meeting for atonement in the holy place; it shall be burned with fire' (cf. Lev. 10.16-18). However, the mention of the high priest and the use of *hagia* elsewhere to denote the most holy place (or 'Holy of Holies'; see 9.8, 12, 25) show that the author has the Day of Atonement specially in mind (cf. chs. 9–10). On the occasion of this annual fast a bull and a goat were killed as sin offerings, for the high priest and the people respectively, their blood was carried into the most holy place by the high priest, and their bodies were burned outside the camp (Lev. 16.11-17, 27). Thus there was no opportunity for the priesthood to have parts of such animals as food perquisites. By beginning a new paragraph at v. 11 and disregarding the conjunction *gar* ('for') NIV misses this essential connection between vv. 10 and 11. It is true that *gar* in *koinē* Greek should not always be translated by 'for', nevertheless in this instance it is clear that v. 11 connects as much with v. 10 as with v. 12, however the word is treated.

The point of the comparison with the sin-offering becomes clearer in v. 12, where Christ is seen providing an 'antitype' to the Atonement ritual: 'by his own blood', in contrast with the animal blood of the Atonement ritual, he is said to have sanctified his people. In that Christ suffered 'outside the city gate' of Jerusalem the writer is able to exploit a comparison with the sin offerings whose carcasses were burned 'outside the camp'. (The expression 'outside the city gate' does not occur in the Gospels tradition in connection with the crucifixion, but is entirely consonant with it [cf. Mk 15.21; Lk. 23.26; Jn 19.17, 20]. In the parable of the wicked husbandmen the corpse of the owner's son is thrown outside the vineyard by the tenants [Mk 12.8], while in the Matthaean and Lukan versions of the parable the actual killing takes place outside the vineyard [Mt. 21.39; Lk. 20.15]. In a variant Targumic rendering of Zech. 12.10 the Messiah son of Ephraim—a figure of little importance in Jewish messianism and perhaps developed partly in response to the Christian doctrine of the messiah—goes out to do battle with Gog but is killed by him 'before the gate of Jerusalem'.) The implication is that, just as the priesthood, here representative of the Jewish people, had no share in the Atonement sin offerings, so they have no part in Christ whose death is believed to answer to, and fulfil, the Atonement ritual.

There is, of course, some asymmetry in the comparison with the ritual of the Day of Atonement, since the crucifixion of Christ naturally took place away from the temple temenos, in a place that, strictly speaking, would correspond to the location of the burning of the Atonement carcasses—a place regarded as profane and unclean in Old Testament law (cf. Lev. 16.27-28; Deut. 23.9-14). This did not worry the author, for whom Golgotha was truly a place of sacrifice and for whom the blood ritual of the cross had to do with a heavenly sanctuary into which Christ entered 'by his own blood' (9.12). The purpose of Christ's suffering, as expressed in v. 12, was to 'sanctify the people', where the reference to 'people' may reflect the national dimension of the annual Atonement ritual (cf. 9.7, also in the context of the Day of Atonement). As in earlier references, sanctifying represents that purifying of human hearts that makes people acceptable to God the source of all holiness (cf. 2.11; 9.13-14;10.10, 14). There is, then, a great paradox at the heart of these claims about the significance of Christ's death. The addressees were being asked to recognize a profane execution plot outside the holy city as the place where Christ suffered in order to make his people 'holy'; and their cherished views of what was holy may have been stood on their head in consequence.

Verses 13-16 show in what way those who have been 'sanctified' through Christ have access to the altar that he has provided for them. In 9.14, where 'purify' is a synonym for 'sanctify' in the preceding verse ('sanctifies those who have been defiled'), the effect is that those purified are enabled to worship the living God. So too for the beneficiaries of Christ's suffering there is the possibility of a round of unceasing praise and service to God (vv. 15-16). First, there is the requirement to go 'outside the camp'—in a kind of inverted entrance liturgy (cf. on 10.22)!—to identify with the crucified Christ and 'bear the abuse he endured' (v. 13). The contrast with the directional language of 10.22 ('let us approach [*sc.* the sanctuary]') is the more striking when it is considered that the purpose is the same in both instances, namely worship and its particular manifestations of love and goodness (cf. 10.24-25). This the writer seeks to promote by means of exhortation and moral challenge, for, although it may be said of the addressees that they had already come to 'Mount Zion...and to Jesus' (12.22-24), their 'going outside' will require still further resolve on their part.

The goal of the consequent activity is personalized: they are exhorted to go out 'to him', which phrase is meant to put in a different light the uncongenial terrain that they must occupy. In so doing they will 'bear the abuse he endured', which expression echoes what has been said of Moses in 11.26 and therefore reminds them of a venerable role model, and the more so since Moses is there described as having endured 'abuse suffered *for the Christ*. There may be in the reference to 'carrying' (*pherontes*) the abuse a hint of a comparison with Christ's carrying of his cross (cf. *bastazōn* in Jn 19.17), though more attention is paid in the Gospels tradition to the part played by Simon of Cyrene in the shouldering of Christ's cross. There is also the possibility that Christ's own call to discipleship by 'taking up one's cross' (cf. Mk 8.34) is echoed here. Other ways of expressing the idea of sharing in Christ's reproach certainly were available to the author. It is also difficult in this context, and the more so after the back-reference to Moses in 11.26, to overlook the situation described in Exod. 33.7-11 when, following the apostasy at Sinai, Moses 'used to take the tent [of meeting] and pitch it outside the camp… And everyone who sought the Lord would go out to the tent of meeting, which was outside the camp' (v. 7). The comparison makes no concessions to historical-critical considerations in Exodus 33, but then the author would not have had to concern himself with such, and would have been at least as alert as a modern reader to the parallels between his text and the Exodus pericope.

Then, in v. 14, the writer encourages his readers to think that, although following Christ means remaining outside the city that has encapsulated so many of the hopes of the faithful, they are not now rootless and disfranchized; they belong to a city that is not of the present order. Again the parallel with Moses is valid, since his willingness to suffer abuse 'for the Christ' rested on the conviction that present loss was future gain (11.26). At the same time, v. 14 clearly points back to others whose faith is commemorated in ch. 11, and especially to Abraham and Sarah, who are said to have left their homeland in search of 'a heavenly country', and for whom, says the writer, God himself had prepared a city (11.13-16). The verse is also notable for its ringing of the changes on the twin themes of possession and permanence that have featured in this chapter. For once, the message is that 'we do *not* have', and, whereas the idea of the continuance of things that cannot be shaken has resonated since 12.27, here it is confessed that there is no earthly 'city that remains (*menousan*, which sets up an assonance with *mellousan* ['that is to come'])', and so Christians look for one beyond the present order.

Having laid the ground for his exhortation, the author seeks to enthuse the 'Hebrews' on the subject of Christian worship (vv. 15-16). His previous discussion of the once-for-all sacrifice of Christ (cf. 9.26; 10.12) does not deter him from using the language of sacrifice for

Christian worship; he has, after all, asserted that Christians 'have an altar' (v. 10). His approach to the subject of worship is hierarchical, or at least functionalist: essentially, Christian worship is offered to God through Christ (*di' autou* [v. 15]; cf. Eph. 5.20). This cultless sacrifice of praise can, moreover, be offered without regard to time or place, which suggests an ease of access and opportunity not possible within the confines of the old cultic order, though always available to individual piety. The 'sacrifice of praise' is a category of communion offering in the Levitical sacrificial tariff (cf. Lev. 7.12), but the idea of offering praise as a sacrifice in its own right is also known in the Old Testament (e.g. Ps. 50.14, 23). The words *tout' estin* ('that is') introduce an explanation that seems to reflect Hos. 14.2(3) in its Septuagintal form, 'we will offer the fruit of our lips', which may be more pristine than the standard Hebrew text ('so will we render the calves of our lips', AV). Again, in 'that confess his name' an Old Testament phrase is used to help explain the nature of the 'sacrifice of praise' (see, e.g., Ps. 7.17). In its Old Testament setting, to praise the name of the Lord may also imply the rejection of other gods worshipped by Israel's neighbours (cf. Ps. 16.2, 4).

The structure of v. 16 quite closely parallels that of v. 2 as the subject of worship is taken a stage further. The 'Hebrews' are not to forget, and again a reason is given. Here the concept of worship is extended to include the doing of good and the sharing of one's possessions, which things are said to be 'pleasing to God' in the manner of the sacrifices laid down in Old Testament priestly law. The theme of exemplifying Christian faith by the performance of good deeds is commonplace in the New Testament, partly as representing a proper expression of the faith and partly because of its apologetic value in the face of hostility from non-Christians. (We might compare, for example, the letter to Titus, which has a series of references to 'good works' running through it like the fabled thread of Ariadne, itself associated with the island of Crete where Titus had special pastoral responsibilities.) In vv. 15 and 16, therefore, the non-cultic offering of praise and the doing of good are alike described in sacrificial language, and in that sense the assertion 'we have an altar' (v. 10) is both illustrated and justified. Christians may be 'outside the camp', our author implies, but they are not to imagine that they cannot engage in the worship and service of God. On the contrary, they may satisfy a criterion of great importance for the author—the pleasing of God (cf. 11.5-6; 12.28; 13.21).

Such a conception of 'sacrifice' fits well with a major argument of *Hebrews*, namely that the old cultus has fulfilled its purpose and that the proper approach to God no longer relies on the apparatus of priesthood and sacrifice. It is a position that is maintained elsewhere in the New Testament, not just in specific statements about the old cultus but also in references to the role of 'sacrifice'—for the concept is by no means abandoned—in the Christian scheme of things. So Paul may speak of the presentation of the body, in the form of a sanctified life, as a 'living sacrifice' to God (Rom. 12.1), and when he refers to priestly activity within a Christian context it relates to his preaching of the Gospel (Rom. 15.16; cf. also 1 Pet. 2.5, 9; Rev. 1.6). Neither in the present text nor in any other is it envisaged that the offering of worship is the prerogative of individuals considered more 'priestly' than others within the church. It is, moreover, ironical indeed that in much ecclesiastical discussion in relation to women and the priesthood what is regarded as 'priestly' in the New Testament is commonly permitted to women, while what is nowhere so described (notably in relation to eucharistic practice) has tended to be forbidden to them. Finally, as regards vv. 15-16, it is important to observe that the 'dematerializing' of the cultus and the futuristic perspective of v. 14 are not interpreted to mean that Christians may opt out of working for the good of their own communities, or of society, in the world of the present.

The second mention of leaders in this chapter (v. 17) refers to the current leadership, whom the addressees are enjoined to obey. Although the language of shepherd and sheep is not used, as it will be in relation to Christ as the 'great shepherd of the sheep' (v. 20), something of the metaphor is suggested in the idea of the leader who watches out for the congregation and who also will give account for its spiritual condition. It is likely that in the purpose clause beginning 'so that they may do this' (lit.) the writer is thinking not of the future giving of account, as something that will have to be done with either regret or pleasure, but of the discharge of pastoral duty in the present (*pace* AV, 'for they watch for your souls, as they that must give account, that they may do it with joy'). At first NRSV ('Let them do this') seems ambiguous, but its translation of *mē stenazontes* by 'and not with sighing' strongly suggests the down-to-earth struggles of church leadership rather than a sorrowful accounting by and by (cf. NIV, with resumptive use of 'obey': 'Obey them so that their work will be a joy'). This does not mean that the idea of an eschatological giving of account with or without joy would be inappropriate to the context; what applied to an apostle (cf. Phil. 2.16) could apply *a fortiori* to a local church leader. In the same way it would be possible to defend the last clause of the verse ('for that would be harmful to you') as referring to loss sustained at Christ's judgment seat.

More Personal Touches (13.18-25)

In the closing verses that frame the benediction and doxology of vv. 20-21 the writer adopts a more personal tone, although he begins in v. 18 with the first person plural before using the more direct first person singular in v. 19 (cf. 11.32). He has not included himself among the leadership of which he has just spoken, yet he obviously has had some standing in relation to the community to which he is writing. His absence from them may have been a problem, and the defensive way in which he writes suggests that he or they, or both, regarded it as regrettable in the circumstances. He chooses his words carefully: he 'is persuaded' (lit.) that he has a clear conscience and he 'desires' to act honourably. Despite his anxieties about their spiritual state, he is not above soliciting their prayers on his behalf—or even suggesting that their requests will be well-directed since he has a good conscience about the motives that underpin his Christian service. Noticeably, he asks for their prayers and then pronounces his own blessing on them (vv. 18-19, 20-21).

If this letter is a kind of homily (see on v. 22), then vv. 20-21 function as the benediction—rather as they have tended to be used down the centuries. The basic structure consists of invocation, participial clause descriptive of an action of God, request and ascription. The title 'God of peace' is sufficiently common in epistolary benedictions (e.g. Rom. 15.33; 1 Thess. 5.23) for it to be unnecessary to seek to prove its special relevance to the circumstances of the 'Hebrews'. Two novel features as far as *Hebrews* is concerned appear in the descriptive clause. First, God is the one who brought up (participial *anagagōn*) Christ from the dead, and there has not been, hitherto, an explicit reference in the letter to Christ's resurrection. Secondly, Christ and his relationship to his people are described in terms of shepherd and flock. The writer does not use the standard New Testament verb (*egeirein*) in connection with the resurrection; 'bring up' is a little suggestive of the exaltation motif that predominates in the letter (cf. the rare, spatial use of *anagein* in Rom. 10.7). *Hebrews*, on the other hand, is at one with the majority of New Testament texts in viewing the resurrection as an act of God in relation to Christ—partly by way of vindication of his suffering—rather than as the act of a self-sufficient sufferer. The participial mode of referring to God's raising of Christ (lit. 'the one having brought up from the dead the great shepherd of the sheep') parallels other New Testament texts in this respect (cf. Rom. 4.24; 8.11) and recalls the doxological participles of certain Old Testament texts already noted in connection with 1.3.

In the description of the shepherd of the sheep as 'great' there is just a hint of the superiority that the writer finds in relation to Christ and his new order, elsewhere represented in the use of 'better' (e.g. 7.19, 22). The terms 'great high priest' (4.14) and 'great priest' (10.21) have already been used in relation to Christ in this letter, though perhaps with more of a basis in Old Testament priestly terminology. The title 'chief shepherd' in 1 Pet. 5.4 is superficially parallel but is used to distinguish Christ from church leaders who, as his under-shepherds, owe responsibility to Christ the chief shepherd (see v. 2). There may also be a recollection of Isa. 63.11 in one of its Septuagintal forms: 'Where is he that brought up (*ho anabibasas*) the shepherd of the sheep from the earth (var. 'sea')?', though this is far from certain. There the reference is to Moses as the leader of the flock of Israel; the use of 'great' here would gain a certain point if a comparison with Moses were involved (cf. 3.1-6). The benediction, at any rate, makes its contribution to the theme of death, and the fear of it, having been overcome in Christ and through faith in him (see on 2.14-15).

This 'raising up' is said to have been in virtue of 'the blood of the eternal covenant', meaning that Christ's covenant-ratifying death had secured acceptance with God who accordingly raised him from the dead. That it is the shepherd whose covenant blood is in question recalls the Johannine picture of the 'good shepherd' giving his life on behalf of the sheep (Jn 10.11). In 9.20 the expression 'blood of the covenant' occurs in a quotation from Moses' speech in Exod. 24.8, in demonstration of the point that under 'the law' almost everything was cleansed by means of a blood ritual. Also influential in the present passage are those Old Testament texts that look forward to the inauguration of an everlasting covenant between God and his people (Isa. 55.3; Jer. 32.40; Ezek. 37.26, where 'covenant of peace' is in parallel to 'everlasting covenant'). In the present chapter the idea of permanence and continuance already noted (see on v. 1) is, therefore, consolidated in the delineation of this covenant as 'eternal'. The instrumental clause 'by the blood of the eternal covenant' is followed in the Greek by a fullish title for Christ ('our Lord Jesus'), by *Hebrews'* standards. The petition itself comes in v. 21, beginning with the optative *katartisai* ('make [you] complete'), and requests God to equip his people for the doing of his own will (cf. Phil. 2.13) and of what is pleasing before him—a matter of no little concern in *Hebrews* (cf. on v. 16). This is the ideology, if not the language, of Jeremiah's 'new covenant', according to which the law of God would be within, written on the heart (Jer. 31.33). Finally there is the ascription, the focus of which is uncertain, for while it is true that 'to whom' has 'Jesus Christ' as its immediate antecedent, God is the main subject of the sentence. Given the generally 'high' christology of *Hebrews* (though see 2.16-18; 5.7-8) it is a choice that we may not be required to make.

It is appropriate that a letter that lacks an epistolary introduction should locate its particularly personal comments—saving the presence of vv. 18-19—after the benediction in vv. 20-21. The writer seems to apologize in v. 22 for the length of what is not an unduly long letter, possibly because of its sometimes critical tone (e.g. 5.11-14). He describes what he has written as a 'word of exhortation', which expression is used in Acts 13.15 for the homily that followed the lections in the synagogal liturgy, and hence the common characterization of *Hebrews* as a written-down homily. However, the reference to (relative) brevity is also to be read along with v. 23 and its promise of a visit in company with Timothy if the latter joins the writer in the near future. In other words, long as his exhortation may have seemed, it could have been longer (cf. 9.5)—but his expectation is that he will soon be able to speak to the addressees face to face. This is, then, *Hebrews'* equivalent of the 'pen and ink' references in the shorter Johannine letters (2 Jn 12; 3 Jn 13-14). Finally come words of greeting for the church leaders and the members generally (v. 24). The special greeting for the former serves to reinforce the exhortation to obey them in v. 17, while the use of 'all' in relation to both groups is possibly meant to discourage a partisan spirit in the community or its sister communities. The same may apply to the final short benediction in v. 25 (cf. Rom. 15.33; 2 Cor. 13.13; 2 Thess. 3.18). The particular mention of 'those from Italy' (v. 24) connects the letter with Italy (Rome?) in some way, whether as its place of origin or as its destination, but more probably the latter, since a comprehensive term like 'those from Italy' would mean little if coming from Italy, and so much more if applied to an expatriate group wishing to be remembered among friends back in their home country.

Bibliography

Alford, H., *The Greek Testament*. IV.1. *The Epistle to the Hebrews, and the Catholic Epistles of St. James and St. Peter* (London: Rivingtons; Cambridge: Deighton, Bell and Co., 1864).

Attridge, H.W., *The Epistle to the Hebrews* (Hermeneia; Philadelphia: Fortress Press, 1989).

Bockmuehl, M.N.A., 'The Church in Hebrews', in M.N.A. Bockmuehl and M.B. Thompson (eds.), *A Vision for the Church: Studies in Early Christian Ecclesiology in Honour of J.P.M. Sweet* (Edinburgh: T. & T. Clark, 1997), pp. 133-51.

Braun, H., *An die Hebräer* (HNT, 14; Tübingen: Mohr [Siebeck], 1984).

Bruce, A.B., *The Epistle to the Hebrews: The First Apology for Christianity* (Edinburgh: T. & T. Clark, 1899).

Bruce, F.F., *The Epistle to the Hebrews* (New London Commentaries; Grand Rapids: William B. Eerdmans, 1964; London: Marshall, Morgan and Scott, 1965).

Bruce, F.F., 'Hebrews: A Document of Roman Christianity?', *ANRW* II.25.4, pp. 3496-521.

Bruce, F.F., *The Acts of the Apostles: Greek Text with Introduction and Commentary* (Grand Rapids: Eerdmans, 3rd edn, 1990).

Gall, A.F. von, *Der hebräische Pentateuch der Samaritaner* (Giessen: Alfred Töpelmann, 1918).

Gooding, D.W., *The Account of the Tabernacle: Translation and Textual Problems of the Greek Exodus* (Cambridge: Cambridge University Press, 1959).

Gooding, D.W., *An Unshakeable Kingdom: The Letter to the Hebrews for Today* (Leicester: Inter-Varsity Press, 1989).

Gordon, R.P., 'Better Promises: Two Passages in Hebrews against the Background of the Old Testament Cultus', in W. Horbury (ed.), *Templum Amicitiae: Essays on the Second Temple presented to Ernst Bammel* (JSOTSup, 48; Sheffield: JSOT Press, 1991), pp. 434-49.

Hawthorne, G.F., 'The Letter to the Hebrews', in F.F. Bruce (ed.), *The International Bible Commentary* (Basingstoke: Marshall Pickering, 1986), pp. 1500-32.

Horbury, W., 'The Aaronic Priesthood in the Epistle to the Hebrews', *JSNT* 19 (1983), pp. 43-71.

Horbury, W. (ed.), *Templum Amicitiae: Essays on the Second Temple presented to Ernst Bammel* (JSNTSup, 48; Sheffield: JSOT Press, 1991).

Howard, G., 'Hebrews and the Old Testament Quotations', *NovT* 10 (1968), pp. 208-216.

Hughes, G., *Hebrews and Hermeneutics: The Epistle to the Hebrews as a New Testament Example of Biblical Interpretation* (SNTSMS, 36; Cambridge: Cambridge University Press, 1979).

Hurowitz, V., *I Have Built You an Exalted House: Temple Building in the Bible in Light of Mesopotamian and Northwest Semitic Writings* (JSOT/ASOR Monograph Series, 5; JSOTSup, 115; Sheffield: JSOT Press, 1992).

Lane, W.L., *Hebrews* (2 vols; Word Biblical Commentary 47a, 47b; Dallas: Word Books, 1991).

Lindars, B., *The Theology of the Letter to the Hebrews* (Cambridge: Cambridge University Press, 1991).

Manson, W., *The Epistle to the Hebrews: An Historical and Theological Reconsideration* (London: Hodder & Stoughton, 1951).

Metzger, B.M., *Manuscripts of the Greek Bible: An Introduction to Greek Palaeography* (New York: Oxford University Press, 1981).

Michel, O., *Der Brief an die Hebräer* (12th edn; Göttingen: Vandenhoeck & Ruprecht, 1966).

Peterson, D., *Hebrews and Perfection: An Examination of the Concept of Perfection in the 'Epistle to the Hebrews'* (SNTSMS, 47; Cambridge: Cambridge University Press, 1982).

Porter, S.E., *Verbal Aspect in the Greek of the New Testament, with Reference to Tense and Mood* (Studies in Biblical Greek, 1; New York: Peter Lang, 1989).

Porter, S.E., 'The Date of Composition of Hebrews and Use of the Present Tense-Form', in S.E. Porter, P. Joyce and D.E. Orton (eds), *Crossing the Boundaries: Essays in Biblical Interpretation in Honour of Michael D. Goulder* (BIS, 8; Leiden: E.J. Brill, 1994), pp. 295-313.

Spicq, C., *L'épître aux Hébreux* (2 vols.; Paris: J. Gabalda, 1952–53).

Westcott, B.F., *The Epistle to the Hebrews: The Greek Text with Notes and Essays* (London: Macmillan, 3rd edn, 1889).

Walker, P., ' "Fireworks in a Fog"? New Insights into the Book of Hebrews', *TynBul* 45.1 (1994), pp. 1-47.

Wilson, I., *Out of the midst of the Fire: Divine Presence in Deuteronomy* (SBLDS, 151; Atlanta, GA: Scholars Press, 1995).

Index of References

Index of Authors